LARRY BROWN

and the Blue-Collar South

LARRY BROWN

and the Blue-Collar South

Edited by Jean W. Cash and Keith Perry

University Press of Mississippi
Jackson

www.upress.state.ms.us

The University Press of Mississippi is a member of the Association of American University Presses.

First printing 2008

∞

Library of Congress Cataloging-in-Publication Data

Larry Brown and the blue-collar South / edited by Jean W. Cash and Keith Perry.
p. cm.
Includes bibliographical references and index.
ISBN 978-1-934110-75-1 (cloth : alk. paper) 1. Brown, Larry, 1951–2004—Criticism and interpretation. 2. Working class In literature. 3. Rural conditions in literature. 4. Southern States—In literature. 5. Mississippi—In literature. I. Cash, Jean W., 1938– II. Perry, Keith Ronald, 1967–
PS3552.R6927Z75   2008
813'.54—dc22
2007036238
British Library Cataloging-in-Publication Data available

CONTENTS

CONTENTS

FOREWORD

A Tribute to Larry Brown

RICK BASS

My friend Larry Brown, whom I admire as much as any writer I've ever known, was beloved by so many for his innocence and tenderness, for his thoughtful consideration for the voiceless, the disempowered, and the disenfranchised: for children, dogs, wild nature under assault, and, always, the poor. He was a complex man, extraordinarily gentle-hearted even though steeped in the practices and traditions of a culture well-versed in the functional and pragmatic and daily execution of brutality and violence. With the moral precision of our greatest novelists, he wrote not just of the world he inhabited but of a world he believed we *ought* to inhabit, one often sharper, more vital and consequential than this one, a world that reflects the fullest potential of our own, a world with no slack spots and few inconsequentialities: a truly sacred and moral world, in other words.

The essays that follow this foreword are scholarly treatises, not personal ones, but because Larry was my friend, it's important to me to tell future readers what I know, what I worry they may not otherwise discern: that his novels are novels of manners, of deeply moral values, works in which every action has profound consequence and in which every description is either laced—if not fraught—with beauty or laments the absence thereof. Consider, for instance, the following, from his posthumous novel *A Miracle of Catfish* (2007): "Each evening," he wrote, Cortez Sharp "stood on the porch and studied the sky. On the prettiest evenings the gray patches of clouds reddened in the wake of the sinking orange ball and were backlit in some kind of old beauty that fell behind the curve of the world and turned the sky into a painting he never tired of watching" (66). What Cortez looks for is rain to fill his pond; soon, he begins to see it: "He stood there and felt the wind stirring in his thick hair. The leaves on the big pecans were starting to waft up and show their paler undersides, and he saw a bolt of pure white light up the inside of a gray cloud far off. Deep thunder rolled booming out of the sky echoing again and again and the wind picked up as the ceiling blackened and moved his way. Birds fled before it, scattering in the wind, wavering, dodging in its path. The sky rumbled and Cortez saw the beauty of the world God made" (68–69). I have always found great affinity with Larry's keen regard for a certain rightness of things, his respect for the fitted elegance and sophistication and just plain mystery of a wilder, farther nature so much older than our own.

And as a writer, I'm certain that such passages—singular, graceful, hypnotic—will stand on their own as markers and testaments to the era in which he lived: a historical time, a transition period of profound socio-economic stratification, colonization, dissipation, and fracture. The Old South hurtled into the New within a single generation and then—carried headlong by its own momentum—hurtled still faster into the No-South as the commerce of corporate homogeneity swept across the region. (In the next generation, a Faux-South would be erected, with decorative signposts and commercial pressure points that, sadly, would be the last remnants of what was previously a place of ecological integrity.)

What I lament is the loss not of the sociocultural legacy of the Old South but its older, more intact and, to my way of thinking, diverse, graceful, and cohesive physical landscape. In that now bygone South, that land of physical integrity, there was still an ungoverned wildness. In stories—perhaps most famously Faulkner's "The Bear" (1942)—that wildness becomes an innate refusal to be governed, a willful refutation of structures, covenants, communal sensibilities, a standing defense against the forces of change and attacks against the integrity of place. We often witness that same wildness in Brown's work, a wildness familiar to those increasingly few observant enough to have fully experienced any ecosystem not yet completely beset by fragmentation: a landscape in which significant and elegant connections and relationships have not yet been wholly truncated.

Not even a numb-nuts fuckup like Jimmy's daddy, also from *A Miracle of Catfish*, can vanquish that bright-burning fire found far back in the remnant country of ecological integrity. Drunk and stumbling of a wild, snowy, December midnight, he follows a pack of ravening hounds deep into the forest: "They had been running through the woods in the river bottom and they were still running, dodging past the trees and past the big hanging wild grapevines and over the dead leaves with their guns and following the sounds of the dogs and the squealing of the hog as he turned occasionally and stopped to fight. Jimmy's daddy was almost out of breath and he hadn't known it was going to be like this. The snow was still falling and everything was dusted in this surprising December white" (421). The hunters eventually force the last-gasp stand of a feral European beast that is the essence of this same wildness:

> He ripped his way through the hanging vines and tried to bat away the clinging thorny vines and felt one of them rip his cheek. He dabbed the back of one hand against his face and it came away slick with blood. Fuck it. And then he saw them. And it was something he would never forget. The hog had backed himself against the trunk of an enormous cypress and he was cutting at the dogs that had encircled him, dogs that were almost unrecognizable because of the mud on their hides, and they were dashing in and out and nipping at the hog. The lost dog had somehow found them so that there were four of them in a ring around the beast, who was enraged and snapping his jowls at the dogs, the hair raised on their backs, their fangs long and white and exposed. The hog had sunk to his hocks in the soft ground and he was struggling to keep his footing and still make a fight and it was still snowing. Every time he turned his head to cut at a dog, the other three rushed in and slashed at him with their teeth, and the hog was dripping blood from his face, and Jimmy's daddy was scared of it just standing there looking at it. (425)

The boar charges Jimmy's daddy, and in the raw presence of such elemental fortitude, the corrupted, drunken, softbellied man of the present, vomiting from his long run through what once had been his home, is humiliated again as he fires blindly at the mythic beast, missing the wildness entirely, killing instead his domesticated and servile dog.

This same inner spark of indomitable wildness lives in much of Brown's work, and there as in *A Miracle* it makes the land, as well as those rare inhabitants of it fully attuned to it, whole again. Such values, when enacted upon behalf of an indigenous landscape or nature, I posit, are moral values, and by coupling this moral vision with literary excellence Brown produced several great works. My personal favorite, though—despite my great passion for *On Fire* (1994), *Billy Ray's Farm* (2001), and *A Miracle of Catfish* in particular—is his 1991 novel *Joe*.

Many years have passed since I have heard someone refer to the Great American Novel—not for a lack of great novels being written, I suspect, nor for an absence of writerly ambition, but perhaps from a healthful fragmentation and diversification of the American experience. I have heard the case made often that F. Scott Fitzgerald's *The Great Gatsby* (1925) is as fine a candidate for the title as any, but I've always been partial to Robert Penn Warren's *All The King's Men* (1946), with its theme of lost innocence concurrent with the corruption of absolute power. On that novel's luscious first page, the fecund rot of love vine claims so eagerly the wrecked carcass of an imaginary vehicle whose driver, in a spate of dreamy inattentiveness behind an engine of too-much power, has spun off the blacktop and careened into the ditch to be forgotten and passed by:

To get there you follow Highway 58, going northeast out of the city, and it is a good highway and new. Or was new, that day we went up it. You look up the highway and it is straight for miles, coming at you, with the black line down the center coming at and at you, black and slick and tarry-shining against the white of the slab, and the heat dazzles up from the white slab so that only the black line is clear, coming at you with the whine of the tires, and if you don't quit staring at that line and don't take a few deep breaths and slap yourself hard on the back of the neck you'll hypnotize yourself and you'll come to just at the moment when the right front wheel hooks over into the black dirt shoulder off the slab, and you'll try to jerk her back on but you can't because the slab is high like a curb, and maybe you'll try to reach to turn off the ignition just as she starts the dive. But you won't make it, of course. Then a nigger's chopping cotton a mile away, he'll look up and see the little column of black smoke standing up above the vitriolic, arsenical green of the cotton rows, and up against the violent, metallic, throbbing blue of the sky, and he'll say, 'Lawd God, hit's a-nudder one done done hit!' And the next nigger down the next row, he'll say, 'Lawd God,' and the first nigger will giggle, and the hoe will lift again and the blade will flash in the sun like a heliograph. Then a few days later the boys from the Highway Department will mark the spot with a little metal square on a metal rod stuck in the black dirt off the shoulder, the metal square painted white and on it in black a skull and crossbones. Later on love vine will climb up it, out of the weeds. (3)

All the King's Men retains this power all the way through to its final page, on which the protagonist is brought, like a reluctant birthling, into the full awareness of "the convulsion of the world, out of history into history and the awful responsibility of Time" (464). And in that time's passage we are reminded, almost by cadence if not by voice alone, of *Gatsby's* final line: "So we beat on, boats against the current, borne back ceaselessly into the past" (189). The insularity and romance and aggression of the old American experience—or at least those of the ruling white folk of the time—are all magnificently rendered, beautifully embodied.

I'd argue that Brown's *Joe* is the second Great American Novel, a direct descendant of the first—and, likewise, the Great Southern Novel. With innocence in the world long-lost, ceded at least a quarter-century ago, the next casualty is the last of the old American virtues—personal freedom, with all its rights and responsibilities—and, in such a deeply place-based existence as that of rural Southerners, such loss translates into the loss of identity itself: a fate infinitely worse than the rot and senescence of Warren's bittersweet denouement.

Joe's opening notes even sound like those of *All The King's Men*: human transience; an indefinable mood of yearning and dissatisfaction; solitary figures sketched sharp but tiny against an overpowering, overwhelming tableau of elemental nature; the primal passage of time (and hence history) one of the residual side-effects of the disparity between big Nature, little Mankind, and Time immemorial.

> The road lay long and black ahead of them and the heat was coming now through the thin soles of their shoes. There were young beans pushing up from the dry brown fields, tiny rows of green sprigs that stretched away in the distance. They trudged on beneath the burning sun, but anyone watching could have seen that they were almost beaten. They passed over a bridge spanning a creek that held no water as their feet sounded weak drumbeats, erratic and small in the silence that surrounded them. No cars passed these potential hitchhikers. The few rotting houses perched on the hillsides of snarled vegetation were broken-backed and listing, discarded dwellings where dwelled only field mice and owls. It was as if no one lived in this land or ever would again, but they could see a red tractor toiling in a field far off, silently, a small dust cloud following. (1)

As in *All The King's Men*, most if not all of *Joe's* major concerns announce themselves on the novel's first page, as does even the concurrent imagery: rot; the dazzling Southern heat (nature as ultimate arbiter and character); the newer American (and more specifically Southern) themes of the threat and fear of intransigency; and yet, at the same time, a ceaseless opportunity for growth, or at least re-growth, with the repetitiveness of the cycling seasons—new growth emerging from old rot, even if according to the same patterns.

The villain in Joe Ransom, the title character, is the forward momentum, the short-term economic muscularity, of America itself, as well as the fear-driven societal pressure toward homogenization. Joe makes his living by killing, in part, that wildness I mention above, that rank spirit of the Southern swampland that is tragically and at the same time his home and heritage, the landscape that has shaped him, that accepts him, and in which he finds solace from his failures, marital and economic, among others. He barters, trades—ransoms, in other words—his own independence for cash.

Dense also in *Joe* is the theme of horrific waste. We learn that, for timber companies, it's cheaper to hire Joe and his crews to inject poison into hardwoods and then wait for them to die than it is to expend the energy of sawing them down. For Joe, the changing world—police vigilant to his every move, the passing-by of a rural life and rural objects—so conspires against his old freedoms that he may as well be one of those hardwoods himself.

Again and always, however, the land remains steadfast, even against Joe's own depredations, stands as refuge and harbor, sanctuary and emotional firmament against the shifting substratum of his life, as well as that of Gary, the young wastrel-boy he takes under his wing. Gary's perspective recognizes and identifies nature as balm early in the book:

It was that part of evening when the sun has gone but daylight still remains. The whippoorwills called to each other and moved about, and the choirs of frogs had assembled in the ditches to sing their melancholy songs. Bats scurried overhead, swift and gone in the gathering dusk. The boy didn't know where he and his family were, other than one name: Mississippi.

In the cooling evening light they turned off onto a gravel road, their reasons unspoken or merely obscure. Wilder country here, also unpeopled, with snagged wire and rotten posts encompassing regions of Johnsongrass and bitterweed, the grim woods holding secrets on each side. They walked up the road, the dust falling over their footprints. A coyote lifted one thin broken scream down in the bottom; somewhere beyond the stands of cane they could see a faint green at the end of the plowed ground. They turned in on a field road at the base of a soapstone hill and followed it, stepping around washed-out places in the ground, past pine trees standing like lonely sentinels, where doves flew out singing on gray-feathered wings, and by patches of bracken where unseen things scurried off noisily through the brush. (5)

The urge in Joe to do good, to be good, wrestles with his at times uncontrollable dark urges, which are not limited to an alcoholism of wild amplitudes. If such individual wildness—such volatile conflict—was ever sustainable in Joe's life, it surely seems less so as the novel progresses. And as the swamp's rank richness is sacrificed, it seems that the uncontrollable in him surges evermore.

We watch with fascinated horror, strange and conflicting emotions, as Joe increasingly "adopts" Gary, giving him vital guidance and values. Under his attention the boy blossoms, even as we fear also that the world into which Joe indoctrinates him is a wretched dead-end. There's something particularly horrific about the innocence and enthusiasm with which Gary all but leaps into this world of boozing, whoring, and drinking-and-driving. And yet for Gary, who even as a barely adolescent boy has assumed the work and responsibilities of a grown man, a breadwinner, it is a step up, a forward movement, to enter this doomed world. And in this transformation, even as Joe succumbs increasingly to a kind of inevitable, almost predestined personal rot, Gary seems increasingly salvaged—if not saved, then redeemed—rather than wasted.

Another of the now-crumbling foundations on which Joe's older South once rested is the traditional role of the father or husband as breadwinner, and indeed the general loss of freedom—the virtual imprisonment—wrought by economic disintegration. Stranded between the wild yaws of his life—the deep urge to do great good, with, yet, the powerful urge to do great harm—and beset by that wild refusal to be controlled, he repeatedly tries to use the strange new god of the times, cash, as intermediary between these two lands—between these two Joes—and as communication and mitigation for the emotional absences caused, in part, by that same wildness and the failures in his case attendant to it. On the unpredictable, windfall occasions in which he does come into financial bounty, he tries to pass wads of money to his ex-wife and daughter, as well as to Gary. (He's unsuccessful with the first two, though with Gary he is able to exorcise this desire to help—to control or mitigate, briefly—some of his demons.)

What are his demons? Reading *Joe*, I'm struck by the notion that they may be largely innate: that innate wildness, again, once present in many, perhaps, which might have been nurtured in certain cultures (such as the backwoods or deeply rural South) but which is now somehow rendered more dangerous, even toxic—as poisonous as the elixir that Joe and his crew pump into the native and yet non-economic hardwoods—by an increasing cultural estrangement from a wilder, stronger, and above all uncontrollable natural environment. I wonder if, in a wilder nature, the rank forest could at once soothe and calm the demons of men like Joe, leaving their communities and cultures to benefit from the equally powerful but oppositional urges to be generous and to do great good.

In this regard—with its quintessentially American paradoxes—the seeming paradox of strength combining with weakness, right combining unblinkingly with wrong—I believe that *Joe* is, while one of a small handful of great American novels, and one of the great Southern novels, a great American nature novel as well. Who can forget the memorable and lyrical, yet unintentional solace of the epilogue, following Joe's final act of redemption—the gift of his beloved freedom in final defense of good versus evil?

That winter the trees stood nearly barren of their leaves and the cold seemed to settle into the old log house deep in the woods. The old woman felt it seep into her bones. Each morning the floors seemed colder, each day it was harder to crank the truck. The boy piled wood for colder days to come. At odd times of the day they'd hear the faint honking, and they'd hurry out into the yard to see overhead, and far beyond the range of men's guns the geese spread out over the sky in a distant brotherhood, the birds screaming to each other in happy voices for the bad weather they were leaving behind, the southlands always ahead of their wings, warm marshes and green plants beckoning them to their ancient primeval nesting lands.

They'd stand looking up until the geese diminished and fled crying out over the heavens and away into the smoking clouds, their voices dying slowly, one last note the only sound and proof of their passing, that and the final wink of motion that swallowed them up into the sky and the earth that met it and the pine trees always green and constant against the great blue wildness that lay forever beyond. (345)

I can recall no more descriptive passage of nature writing than any number of the scenes in *Joe*, providing almost always tonic against the turmoil of

Joe's life, and yet standing also as their own sentinel, independent of his turmoil.

It is said of *All The King's Men* that when someone complimented Warren on the elegance, the fittedness, of its structure—particularly in a narrative all but bursting with lyricism, the genius of corollary and metaphor—the author replied testily that it was "built like a goddamned Swiss watch." I get the sense, reading *Joe*, that it is much the same. Just as Joe needs the sanctity or stabilizing influence of a larger, wilder nature to buffer his own struggles, so too does Joe's relationship to the reader benefit from, and achieve a necessary balance and reference because of, the truly awful standard or yardstick that is Gary's father.

Doubtless there are thousands of such connections, far more subtle and intricate, yet vital in their cumulative effect, that help give the novel much of its density and power. It's a novel I love to re-read, admiring character in one reading, plot in another, dialogue in another, and yet, always, its use of language.

A little less than halfway through the novel, Brown lays in a beautiful stand-alone chapter, only three pages in length—seemingly, at first, a set piece, a kind of intermission—in which Gary is trapped, away from home and shelter, in the most torrential thunderstorm he's ever experienced, a storm beyond his imagination. In a beautifully presented scene, rather than fretting over or fighting the storm, Gary gives himself over to it, hunkering for cover finally in a road culvert, though even this slight protection soon yields to none at all. In a joyfully written, birth-like passage, he is expelled from the canal by the floodwater, gushed out into the new world of opportunity and respect that Joe has helped provide for him—carried along by Joe's muse, that natural wildness yet again—and in this second birth, Gary is gleeful, a child once more: twice-redeemed, and both times without having sought such redemption.

The roar was a din and the color of the water was like pure mud. One foot slipped, then one hand, and he flew out of the culvert and landed churning in the middle of a creek rising to an angry level, foaming with bits of straw and trash and sticks. He pawed his way through the brown water to the bank and clambered up over the edge of it, his knees coated with mud, his shirtfront and his hands slick with it. The water was cold and the wind was a solid thing he could push against and feel it push back. There was nothing for shelter. Leaves were wafting across the road as they were torn from the trees and sucked out of the woods. He tried to go up another bank slippery with mud, but it defeated him again and again. His ears were full of water. It didn't seem possible to him, but the rain doubled in intensity. The world was gone, nothing left but gray disaster. He squatted on the side of the bank and dug his heels in, covering his head with his arms and waiting for it to be over. He was washed clean by the rain. Every drop of mud ran from his clothes and shoes. He had never seen such a rain. He had never even imagined that such a rain could come. (157)

Throughout *Joe*, there is the powerful, wonderful sense of a greater and grander, wilder, more sharply felt world—more beautiful, more tragic— moving always just below and above the human participants: and through Larry Brown's mastery, his characters are able to gain access to that more deeply felt world where actions have consequence, and where numbness— the enemy of art—will not be tolerated. The characters enter this world sometimes enthusiastically, sometimes with hesitation, trepidation, even awe—but they always enter it, and in this, become fully human, fully realized, fully *moral*. The courage of such characters and the beauty of the language and tautness of Brown's plot leave a reader feeling invigorated about the business of being human, about the viability of hope: again, attributes which place it in good stead, I think, to be designated a great American novel.

History will assuredly preserve Brown's mantle of excellence; time will only brighten its luster. But what I fear will be lost—particularly as readers of a perhaps more sterile future read of the violence and anger that permeated many of the empty spaces and deep histories of the Deep South of his era—is again what an amazing human being Larry Brown was: far from perfect, but nonetheless amazing. Amazing perhaps for that very disparity. My worst fear is that a casual reader, distanced by time, might come to the assumption that, with his characters so often drinking and fighting and maiming and killing, he might not have been a very kind person. I'll say once more how important it is to me that readers of the future know what we, here in the present—where it seems that he has been gone now only a few moments—still know: what an incredible human being he was, what an utterly sweet man, and what an absolutely loyal friend. The hundreds or thousands of community members who knew and loved him know this about him, but after they/we are gone, no one else will. I still can't quite fully believe or comprehend that; and for that loss—mine, not the future's—I still sometimes grieve.

But perhaps such things do not matter to posterity. Perhaps only the naked words themselves matter, and after all of us are gone—after all of us who were fortunate enough to know him are gone—maybe it won't even really matter. But to overlook his true nature as a human being would be to miss or at the very least underappreciate the generosity and moral compassion that lie sometimes unseen or only suspected beneath the harshness and violence of his fiction. Because there is such harshness, is such violence, I would not be surprised if readers of the future ascertained that Brown himself was a harsh and violent man. Maybe such a mistake would be meaningless, for the dead are dead, but such a misunderstanding would fault not just Brown himself but that reader by steering him or her away from the morality that is both the foundation and essence of his fiction.

I keep thinking he's coming back. I keep thinking that I hear his voice. Lucky readers in the future will discover a great writer, and in his work they will doubtless catch the echoes and resonance of a great man. But they'll never know what a great friend he was. That's the part that usually gets lost to history—and, in my mind, it's the best part—so I'd like to get it submitted here, in this scholarly examination of Larry Brown the Writer, not to dismiss the work discussed herein, but to remind the future that, for all its power and grace, that wasn't the half of it.

Works Cited

Brown, Larry. *Joe*. Chapel Hill: Algonquin, 1991.
———. *A Miracle of Catfish*. Chapel Hill: Algonquin, 2007.
Warren, Robert Penn. *All the King's Men*. New York: Harcourt, Brace, 1946.

LARRY BROWN

An Introduction

JEAN W. CASH

When Larry Brown published his first collection of short stories in 1988, Harry Crews, whose work Brown had read and admired since 1980, announced, "talent has struck." From this propitious beginning—recognition would soon follow from other celebrated writers and critics—Larry Brown, a one-time firefighter from Oxford, Mississippi, emerged as one of the breakout talents in Southern fiction. Brown published *Facing the Music* after spending most of the 1980s training himself to write, then published five novels, *Dirty Work* (1989), *Joe* (1991), *Father and Son* (1996), *Fay* (2000), and *The Rabbit Factory* (2003); a second collection of stories, *Big Bad Love* (1990); and two collections of nonfiction, *On Fire: A Personal Account of Life and Death and Choices* (1994) and *Billy Ray's Farm: Essays from a Place Called Tula* (2001). He was completing a sixth novel, tentatively entitled "The Miracle of Catfish," when he died on November 24, 2004. Algonquin Books of Chapel Hill, Brown's principle publisher, released *A Miracle of Catfish*, calling it "A Novel in Progress," in early 2007.

Following in the tradition of Crews, arguably the first Southern writer to sympathetically depict the region's working class, Brown produced a body of work that still further humanizes its members. Hard-packed, realistic, and heavily fraught with emotion, Brown's work first drew readers from throughout the South, then from elsewhere in the country. Honors followed: Brown received the Mississippi Institute of Arts and Letters Award in 1989 for *Dirty Work*, then twice won the Southern Book Critics Award for Fiction (for *Joe* in 1992, *Father and Son* in 1997). He received the Lila Wallace-*Reader's Digest* Fund Writers' Award in 1998, and in 2001 he received the second Thomas Wolfe Prize, awarded by the Department of English at the University of North Carolina-Chapel Hill. Jonathan Yardley of the *Washington Post*, in his 2001 review of *Billy Ray's Farm*, offered the following summation of the author and his work: "Brown is the real thing: a self-taught country boy who may now make the rounds of the writing conferences but whose heart is obviously, and wholly, in the country he loves" (C2).

Because he was born in Oxford and lived in the more rural area around it for all but about a dozen of his fifty-three years, Brown faced constant comparison with William Faulkner; except for their mutual reverence for place, however, the two writers are quite different, especially with regard to their social origins. Faulkner was of Oxford's upper-middle class, with roots strongly entrenched in the town. His grandfather was president of the First National Bank there, and his father Maury, who moved to Oxford to run the local livery stable, ultimately served as bursar at the University of Mississippi. Brown's family, on the other hand, was of the yeoman class, like Faulkner's Varners, Armisteds, and Tulls. Knox Brown, his father, was a sharecropper in the country surrounding Oxford—he lived outside rather than inside the city limits—when Larry was born in July 1951. Both sides of his family were rural people who worked hard, hunted the land, and fished the local waters.

Of his connection with Faulkner, Brown said, "Mr. Faulkner and I don't have much in common, really, besides dealing with the same kind of people in the same area. I'm writing at a much later date. And he wrote about so much that went back before his time. I don't get into that. I write about the here and now" (qtd. in Summer F4). Brown also asserted that Faulkner wrote mainly about aristocrats, while he himself wrote about "blue-collar folk, the ordinary people I know best" (qtd. in Mantell 2). In spite of these disclaimers, however, Brown admitted that he felt shadowed by Faulkner and sometimes found the burden a heavy one. In a 1992 interview, in fact, he seemed to imply—perhaps unconsciously—the inescapability of Faulkner and his legacy. Describing the raw material of his own fiction, Brown echoed a section from Faulkner's 1962 Nobel Prize acceptance speech: "I found out that . . . the things to write about were the truths of the human heart and people and how they reacted and how they try to do the best they can and get along. And I think that's what all good literature is about, about people struggling through problems and trying to do the right thing" (LaRue 46).

Oxford was not as central to Brown's life as it was to Faulkner's. He told another interviewer that, though he was born "at the old hospital up the street from the courthouse . . . we lived twelve miles out in the country" (Bonetti 234). At that time, his father was sharecropping in a creek bottom at Potlockney (about eight miles south of Yocona, where Brown's survivors live today), and a little farther south of Tula, (where he and his family lived after 1964 and where Brown owned land at his death). A veteran of World War II, he had been wounded at the Battle of the Bulge, and as his son would write in *A Late Start*, the speech he delivered at the 1989 Conference on Southern Literature in Chattanooga, Tennessee, his war experience "left emotional scars on him that were never to heal. He would never mention the war when he was sober, but when he was drinking, which was frequent in the years of my growing up, he would begin to talk about it and about the horrors he had seen, and he would eventually break down" (2). Brown's mother Leona Barlow Brown was a homemaker and mother of four—three sons and a daughter (one brother and the sister continue to live in north Mississippi). When Brown was three years old, the family moved to Memphis, Tennessee, where his father took a job at the Fruehauf Trailer Company. His heavy drinking kept him from holding any job for any extended period, though. His son would later term his family life "troubled . . . but through it all, I loved my father as children will, no matter what happens" (qtd. in Weinraub F4). In Memphis, the Browns lived in a series of rented houses that, in *Billy Ray's Farm*, Brown characterized as "stacked tightly side by side behind their tiny yards." He remembered not having room for a dog or anywhere to fish or roam: "It's one thing to have a life in a place," he wrote, "and to be happy in it is quite another" (10).

In 1964, before Brown finished the eighth grade, his family left Memphis and returned to north Mississippi, where his father found work in an Oxford stove factory. (Later, briefly, Brown would work there himself.) His father's drinking and the consequent lack of money continued to disrupt the family: as Brown told one interviewer, "Let's just say I [had] . . . a childhood that had some hard times" (qtd. in Weinraub F4). His father would eventually conquer his drinking, but he would die shortly thereafter, in 1968. At the funeral, Brown recalled, his mother declared that "she was so proud to have been his wife. This love for him, even in the face of what she lived with in her marriage to him of a little over twenty years, is a testament to the strength of the human spirit, and maybe my early life is why I wrote so many things about drinking and trouble and violence. I know these things well, and I don't have to imagine what life with them is like" (*Late* 3).

Although, as a youngster, Larry Brown had no dreams of becoming a writer—"It never crossed my mind," he once said (LaRue 40)—he was an inveterate reader whose love of books and reading came "[m]ainly from my mother. One of my earliest memories is of seeing her reading. There were always books in our house. I just grew to love it real early, I guess—escaping into stories and discovering other worlds" (Bonetti 235). In another interview, Brown revealed that his father's dislike for "anybody who was reading" (LaRue 40) forced his mother to hide magazines under a chair cushion so as to avoid conflict with him. When he was a child, his mother also bought the family a set of encyclopedias, and with it came a set of ten "classics": works by Edgar Allan Poe, Mark Twain, Zane Grey, Herman Melville, and Jack London. Grimms' fairy tales, a collection of Greek mythology, *The Iliad*, and *The Odyssey* were also part of it. Brown later recalled that, "When I was a child I was a big reader of Greek mythology" (Bonetti 235): "When I read *The Iliad* and *The Odyssey* when I was little, on my own, it got me thinking in terms of myths and dreams; I was really into Greek mythology, all the battles and gods. . . . They formed the core of my belief about storytelling" (Ketchin 138).

Brown could hardly have cared less for his school books, though—but he did read books about hunting, fishing, and cowboys, which he checked out from the school library. He would later dismiss them as "nothing you would call literature. It took me a long time even to learn what literature was" (qtd. in Summer F4). He had few if any aspirations beyond completing high school, his mother's wish for him, and his early enthusiasm for hunting and fishing—the outdoors in general—interfered with even that. "Most of the time I stayed out in the woods, out with my dogs coon hunting when I should have been home doing my homework" (LaRue 55–56), he later said. A self-styled "terrible" student, he failed twelfth-grade English— even earning an F on a term paper about an obvious area of expertise, deer hunting—and was not allowed to graduate with the rest of his class (LaRue 55). As might be expected, his mother was upset with him, but after attending summer school, Brown graduated from Lafayette High School in August 1969. Expecting to be drafted and sent to Vietnam, he wanted only to finish school, get a job, and buy a car. He thought little about his more distant future.

After working a few months at the stove factory, he joined the Marines in 1970 as his birthday was the first drawn in that year's lottery; enlisting in the Marines, he reasoned, was preferable to being drafted by the Army. He trained at South Carolina's Parris Island and served for about a year at North Carolina's Camp LeJeune but was never ordered to serve in Vietnam. Instead, he spent two years at the Marine Barracks in Philadelphia, Pennsylvania, where he met disabled marines "who were in wheelchairs, who had lost their arms and legs and had made that great sacrifice, too" (Bonetti 251). Walter James and Braiden Chaney, the dual narrators of *Dirty Work*, are of course their direct descendents.

Upon his discharge from the Marines in 1972, Brown returned to Lafayette County and soon reencountered Mary Annie Coleman, whom he had first met there in 1969, when she was just fourteen years old. They married in 1974, when she was nineteen, he twenty-three. Of their consequent union, which lasted until his death some thirty years later, Brown once commented, "I've got a happy marriage and I'm crazy about the girl I'm married to. I couldn't ask for anybody better" (qtd. in Weinraub F4). Brown describes in *On Fire* the one time he deserted Mary Annie. When, one night early in their marriage, she objected to his going out alone to drink with friends, they ended up quarrelling, and "she doubled up her little fist and caught me square in the jaw with a decent right hook." He walked out the door, leaving her with their infant son, but returned after only four days: "I crawled back in the window one night and I've been with them ever since" (25).

Their marriage produced four children, including a daughter, Delinah, who died in infancy. "When our baby died in 1977," Brown said, "I didn't think I would survive. It was a very rocky time" (Ketchin 129). This loss of his daughter resonates in *Father and Son*, portions of which depict the suffering of parents who lose young sons. Brown's other children, Shane, Billy Ray, and LeAnne, are adults today; in *On Fire* and *Billy Ray's Farm*, Brown makes clear his love for and devotion to them, and in one 1994 interview he said, "I'm very much concerned with family connections, relatives, and all that. That's like a nest you go back home to every night. You have these people around you who are going to be with you all your life" (Bonetti 244).

Soon after their marriage, the Browns settled into a mobile home on land Mary Annie's parents owned. The only child of a cotton farmer, Mary Annie recalls that she had grown up working the fields alongside her father, declaring herself "born to be a farmer's daughter." When her father died a few years later, in 1977, the young Brown family moved into the home where Mary Annie had grown up, volunteering to provide care and companionship for both her mother and her grandmother. After her husband decided to become a writer and discovered, shortly thereafter, that he could not write in the Coleman house, the Browns in 1986 built a ranch-style home across the road from her mother's, the house where Mary Annie lives today. Their son Billy Ray and his wife and children now live in the old homeplace.

In 1973, Brown became a paid firefighter with the Oxford Fire Department. Unable to support his growing family with the salary he drew there, he pursued for six years a wide variety of part-time work bagging groceries, planting trees, building houses, cleaning carpets, cutting pulpwood, deadening timber, building fences, painting houses, and hauling hay (*Late* 5). In *A Late Start*, Brown described his subsequent decision to become a writer: "When I was twenty-nine, I stopped and looked at my life and wondered if I was ever going to do anything with it" (3–4). Because he had long been an inveterate reader of novels, he decided that he could teach himself to write salable fiction in much the same way that he had learned carpentry and firefighting. His chief aim early on was only financial: he wanted to make sure that his three young children would not have to start their adult lives as he had, working in a factory (5).

In *On Fire*, Brown recalled that, in 1982, when he told "a good friend" about his decision to become a writer (vi), the friend "didn't laugh. He just listened to me seriously and nodded his head" (viii). Mary Annie, however, was uncertain as to whether her husband was serious. In an April 2000 interview she admitted, "I thought it was a whim at first, but he kept at it, month after month. I knew he was serious. He was so determined to make it. . . . We got used to doing things without him around because he was always writing" (qtd. in O'Briant L6). Brown often acknowledged this constant support, revealing that she kept the children out of his way and often went to sleep to the accompaniment of his typewriter: "she believed that I wanted it badly enough," he said, "and she was willing to support and stand by me" (qtd. in Weinraub F4).

Using Mary Annie's portable Smith-Corona typewriter, he set out to write a novel "about a man-eating bear in Yellowstone National Park, a place I'd never been to"—"and it had a lot of sex in it" (*Late* 4–5). Working steadily around his other jobs, Brown finished the novel in five months and sent it out immediately. "Of course, I didn't know what I was doing," he later admitted. "I didn't even know about double-spacing. I typed that whole novel single-spaced, 327 pages" (qtd. in Summer F4). Publishers, as one might imagine, immediately rejected it, editors likewise refusing a handful of "horrible" short stories that he was writing and submitting to magazines at the time (*Late* 5). Of his early lack of sophistication, Brown said, "I didn't have any idea about how much work was involved. I surely didn't think it would take seven years before my first book was published" (qtd. in Ross 89).

In 1982, however, Brown garnered his first publication when the motorcycle enthusiasts' magazine *Easyriders* accepted one of his early stories, "Plant Growing Problems." After that, though, he published nothing else for two years. Yet these initial rejections spurred rather than frustrated his desire: he wrote in *On Fire* that "I had one burning thought that I believed was true. If I wrote long enough and hard enough, I'd eventually learn how" (viii). Seeking to improve his writing, Brown also visited the local library in Oxford, checking out books on writing "by the armload" and "read[ing] them cover to cover" (*Late* 6). They helped him understand how bad his own efforts were, but this realization only increased his determination: "I still had the belief that if I hung in there long enough and wrote enough, I would eventually learn how" (*Late* 7). Essays by writers who had begun in similar situations but succeeded after long struggles—Crews chief among them (*BRF* 20)—he found "tremendously heartening" (*Late* 7). Support also came his way when Brown began frequenting the newly-opened Oxford Square Books. He quickly caught the attention of its founder, Richard Howorth, who remembers, "When we had book signings, he'd come in and sort of hang around. I don't know that he felt real comfortable. But gradually he began to feel at home, and was one of the regulars who came in. For a long time, I didn't know he was a writer. And then, of course, his own book was published" (qtd. in Skube 4). Howorth soon assumed the role of mentor, suggesting novels and short story collections by Faulkner and other writers whom he thought Brown should read (O'Briant L6). In return, Brown would later credit Howorth and his bookstore with guiding him toward works by contemporary writers he would soon come to greatly admire, among them Crews, Cormac McCarthy, and Raymond Carver.

By 1982, Brown had produced three novels and roughly ninety stories, all without much success. After the novel about the man-eating grizzly bear, he had written a second, about Tennessee marijuana growers; a third, a tale of the supernatural; and a fourth, about boxing. Everything he sent out came back, not just rejected but almost always without comment. In *On Fire*, he described his feelings of discouragement, now beginning to mount: "I am wondering if it ever will be, if the rejection slips will ever stop coming, how much longer it will take to learn what I want to learn. The most frightening thing to think is that it might never come, but I never allow myself to think about that very much" (153). He therefore decided to study writing more formally: "I'd been plugging along all by myself there without any kind of guidance—just what I could get out of books about writing and what I could learn from reading, trying to see how good writers put it together" (qtd. in Ross 89).

In the fall of 1982, Mississippi novelist Ellen Douglas was teaching a creative writing course at the University of Mississippi. She describes her first encounter with Brown, as he came to solicit a place in her class: "When he came to interview for my graduate writing class at Ole Miss, he had not had any college. He had been admitted as a special student. I asked him if he had done any writing and he said, 'Yes, ma'am'—he had that Mississippi deference to older women. I asked him what he had written and he said about a hundred short stories. And he said he had drafts of three novels. I said, 'Come to class'" (qtd. in Skube 3). After reading some of his fiction, Douglas told him that she had no problem with his sentence structure, just his subject matter—which soon became, under her tutelage and his continued efforts, more sophisticated. Brown said that his fifth novel, about a man lost in the Mississippi woods, came close to publication (Bonetti 250). He would ultimately credit Douglas with introducing him to the work of writers from Conrad and Dostoevski to Katherine Anne Porter and Flannery O'Connor, and with being "really a great teacher. She had all this accurate insight into your manuscript. And she kind of pointed me in the right direction" (LaRue 43). Douglas herself has eschewed such praise, claiming that she was "impressed" with Brown all along, with his "sense of voice" in particular. "He had a natural talent" (qtd. in O'Briant L6), she remembered. In an interview in 2006, she added, "Even more important and memorable is his . . . honesty, the way he 'faces the music' (to borrow one of his titles) of the human condition."

Although by 1985, Brown had published just three stories—the one in *Easyriders*, a second in *Fiction International*, and a third in *Twilight Zone*—just two years later, Frederick Barthelme at the *Mississippi Review* accepted and published a fourth, "Facing the Music." Barthelme recalls that when he first read the story, which tells of a husband's struggle to accept his wife's mastectomy, "My hair just stood up on end" (qtd. in Richardson 56). Shannon Ravenel, then senior editor at Algonquin Books of Chapel Hill, soon read the story and quickly contacted the author. As Brown recalled, "she wanted to recommend it for the Best American Short Stories [series]. And she asked me if I had enough stories for a collection. I wrote back and said, 'I've got a hundred. How many would you like to see?'" (qtd. in Weinraub F4). A year later, Algonquin published *Facing the Music*; Ravenel says that Brown's fearless perspective is what most attracted her attention: "What Larry does that other people don't is not look away. He is willing to take a sharp knife, stick it in, and expose things without flinching. The music is faced in his work. He finds beauty in other people's pain. There's a big streak of compassion in him that he's able to express" (qtd. in Weinraub F4). Brown, over the next two decades, would often express his strong appreciation for Ravenel's role in his career, and although he would later publish *The Rabbit Factory* at The Free Press, a division of Simon and Schuster, Ravenel and Algonquin published all of his first eight books, as well as his posthumous novel *A Miracle of Catfish*.

Brown has often cited the many writers who influenced his outlook on writing, his focus as a writer, and his use of Southern settings and themes. Among them are Faulkner, O'Connor, Carver, McCarthy, Charles Bukowski, Tobias Wolff, and Stephen King. In one 1990 interview, he elaborated on this debt: "From them I learned how to make strong characters, how to move them around and motivate them. I learned that story was all-important, and I learned about narrative hooks. I learned about using the language, and the different things you can do with it" (qtd. in Ross 89). Brown held deep admiration for the work of O'Connor especially, whom he called "one of my idols" (*Late* 3). He particularly appreciated her assertion that the early experience of writers is all they need as subject matter for their fiction. O'Connor made him realize that, even though he didn't know how to use it until he was almost thirty, he had had "plenty of material for a long time" (*Late* 3).

The writer with whom Brown claimed the strongest kinship, however, is Crews; Brown dedicated *Fay* to him, writing, "For my uncle in all ways but blood: Harry Crews." Critics have characterized Crews as the first working-class Southern writer, and his work empathetically reveals the harshness of lives others have often overlooked. Of his enthusiasm for Crews and his work, Brown said, "I've read everything Harry Crews has ever published. I reckon all of his novels and even his first story, which was published in about 1963" (Parsons 3). One of the strongest essays in *Billy Ray's Farm* is Brown's tribute to Crews, originally published in a 1998 issue of *Southern Quarterly*. Here Brown writes that, upon beginning to read Crews's 1976 novel *A Feast of Snakes* around 1980, he realized that "I'd never read anything like it and didn't know that such things could be done in a book.... It was a combi-

JEAN W. CASH

nation of hilarity and stark reality and beauty and sadness" (17–18). His affinity with Harry Crews and his writing shows clearly throughout Brown's own work.

In his *Southern Culture* article "The Rise of Southern Redneck and White Trash Writers," Erik Bledsoe discusses changes in the treatment of lower-class characters beginning with Crews and continuing through the fiction of Dorothy Allison, Tim McLaurin, and Larry Brown. He asserts that white, lower-class characters had long appeared in Southern fiction, but without realistic treatment. Traditionally they have been comic entertainers, villains, or victims because their creators were of the middle or upper classes and were able to look at them only from above, only from the outside (70). Bledsoe argues that Faulkner, for instance, introduced his Snopeses as comic evocations, but as they eventually gained social and economic power, they stopped being funny and became villainous. "The narrative perspective of the Snopes Trilogy," he writes, "is that of the middle classes who watch in horror as they lose ground to the white trash that seeks to displace them" (72).

Writers like Allison, McLaurin, and Brown were born in and write about the so-called Rough South, a term originated by documentary filmmaker Gary Hawkins. Bledsoe suggests that these writers, Crews and his disciples, force readers "to reexamine long-held stereotypes and beliefs while challenging the literary roles traditionally assigned poor whites" (68). Brown never gets far from the poor-white world in which he grew up, and, "unlike Faulkner," as Bledsoe asserts, "he does not fear that world" (75). Brown himself said, "I write about characters who are from the poor side of town because that's what I know best" (qtd. in Ross 89). Among the many who praise Brown's ability to depict these characters is fellow Mississippi novelist Barry Hannah: "Larry doesn't have the problem that overeducated writers have," he commented. "He gets down to the gutsy level right away. I don't know of anybody as good who started right from scratch" (qtd. in Hudson 7).

Brown's major concern, then, is with lower-class northwest Mississippians—and, on occasion, southwest Tennesseans—whom he invariably presents with realistic detail and forthright empathy. He explores both their daily pleasures and the consistent woes that often accompany them. Brown's men (and some of his women) thrive on drinking alcohol, smoking cigarettes, frequenting bars, and looking for sex. His male characters own pickup trucks— always equipped with coolers full of cold beer—that they

xxviii

love driving through the backwoods, particularly during the early evening. In *On Fire*, Brown resurrects James Street's word for this slice of time: the "gloam," as he puts it, comes when the sun has gone down but there is still "about an hour of light before dark. It's the very best time to ride around and listen to some music" (25).

Of his realistic treatment of working-class Southerners, Brown said, "The people that I write about are very much like the people that I know best. All I really do is just kind of watch the people around me, watch what goes on. That's where all my characters come from" (qtd. in Weinraub F4). He has often talked and written about spending time in bars himself, drinking and watching the behavior of those under the influence of alcohol. Brown is equally concerned that his stories seem realistic: "I build my stories, and I try to be authentic in them. The events have to be authentic, too, no matter how painful the endings might be. I sometimes get accused of being brutal and having a dark vision.... Tragedy is inevitable in my stories because of the circumstances people live in" (Bonetti 244). In his fiction, the circumstances of his characters' lives—particularly their poverty, lack of family and/or social connections, and failure to find positive senses of self—invariably lead them to conflict and violence; resolutions are not always positive. Brown once said, simply, "There is just no way for some lives to have a happy ending" (qtd. in Weinraub F4). One reviewer asserts that Brown "takes nothing for granted. The people he writes about have nothing to take for granted, but a few hold onto a hairline of hope" (Skube 5). Brown commented in *A Late Start* that, "I try to write as close as I can to the heart of the matter. I write out of experience and imagination, toward blind faith and hope" (2–3).

Like other Southern writers, Brown also concerned himself with the importance of family, a value that remains strong in his working-class characters. Such concerns have long been a staple of Southern fiction, but seldom have writers shown its significance to the lower classes; in the Snopes novels, for example, Faulkner shows how little family loyalty Flem holds. He uses family connections to advance his economic aims, but when family members—his cousin Mink, for instance, in *The Hamlet* (1940)—need his help, he denies any connection. Brown, on the other hand, shows loyalty even in families as corrupt as that of Wade Jones and his abused children in *Joe*. When Joe Ransom, knowing how depraved the boy's father is, invites Gary Jones to come live with him, the boy says, "Well. I'd kind of hate to just go off and leave em" (342). This need for family connection is vital to his characters, and when they are unwilling or unable to forge these bonds—as is Glen Davis of *Father and Son*—they invariably destroy themselves. Still, Brown applauds the strength of family in *Father and Son* and extends hope that Virgil Davis's remaining son and grandchild will ultimately resurrect the Davises as a cohesive unit. Family remains a vital concern in *A Miracle of Catfish* as well. Two fathers, Cortez Sharp and Cleve, are willing to commit murder to maintain the integrity of their families, and its central character Jimmy spends much of the novel longing for a father more ambitious and caring than the one he has.

Alongside this concern with family is another focus of Brown's work: strong women who possess extraordinary power to nurture. Brown's sympathy with these women is clearly the result of his own interaction with strong women. His mother, Leona Barlow Brown, held the family together during the rough years the Browns lived in Memphis, and Brown's wife Mary Annie was the mainstay of Brown's own family, particularly during the years he was working so hard to become a writer. Although some reviewers (men, primarily) have seen his fiction as brutal, aimed mainly at male readers, perceptive readers notice that even in his earliest fiction, his female characters are vital women able to make lives for themselves and their families in spite of poor health, alcoholic partners, and emotional deprivation. The alcoholic Angel in *Facing the Music*'s "Kubuku Rides (This is It)" seems entirely real as wife, mother, and helpless victim of her alcoholism. Mary Blanchard, in *Father and Son*, goes on to live a positive life even after the loss of both lover and husband, raising a son who becomes one of Brown's most admirable characters. In *Fay*, Brown created his most resolute female character, a young woman ignorant but possessing the strength and determination of an ultimate survivor.

Somewhat like O'Connor, whose outlook on race has recently received renewed attention, Brown did not aggressively explore racial issues in his fiction. Whatever mars the lives of his white characters—poverty, alcoholism, violence—also blights the lives of his black characters. Angel, again, from "Kubuku Rides (This is It)," confronts but cannot overcome her addiction to alcohol. The black workers in *Joe* hate the hazardous work of poisoning trees, but they don't blame their problems on their white boss. Brown's most poignant black character is the Vietnam veteran Braiden Chaney in *Dirty Work*, a novel in which Brown clearly asserts that war respects members of no race: both Braiden and Walter, his white co-narrator, suffer equal ruin.

Brown, who grew up in north Mississippi during the Civil Rights era, has said that he was aware of racial prejudice as a young boy, but leaving the South and serving in the Marines helped to make him aware of racial injustice: "There's one word that's not allowed to be said in my house, and all my children know what that word is. It was common when I was raised, but I said, 'I'm going to change things.' It was simply I think from getting older and getting out of here, and then coming back and seeing things don't have to be this way. Things can be okay. I met all these great black guys on the Fire Department that I worked with, all these guys I really cared about. I think it's just a process of growing and getting older and finding out about the world around you" (qtd. in Bonetti audio). His novel *Dirty Work* centers on two Southern characters, Braiden Chaney, an African-American, and Walter James, a Caucasian. Though Walter is an obvious member of the lower class, the group most associated with intense racial prejudice, he expresses immediate concern for Braiden's helplessness. He knows about suffering, having had his face blown away and his brain permanently damaged. His concern for Braiden, therefore, has no racial component, is based only on shared humanity and mutual suffering and despair.

Suzanne Jones associates the bonding between the two veterans with that of Faulkner's Bayard Sartoris and Ringo Gibson in *The Unvanquished* (1938). Their friendships end when the young men mature, though; in *Dirty Work*, Braiden and Walter's friendship develops between them as adults because of their similar "war experiences, but more immediately [up]on coping with their debilitating injuries and their frustrated desires for more normal lives" (Jones 108). Brown, therefore, treats his black characters much as he does his white: their problems are not ones of race as much as of the socioeconomic characteristics of the area in which they live. Essentially the same, again, can be said of the lower-class whites with whom they interact.

Brown also depicted in his fiction the natural beauty of the South in which he was raised. He told one interviewer that living in the country shaped both his life and his writing. He particularly appreciated the enticements of rural life: "I love the land I was born to and I never tire of seeing the seasons and the weather change over" (Ketchin 112). On a similar note, he wrote in *On Fire* that "I live out in the county, out here in the land of the Big Sky country. I live at the edge of a river bottom, and the clouds can go all mushroomy and marshmallowy late in the afternoon and loom up big and white in the sky so that they can capture your attention" (26).

Brown also supported his son Billy Ray's desire to continue the tradition of farming on his grandparents' land, later even suffered alongside him as he struggled to establish a herd of cattle. Yardley has written that "Brown's view of animals is part utilitarian, part cold-eyed realist, part romantic. He knows that a steer will end up on the chopping block and then be ground into hamburger, he knows that that's the way of the world, and he hates it anyway." (C2).

Without nostalgia, Brown also admitted human responsibility for changes in the natural world. In *On Fire*, he writes, "Faulkner was right. He said the land would accomplish its own revenge on the people. I just wish it hadn't happened in my time" (64). Just as *Joe's* Joe Ransom knowingly destroys good trees in order to meet the demands of the Weyerhauser Corporation— which plans to "replace" the old hardwoods with scrub pines—Brown regretted his own role as a destroyer of the forest: "I used to do that for a part-time living. I'm not proud of what I did. I did it simply for the money, to feed my family" (Bonetti 242). In *Billy Ray's Farm*, Brown writes of the concern of Southern writers, himself included, with the land, as well as of their attempts to depict it and its inhabitants: "What we had in common was that we loved the land and the people we came from, and that our calling was to write about it as well as we could, to find our own voices through the years of learning, and to bring forth whole people whose lives surrounded us, whose stories were told by us, and who, for whatever length of time it took to compose a piece of fiction, *were us*" (37–38).

Larry Brown wrote with the kind of consummate ease that evolves from practice, a constant striving to improve. He often insisted that his writing ability was not innate but developed through dedicated effort. He said in one interview that "I do not see myself as naturally talented. Whatever talent I have has been developed through years of writing. I do not believe that anyone is born with a natural talent to write; I think it has to be developed. I also believe that simple language is most effective" (Robinson 3). One review of *Father and Son* seems to agree with his final point: "Brown writes in a sparse, lean and simple declarative English and his ear for dialogue doesn't miss a beat" (Levins C5). Brown also believed that the writer must always be concerned about the effect specific words create for the reader: "I want him to be right in the middle. I want it to be like a movie he's watching in his head and I'm the one who's supplying the pictures. I want him to be seeing everything and visualize everything; and whatever happens, I want him to feel it as fully as he can, as much as black words on white paper will transmit that. I want it to be as strong as possible" (LaRue 52–53).

Another area of particular interest to Brown as a writer was control of narrative voice. In his first collection of stories, *Facing the Music*, he experimented fairly widely with methods of getting his stories told. Four stories feature the working-class male narrators that readers have come to associate with him; he wrote "Kubuku Rides (This is It)," however, from the perspective of a young African-American alcoholic. "The Rich" and "Old Frank and Jesus" are written from the third-person-limited perspective, "Boy and Dog" is voiced by the young narrator of the story, and "Julie: A Memory" features stream-of-conscious narration. The dual perspective of *Dirty Work* shows something of Faulkner's influence; *Big Bad Love* features a variety of narrators similar to those in the first collection, but Brown ultimately became most comfortable with versions of shifting third-person-limited narration, as all of his later novels show.

Another stylistic feature that interested several critics, including Matthew Guinn in his chapter on Brown in *After Southern Modernism: Fiction of the Contemporary South*, is Brown's possible use of literary naturalism. Whether that use is conscious or not remains debatable, primarily because the kind of people Brown writes about live lives that seem naturalistic to educated readers. If the elements are there, they exist not because Brown said to himself, "I plan to use qualities of literary naturalism here," but because his characters—realistically presented—lead Southern versions of lives similar to those deliberately created by Frank Norris.

Working-class characters with immediate appeal—because of their skillful narrative presentation—Brown's ability as a storyteller, his strong and direct language, his powers of description, and his ability to maintain suspense are the qualities that drew readers to Brown's work in 1988 and have held their interest through a writing career that, sadly, ended all too soon.

The essays that follow address all ten of Brown's books, their relationship to the work of his literary forebears and contemporaries, their sympathetic portrayal of hard-luck Southerners in search of fulfillment, and of course, an array of other related subjects. Each essay, in one way or another, takes up the central concern of the collection, Brown's realistic and yet sympathetic portrayal of his blue-collar denizens of the Deep South. As my own essay details above, Brown himself spent much of his own life as part of this same demographic; his knowledge of its characters, their lives, their desires and their regrets is therefore unmatched in American fiction.

Darlin' Neal's essay on *Facing the Music* focuses on Brown's female characters, many of whom she finds victims of both the patriarchy in general and concepts of Southern masculinity in particular. Neal looks closely at how Brown's first collection overturns "the still-present Victorian mythologies of the angel in the house and the heroic male whose role it is to protect her": many of its stories, "by revealing the suffering still hidden beneath these myths, call into question the ethical and behavioral codes that govern a contemporary working-class vision of an idealized society." Robert Donahoo then examines *Dirty Work*, illustrating how the novel asks readers to willingly identify with the appalling situation that Walter James faces toward its end. Brown, Donahoo finds, not only "lays out a pattern of morally authorized involvement that demands Braiden's murder as its most logical culmination," but in so doing forces readers to confront "one of the central issues of Southern history." In my own essay on *Big Bad Love*, I argue that its often autobiographical stories ultimately characterize narrative art as a means to rare and hard-won fulfillment, a means by which a certain kind of man can save himself from what otherwise might be a life of hard drinking and desperate womanizing. As the narrators of three particular stories find out, though, attempting the leap from storyteller to published author can easily and perhaps irredeemably upset lives on several fronts, not the least of which is the domestic.

Jay Watson then examines Brown's novel *Joe*, in particular its focus on Southerners struggling to survive amid a landscape increasingly despoiled by an extractive timber industry. *Joe* is hardly the "straightforward poor-white fable of surrogate fatherhood and sonhood" it may seem, Watson argues, is instead a novel that contends that "conditions of economic stress and deprivation work not only to inhibit environmental awareness . . . but also, perhaps surprisingly, to create it." Thomas Ærvold Bjerre then situates *Father and Son* amid a literary and cinematic tradition rooted hundreds of miles west of Brown's Mississippi, asserting that the novel first adopts conventions of the Western—the indomitable landscape and a "distinct set of moral codes" among them—but ultimately subverts them in an effort to call readers' attention to "the value of the lives of the overlooked 'white trash' of America." Robert Beuka then focuses on *Fay*, treating its pervasive violence as a defining characteristic of Brown's postmodern South. "Adrift and isolated" as she walks its "unforgiving" highways, Fay ultimately becomes a symbol, Beuka finds, "of the South's forgetting itself," of "what happens when the shared traditions of the past fade away and ultimately dissolve into the random, aggressive, valueless contemporary environment."

Robert G. Barrier, in an essay on *On Fire* and *Billy Ray's Farm*, emphasizes Brown's lifelong search for balance between work, play, and rest, arguing that his many rides through the gloam in both nonfiction volumes embody elements of all three pursuits: in that they are journeys "to the farthest reaches of home, just close enough for familiarity and yet far enough away for independence," they represent themes of "controlled exuberance and testing the open road, yet returning home when it's all over." In his essay on *The Rabbit Factory*, Richard Gaughran contends that the novel "presupposes but ultimately disproves the argument that contemporary life inevitably and irreversibly reduces the individual to pure commodity." Even in its "most grotesque images, its most darkly comic passages," Gaughran finds, the novel "celebrates the basic human desire for connection—even as, at the same time, it acknowledges the profound obstacles that can make such connections . . . difficult to achieve, much less maintain." John A. Staunton then takes up Brown's "final and forever unfinished" novel *A Miracle of Catfish*, characterizing its author as both "an ethnographer of those struggling to negotiate life at the edge" and a "participant-observer . . . invested in the outcome of his characters." Brown, Staunton argues, wants his readers invested in those outcomes as well—for his characters' fates, he contends, could also be our own—"so we can possibly save ourselves from going along with or giving in to" the forces that so disrupt their lives.

My co-editor Keith Perry then tracks the evolution of the Larry Brown(s) that Algonquin Books of Chapel Hill "built" for promotional campaigns and that reviewers and journalists then "built" for author profiles and book reviews. Perry finds that "one of the best gauges of [Brown's] reputation as a writer is . . . the lack of representation that references his early years and all but one of the ways he made his living as an adult, is thus his publicists' and reviewers' abilities to bypass 'Larry Brown, the fireman writer'—if not the Oxford native, the sharecropper's son, the former marine, or any of his other extraliterary incarnations—to tell their readers about 'Larry Brown, writer.'" The collection concludes with the transcript of a 2003 interview with filmmaker Gary Hawkins concerning his award-winning documentary *The Rough South of Larry Brown* (2002). As does the entire collection, the Hawkins interview, conducted by Katherine Powell, offers insight into Brown's life and work as well as the north Mississippi milieu of them both.

Works Cited

Bledsoe, Erik. "The Rise of Southern Redneck and White Trash Writers." *Southern Culture* 6.1 (Spring 2000): 68–90.

Bonetti, Kay. *Larry Brown: A Conversation with Kay Bonetti*. American Audio Prose Library, 1995.

———. "Larry Brown (1995)." *Conversations with American Novelists: The Best Interviews from the Missouri Review and the American Audio Prose Library*. Ed. Bonetti, et al. Columbia: U of Missouri P, 1997. 234–53.

Brown, Larry. *A Late Start*. Chapel Hill: Algonquin, 1989.

———. *Billy Ray's Farm: Essays from a Place Called Tula*. Chapel Hill: Algonquin, 2001.

———. *On Fire: A Personal Account of Life and Death and Choices*. Chapel Hill: Algonquin, 1994.

Brown, Mary Annie. "Our Family Farm." *Algonquin Books of Chapel Hill*. 1 Apr. 2001. http://www.algonquin.com/larrybrown/larry17a.html.

Douglas, Ellen. Personal interview. 5 July 2006.

Guinn, Matthew. *After Southern Modernism: Fiction of the Contemporary South*. Jackson: UP of Mississippi, 2000.

Hudson, Berkley. "Country Boy Hits Big Time." *Los Angeles Times* 17 Sept. 1989: VI, 1+.

Jones, Suzanne. "Refighting Old Wars: Race Relations and Masculine Conventions in Fiction by Larry Brown and Madison Smartt Bell." *The Southern State of Mind*. Ed. Jan Nordby Gretlund. Columbia: U of South Carolina P, 1999: 107–20.

Ketchin, Susan. "Larry Brown: Interview." *The Christ-Haunted Landscape: Faith and Doubt in Southern Fiction*. Ed. Ketchin. Jackson: UP of Mississippi, 1994. 126–39.

LaRue, Dorie. "Interview with Larry Brown: Breadloaf '92." *Chattahoochee Review* 13.3 (Spring 1993): 39–56.

Levins, Harry. "This Year's Best Thriller Has Arrived." Rev. of *Father and Son*, by Larry Brown. *St. Louis Post-Dispatch* 22 Sept. 1996: C5.

Mantell, Suzanne. "Larry Brown: Son of the Literary South." *Publishers Weekly Online*. 2 June 1997. http://www.bookwire.com/Expo97/Interviews.article$1091.

O'Briant, Don. "Writer Larry Brown: In Faulkner's Footsteps." *Atlanta Journal-Constitution* 9 Apr. 2000: L1+.

Parsons, Alexander. "Waiting in the Gloam: An Interview with Author Larry Brown." *UNoMAS*. 31 May 2003. http://www.unomas.com/features/larrybrown.html.

Richardson, Thomas J. "Larry Brown." *Contemporary Fiction Writers of the South*. Ed. Joseph M. Flora and Robert Bain. Westport: Greenwood, 1994. 55–66.

Robinson, Charles. "Interview with Larry Brown." *Mississippi Writers and Musicians Project of Starkville High School*. 31 May 2003. http://shs.ee.msstate.edu/mswm/MSWritersAndMusicians/write.html.

Ross, Jean W. "*Contemporary Authors* Interview with Larry Brown, 13 March 1990." *Contemporary Authors*. Vol. 134. Ed. Susan M. Trosky. Detroit: Gale, 1992. 88–91.

Skube, Michael. "Straight from the heart." *y'all.com*. 1 Feb. 2001. http://www.accessatlanta.com/global/local/yall/culture/quilll/brownl/brown2.html.

Summer, Bob. "Author's popularity is poised to expand." *Richmond Times-Dispatch* 3 Nov. 1991: F4.

Weinraub, Judith. "The Back-Roads Blue-Collar Artiste: Mississippi's Larry Brown, Bent on Becoming a True Voice of American Fiction." *Washington Post* 9 Dec. 1990: F1+.

Yardley, Jonathan. "Cow Sense." Rev. of *Billy Ray's Farm: Essays from a Place Called Tula*, by Larry Brown. *Washington Post* 29 Mar. 2001: C2.

LARRY BROWN

and the Blue-Collar South

Facing the Music

What's Wrong with All Those Happy Endings

DARLIN' NEAL

> Our propaganda machines are always trying to teach us, to per-
> suade us, to hate and fear other people on the same little world that
> we live in. (92) —**Tennessee Williams**

Reviews of *Facing the Music* (1988), Larry Brown's debut collection of short stories, rarely make more than passing mention of its female characters. When anonymous reviewers wrote in *Publishers Weekly* that its contents "pierce the macho armor" (40) or in *Antioch Review* that the stories are "uncluttered by any attempt at literary effect" (115), they ignored Brown's deliberate use of Southern gothic narrative strategies to deconstruct the still-present Victorian mythologies of the angel in the house and the heroic male whose role it is to protect her. The stories in *Facing the Music*, by revealing the suffering still hidden beneath these myths, call into question the ethical and behavioral codes that govern a contemporary working-class vision of an idealized society. The collection focuses on the private lives of lower-class Mississippians who fail to find meaning through adherence to the rigid roles this mythology prescribes. Brown, furthermore, sets a stage of gothic confinement in which the mythology traps characters in front of television and movie screens and reveals how the rigid divide of the other, in the spheres of both rich and poor, both male and female, serves as a continuing means of imprisonment. In piercing that macho armor, he does not represent female otherness as a threat to be conquered along the way to story resolve, nor do male characters sweep women aside as objects obstructing the path toward defending male honor. Instead, in such stories as "Night Life," "Leaving Town," and "Kubuku Rides (This Is It)," women remain strong forces. Brown foregrounds these women's pain to reveal the home as something indeed other than that Victorian notion of a haven; nor do the homes

3

in these stories serve as enriching forces for the working-class society they ideally uphold.

Clancy Sigal has argued in *Washington Post Book World* that Brown finds no "redemption" possible for these "Third-World Americans" (11), but I disagree. By directing our gaze toward the afflicted lives of those imprisoned in rural towns, Brown invariably humanizes them. Barry Walters, reviewing the collection for the *Village Voice*, noted the startling complexity that readers discover within these lives, concluding that he found within them the reality that the underclass is just as troubled as the rest of "us" (56). As that anonymous reviewer, again, wrote in *Antioch Review*, when Brown captures "in flashlight photos" a "homeless mother, a man contemplating suicide, a wife-beater, a teenaged killer," it "mak[es] for blinding recognition" (115), recognition he uses to problematize his readers' assumptions about class and gender. The redemption Sigal missed thus comes, and not only from the humanization of these characters but through what we as readers learn about the common nature of human suffering. Close inspection of these "flashlight photos" in *Facing the Music*, then, exposes the discontent hidden beneath pop-culture fantasies of the American dream.

In "Facing the Music," the collection's first story, the marital bed itself becomes the scene of gothic confinement. What drives the story is the fact that the husband, because of his wife's recent mastectomy, would rather watch television than make love to her. She believes herself undesirable—she tells him, "I'm not a whole woman anymore. I'm just a burden on you" (8)—but she also believes that if she can lose weight, she will be attractive to him again. The husband/narrator talks to the reader from the bed he shares with her and tells us that, because of his inability to make love to her, he sees himself as low as Ray Milland's character in Billy Wilder's *The Lost Weekend* (1945)—the movie he is watching on TV—a man who would sell his own children for a drink. "Don't feel like a lone ranger, Ray," he says (8). "That old boy, he's trying to do what he knows he should." Ray, obviously, is not the only one who has "responsibilities to people who love him and need him" and is at the same time "scared to death" (9). Recalling his honeymoon in Hattiesburg, however, the husband then tells us that nothing has changed in the way his wife gives herself so wholly to him. Like the iconic domestic angel, she is giving; unlike that domestic angel, though, she does not suffer silently. In that "Facing the Music" is filled with this pain of the wife's desire and the need and tension it creates—the husband knows neither how to meet it nor how to be a hero with the painful reality of that moral center laid so bare—the woman's pain humanizes her for the reader as the narrator loses belief in his ability to be heroic in the face of his sexual responsibility. The story thus dispels the happily-ever-after fantasy of the hero and the angel, and for both characters and readers alike. In that it ends with the husband and wife reaching "to find each other in the darkness like people who are blind" (9), though, it adds a new voice to the dominant narrative, reveals a hope in starting over—minus the happily-ever-after fantasy—as the characters grope to meet raw reality. The dominant narrative may blind them, but they reach out to one another through its darkness.

Now, though, the acknowledgement of vulnerability has unmasked the human beings behind the myth. The problem lies not in their love but with the romantic fantasy. There simply is no happily-ever-after: there are only cancer and longing and the struggle to survive. As the husband had put it earlier, "You can lie around the house all your life and think you're safe. But you're not. Something from outside or inside can reach out and get you. You can get sick and have to go to the hospital. Some nut could walk into the station one night and kill us all in our beds. You can read about things like that in the paper any morning you want to. I try not to think about it. I just do my job and then come home and try to stay in the house with her. But sometimes I can't" (4). The myth proclaims the triumphs of the romantic hero and the domestic angel, the haven of the domestic circle, but, in reality, no such triumph takes place, not for either of them. She's no domestic angel, he's no romantic hero, and their domestic circle offers no haven.

The story's narrator, moreover, alludes again and again to the way the television screen conveys the apparent truths of our time and thereby overwhelms our own voices. "I don't say anything when I cut the TV off. I can't speak" (9), he says near the end of the story, and this statement comes after his telling us that "There are probably a lot of people like me, unable to sleep, lying around watching [late-night movies] with me" (1). In the world of popular culture, spectators consume hour after hour of unattainable images on the television screen, images of men who rarely fail as heroes—the detectives on *Dragnet*, which Mr. P. watches in "Old Frank and Jesus"—images of men and women who never fail to find their happily-ever-after—the passengers on *The Love Boat*, which the narrator watches in "Leaving Town." Like gothic novels, moreover, Brown's stories create a voyeuristic affect as readers peer at these spectacles who sit inside their homes in front of these television sets. The underclass continually encounters the accepted truths of their time on the television and in the movies, and as Terry Eagleton explains, the ideologies of these everyday media push their viewers toward "some more desirable state of affairs in which men and women would feel less helpless, fearful, and bereft of meaning" (184).

As pop-culture consumers, these Southerners thus stave off the need to participate in and hold an intangible place in a larger, invisible community. The narrator of "Facing the Music" says that he would feel better if his wife would just watch the movie with him instead of staring out the window or wanting him to look at her. He does not want to see her suffering. Through movies and television, though, Brown's characters feel only one-sided connections. They worship what they cannot have as they search for an escape into a fantasy world where hillbillies find oil and heroic detectives never fail to solve crimes and exact justice. Brown's characters, as collective viewers of this cultural ideology, fail to find true escape or meaning, for the so-called truths that television offers provide no tangible sustenance for the social or spiritual deprivation of the working class. In "Kubuku Rides (This Is It)," when Angel tunes in to televised church services on Sunday mornings, she only gets "all depressed" and "passed out before dinnertime" (19). The male narrator of "Leaving Town" says he can't stay interested in *The Love Boat* because "There were too many happy endings on it. Everybody always found just exactly what they were looking for" (151). They remain unaware of the fact, but their unhappiness derives in part from their continuing imprisonment by the cultural mythology, disseminated by just such media.

In "Kubuku Rides (This Is It)," the second story in the collection, the romantic fantasy has disappointed the aptly-named protagonist, Angel, as well. The narrator tells us that she "[w]ouldn't never think on her wedding night it ever be like this. She in the living room by herself, he in the kitchen by himself. TV on, she ain't watching it, some fool on Johnny Carson telling stuff ain't even funny. She ain't got the sound on. Ain't hear nothing, ain't see nothing. She hear him like choke in there once in a while" (26). Angel remains trapped in inarticulate silence in front of the television even though she knows she will find no meaning there. She sits emotionally paralyzed. Her marriage has not brought her happiness, she has not magically transformed into the iconic domestic angel, and she knows no way out, searching for relief and solace through alcohol. Her failure to heal, as Brown reveals in the final moment of the story, comes in part from her failure to dispel the romantic myth. As she prepares to drive off for yet another six-pack, the porch light illuminates "her home, this warm place she own that mean everything to her. This light, it always on for her. That what she thinking," Brown writes, "when it go out" (31). Part of Angel's stagnation stems from her inability to realize that that light will *not* always be on for her, from her inability to shake her belief in the myth. When the porch light does goes out, the reader not only knows that she is mistaken, but is left to ponder whether, indeed, she will ever make it back or will have another car accident, one she may not survive this time. Once again, by doubting the notion of the angel as domestic moral center, Brown questions the security and stability inherent in the false promises of the dominant narrative. The word "angel" itself even takes on new connotations. Angel's deep unhappiness leaves her anything but the blissful moral center of the story. Brown again reveals the degree to which the dominant American narrative remains Victorian in its definitions of marriage, the hero, and the woman's place in the ideal society. For Angel, as for the husband and wife in "Facing the Music," the Victorian narratives of the conquering hero and the domestic angel are prisons she seeks to escape.

When Angel steps out of her designated role as housewife and mother and into the local bar, though, we see her not as a mere object of the male gaze but as a psychologically wounded woman. Yet as readers enter her perspective, others look upon her as a spectacle. Her friends leave because they refuse to "hang around and watch this self-destruction" (19). Strangers read her intentions incorrectly as they watch the spectacle she creates. "This one wimp done even come over to the table, he just assume she lonesome and want some male company, he think he gonna come over like he Robert Goulet or somebody and just invite himself to sit down" (20). She ponders suicide and thinks of how, if she goes through with it, people will see it from the outside: the community will see it as "[j]ust a tragedy," and her "brief pain" will end the long suffering they/we know nothing of until Brown turns the surface gaze of a tragedy into a shared experience (23). In her contemplation of suicide she expresses a desire to slip away with all her secrets in place. She says that while her husband believes their house to be clean, it isn't: "House ain't clean. Lots of places to hide things, you want to hide them bad enough. Ain't like Easter eggs, like Christmas presents. Like life and death" (26). Her own secrets derive, of course, from pop culture's reading not of spiritual mythology about resurrection and birth, but the shame and suffering that result from secret alcoholism.

The depiction of such women's suffering helps articulate what their language cannot. Angel does not speak a language of protest, but her actions and body do. She does not remain silent and unseen in her house but, by stepping out and becoming a spectacle, she shatters that silence, revealing to the reader her unbearable loneliness, poverty, and pain—even though, according to the dominant narrative, she *should* have everything she wants. She has the child and the loving husband and the house, but, as Brown illustrates by way of her near-inarticulate dialect, her actions, and the disparity between her desires and her reality, she becomes before the reader a broken and devastatingly sad woman.

Brown also reveals in the collection how the causes of women's sadness and confusion affect the men and children around them. When the wife in "Facing the Music" suffers the mutilation of cancer and invasiveness of surgery, her husband wants the reader to understand that the shattering of the illusion of security hurts them both. He speaks of how burdened he feels by everything she wants from him, which on the surface feel like very simple things: to talk to her, to make love to her. But he wants the reader to understand that what has happened has hurt them both. He realizes that he cannot protect her, and it scares him "to death" (9).

Brown's vivid portrayals of such characters as the mutilated wife in "Facing the Music," Angel in "Kubuku Rides," the crippled child in "Leaving Town," and the child who causes the car wreck in "Boy and Dog" all serve to reveal truths beneath class and gender divisions as well as to humanize the inherent suffering that pop culture works to hide. His community of the marginalized—people in bars, bedrooms, workplaces, kitchens, roadsides, and living rooms—forces the reader to even further question the nature of the hero and the suffering woman. In "Leaving Town," Brown shifts back and forth from Myra's to Richard's point of view, allowing us inside each. We find that for Myra, the class barrier is impregnable, for when Richard, beaten and drunken, turns to her as she had earlier turned to him, she pushes him away, seeing him as the monstrous figure from which she must protect herself. As the woman in his home, Betty represents the domestic center in Richard's life, yet we discover that she refuses to work, neglects the home and her child. The narrative solution to their problem does not end up as just hers. Richard thus embodies a new kind of hero, not someone who conquers those weaker than himself but a nurturing center who takes a crippled little girl to find a new home where he can raise her with love in the absence of her callous mother. By putting us inside these two perspectives, Brown again allows readers to see a reality behind the mythologies of the angel in the house and the romantic hero. As he put it himself, he causes readers to question "what really was occurring, what was fantasy and what was reality" (Ketchin 138).

Brown forces us to question the ideological framework of the larger cultural narrative not only by deconstructing the magical thought surrounding the domestic angel and hero but by creating a triangulation that furthers reader involvement in the process. He accomplishes this in two ways: first, by directly addressing the reader, and second, by focusing on the female character, leaving readers to decide her punishment, her literal or figurative "beating." Central to the work are Brown's depictions of women in scenes of suffering, such as Myra in "Leaving Town," who ends up on her knees, picking up shards of glass and longing for tenderness from Richard, or the woman Gary looks for in "Night Life," "one who is sitting by herself, who is maybe a little older than most, maybe even one who doesn't look very good" (101). Brown shows us that we have not moved far beyond either that patriarchal culture of shame and honor in which gothic women are the objects of our gaze or what Foucault defines as the spectacle of the scaffold, that ritual of public execution that historically was a means of establishing hierarchical order. The belief held that torture both reveals truth and demonstrates the workings of power through the body of the condemned. Of course, danger occurs to an established hierarchy when the sentence turns back on itself and reveals an unexpected truth. In the same metaphorical sense, if we look at the bodies of the suffering women in *Facing the Music*, we find the reasons for their condemnation problematized. The title character of "Julie: A Memory" does not ask to be raped. Myra was a good wife, and yet her husband beat her. Unlike a narrative that upholds the traditional mythology and clearly depicts women who step out of traditional roles, Brown's stories do not uphold the status quo's definition of what constitutes shame and honor. If the stories represent the collective culture's fantasies about what constitutes justice, the author leads us to an interpretation that reveals unexpected consequences. When Brown puts women on the scaffold—or, perhaps better said, directs the reader's gaze to women whom traditional beliefs have put on the scaffold—he subverts the traditional message. In all but three stories of the ten (I will later show how "Boy and Dog," "Old Frank and Jesus," and "The Rich" further these themes), Brown presents a gallery of women who step outside the boundaries of traditional roles—alcoholic Angel, divorced Myra, soon-to-be-divorced Connie, raped Julie, and the beggar woman drinking in the bar in "Samaritans." As they step out of these roles, they shake the very foundation, again, of cultural views about the nature of the angel in the house.

Connie, from "Night Life," for instance, embodies both victimizer, a woman who neglects her children, and victim, a woman whom Gary would have beaten regardless of reason. Still, when Gary expresses a reason—that she leaves her children alone—and subsequently acts on his violent urge, Brown creates discomfort in the reader. He deliberately draws us into participating as spectators, deliberately engages us in the question of what Connie deserves and what right Gary has to enact some form of justice in that moment. In blurring this line between spectacle and spectator, Brown also calls into question the detachment and paralysis of observing. What blame does the community in "Julie: A Memory" hold for her rape when they sit listening to their television sets and blot out her cries for rescue? As the onlookers gather in "Boy and Dog," the narrator says, "Somebody needed to get help." The problem, however, is that "Some people won't get involved" (65). As readers peek into cars, bedrooms, and bars, the lines between rape and consensual sex, murder and justice continually blur. Class and gender lines remain largely stable, but Brown's work disputes their validity.

The characters' physical qualities in *Facing the Music* reveal their inner terrors and, as those terrors emerge, Brown reveals what the class system turns the underclass into: men with backs bent from menial labor, little girls who reach out to be carried because they cannot walk, women who wear age and infertility as a scar. When Angel sees herself "in the rearview mirror, she don't know her own self. Look like something in a monster movie. She screaming now. Face cut all to pieces. She black out again. She come to, she out on the ground. People helping her up. She screaming I'm ruint I'm ruint" (24–25). Angel feels guilt throughout the story for her inability to give up her addiction and get on with cooking dinner and cleaning the house, but she feels destroyed when she fears losing her looks. As is also the case for the breast cancer victim in "Facing the Music," becoming undesirable is her greatest fear. Even as the cultural narrative tells her to be selfless and patient and absent of desire, nothing is worse for the domestic angel than becoming physically undesirable.

The suffering women and failed working-class heroes are aware that the class system considers them spectacles, and this awareness only further entraps them. They wish to avoid the spotlight. Myra wants to shop only in uncrowded supermarkets, and only at night, "when the stores aren't full of people." When she encounters in one "a girl with a sweatshirt and blue jeans and fuzzy blue house shoes," she says, "I wouldn't be caught dead out like that" (155). When she sees Richard and becomes so full of longing that she absentmindedly knocks over a display, she says, "people stepped out of the aisles to look at me. I was trying to think of something to say. I didn't look over my shoulder to see if Richard was watching. I was scared of what I might see" (156). What she fears seeing, of course, is herself as a spectacle in his eyes. The narrator of "Facing the Music" relates similarly to Ray Milland's character from *The Lost Weekend*: "I know they're all going to be waiting for him, the whole club. I know what he's going to feel. Everybody's going to be looking at him" (6). Angel knows the spectacle she makes as she thinks of herself as a freakish figure on display. "[S]he look like somebody afflicted. . . . she done gone in the liquor store so many times she ashamed to. She see these same people and she know they thinking: Damn, this woman done been in here four times this week. Drinking like a fish" (21). These characters thus feel the weight and power of all those eyes trying to shame them back into their placated, invisible roles.

Men and women alike in these stories serve and worry about the larger culture that ignores their reality, and in the process they become erased from power by their subservient participation in the hierarchy. Between men and women, a blinding worship of the other obscures reality. Brown's characters search for a place to worship, to understand what worship and powerlessness mean. "I don't mean anything against God by saying this," the husband in "Facing the Music" tells us, "but sometimes I thinks she worships me" (2). Angel "love her husband like God love Jesus" (13). In "Julie: A Memory," the narrator describes the raped girlfriend's body as "the temple where I worshipped" (84). Such worship, based as it is on hierarchical divisions, keeps the rigid divide in place. If men and women appear to each other as heroes or angels, the fantasy continues to shackle and render them incapable of effecting a change of place in the hierarchy.

When men put women on pedestals or women expect men to manage the power, the fantasy and objectification of men and women alike create imprisonment. Conforming to specific gender roles works much the same as conforming to specific class boundaries because, in creating a more complete picture, Brown reveals not only outward but inward forces that create the cultural power system. Women give power to men. The poor give power to the rich. Mr. Pellisher, the travel agent in "The Rich," serves wealthy clients who "don't look back" as he waves (40). He feeds the dream only for those in the upper class who own the nice houses with elaborate security systems and drive off in nice cars, but it's not a dream that he believes can be made real for him, even though he sees the falsity of the arrangement, of the reality foregrounded under current conditions. Mr. Pellisher, that is, "knows the rich are not different from himself. They are not of another race, another creed, another skin. They do not worship a different God" (35–36). Yet the barrier remains. The same sort of servitude and a trust in the system destroy Mr. P. in "Old Frank and Jesus." He "needs to be up and out in the cotton patch, trying to pull the last bolls off the stalks, but the bottom's dropped out because foreign rayon's ruined the market" (42). He serves an economic system that has betrayed him. His isn't a world in which justice makes the kind of sense it does on the TV shows that those who come to his house for haircuts watch. There is no neat, easy justice like that on *Dragnet* or *Perry Mason*. And yet, still, he and his customers continue to watch. They get caught up in the opening credits of *The Beverly Hillbillies* and stay in the house until the shows are over.

Brown's stories destroy the illusion of race, gender, and class boundaries, tearing apart the illusion of domination up and down the chain of being. Hierarchical worship renders all characters powerless. They are as vulnerable and given to worship as their dogs—the dog in "Samaritans" who, if he'd just stayed down, would have been all right, the dog in "Old Frank and Jesus," who didn't see the betrayal coming. Mr. P. shoots his dog "because his wife said the rabies were getting too close to home" (47). The final straw for Mr. P. comes when he realizes what he has done in the name of domestic safety. Mr. P. betrays Frank just as the larger culture betrays him. As Mr. P. prepares to commit suicide, he thinks, "Old Frank has already gone through this. He didn't understand it. He trusted Mr. P. and knew he'd never hurt him. Maybe Mr. P. was a father to him. Maybe Mr. P. was God to him. What could he have been thinking of when he shot his best friend?" (57). The hierarchy Mr. P. trusted has betrayed him, and now he has done the same thing to Old Frank. His grief over the loss of his loyal friend and the realization that he has internalized what oppresses him soon become unbearable.

Figurative violence trickles down as those who are dominant change places with those who are subordinate. In "Boy and Dog," firemen feel shame as "Bystanders muttered about their incompetence." But when the ambulance pulls up, the "firemen acted very important. / They bullied the ambulance attendants" (68). The alternative world of pop-culture offers the bystanders a chance to change places with the stars who have achieved the American Dream or with characters in television shows or movies, where everything works out in the end. The bystanders get excited over the possibility of becoming celebrities interviewed on the evening news. As the narrator explains, "Several people were interrogated live. / They rushed home to brag. / They were almost real celebrities. / They would phone their neighbors. / They would phone their friends. / Neighbors and friends would watch" (69). Interestingly, the spectacle of the man in the Mustang burning to death, a man who was more concerned with finding a hubcap than with killing a dog, mesmerizes them all. None notice the child and his dead dog; even the child's mother cannot see as she calls from her kitchen doorway. They focus on the horror show of the man burning to death. Brown, though, directs his readers' attention to the crowd, their worrying over who is shameful and who is honorable, over what illusion will be played out on television. Not only do they fail to see the child and dog, but they will never know what caused the accident. Through the juxtaposition of the child who has defended his dog and the man who tries to save the burning body, Brown again challenges the nature of the hero. A hero is not someone who merely goes through the outward motions, not merely what we might expect when we see him from the outside. More is required. "He was evidently a hero" describes a man going through the motions but who is too incompetent and too ignorant to save a life (64). Again, we do not witness a reification of the word "hero" as much as we are challenged to define it for ourselves.

The most horrifying moments in *Facing the Music* come when the culture silences characters to the point that they become incapable of affecting the world around them in significant ways or of helping one another avoid the dangerous, shadowy living rooms and motel beds lit now and then by the glow of television screens. While Julie is raped, the narrator says, "People were watching television within sight of us." He cannot "understand why nobody was coming to help us" (77). Mr. Pellisher is filled with murderous rage toward the rich, whose handshakes "are limp, without feeling, devoid of emotion" (34). He dreams of their alternative reality, of what it must be like "to live in a world so high above the everyday human struggles of the race" (37), and his comment, "The rich are rich" (33), compares to that from the woman in "Samaritans": "It's some people in the world that has got thangs and some that ain't" (95). Part of what imprisons these characters, in short, is their belief in the impenetrability of these distinctions.

Brown, again, forces us to question what is real and what is not in the patriarchal model of social relations. "Samaritans" begins with a homeless child stepping over the threshold of a bar. "And of course," the narrator says, "that's not allowed" (87). Try as he does to avoid involvement in the situation, he ends up sitting in the bar, buying drinks for the grotesque woman in the dirty slip and nasty house shoes who thanks him with, "Ain't many men'll hep out a woman in trouble.... Specially when she's got a buncha kids" (95). She questions the hero's motives. Most would not want to help an undesirable lower-class woman with a bunch of kids who belong to someone else. The narrator says, "I felt like I feel when I see those commercials on TV, of all those people, women and kids, starving to death in Ethiopia and places, and I don't send money. I know that Jesus wants *you* to help feed the poor" (99; italics mine). What he sees deceives him: a homeless woman with children out searching for her husband. He reads her as powerless, himself as the hero who will help her, but he ends up being a "dumb sumbitch" (100), as the woman's oldest son puts it, for he gives her money and watches her go back into the bar with her mother. He is a "dumb sumbitch" not because he responds to, but because he misreads, the woman. She is outside the home and wayward, but not helpless, and her natural desires do not lead her to take care of her children. She wants the same thing the narrator wants, a good time and another drink.

Brown seeks to unravel the intertwining of working-class male identity from the elite culture of honor and shame, and, as mentioned earlier, he does so most clearly in "Night Life," by way of the predatory character Gary, who literally looks for a woman to beat. Gary searches in the bar "outside the city limits" for a spectacle/obstacle to put on the scaffold (101). When he finds Connie, he does not realize that it is a wayward, upper-middle-class housewife whom he has put there. She obscures lines of class for both Gary and the reader by being in that bar and by deferring to a man like Gary. When she refuses to have sex with him that first night, she apologizes, and he says, "She's talking like she did something wrong. But all she did was refuse to take her pants off. In a public parking lot. Where anybody could have walked up to the car and looked in, seen her in all her naked glory for free" (111). Upon his visit to her house, the reader shares his surprise at what he finds on Willow Lane: as his friend had said, "there ain't nothing but rich people live up in here" (123). He complicates the code of honor further when he expresses discomfort for standing "[o]n another man's concrete" (124), and as he appears to protest entering that home, he says, "I feel myself to be an intruder in this house, a homewrecker. The husband, the father, could come home and kill me this minute with a shotgun. Nothing would be said. No jury would convict the man. I don't belong here" (124–25). Upon his discovery that Connie has been leaving her two little girls alone, though, the lines completely blur, and he finds what he has been looking for: justification for beating her. A twenty-eight-year-old mechanic, out on probation, who lives with his mother thus becomes the defender of the domestic fantasy. By neglecting her children, upper-middle class Connie gives lowlife Gary a societally condoned reason to punish her. The distinction between observer and observed only *seems* to exist, then. Readers stand aside and watch as Gary again presents his "noble" intentions, promising to keep his hands open so as not to frighten the little girls and give them something terrible to remember for the rest of their lives. He thereby also complicates the code by creating that voyeuristic sense in readers who are part of the community at large, by causing them to step over cultural boundaries that define shame and honor. In this moment, Brown again causes readers to probe the gender/class implications of the scene of the scaffold. Gary may be a poor man in a rich man's territory, but his intention, of course, is still to promote white male dominance.

In each story in *Facing the Music*, the gallery of characters persists in the search for meaningful connection. Upper-class Myra and working-class Richard, from "Leaving Town," come closest to realizing one—but that realization does not come in the form of requited romance. As the point of view shifts from Myra to Richard, the illusion of their uniqueness shatters not only for Myra, but for the reader as well. She says, "Nobody thinks the things I think" (152), as she contemplates her loneliness, but she soon finds that Richard does—this man who, because he comes from the working class, is a stranger to her, and yet is also kin to her because he suffers as she does within the class system. Work as he might, he cannot make enough money to do anything more than survive. And though she has lived angelically in a house that continually looks clean, her husband beat her and finally left her alone. Myra and Richard also break barriers—between rich and poor, between older woman and younger man—impenetrable in the Victorian mythology. She believes herself undesirable, but Richard says, "I wanted to take all her clothes off gently and touch her whole body and make her happy. I wanted to heal her" (150). But they do not make love. The reader experiences the heartbreak the barriers of the mythology cause because, through the turns in point of view, we know how much each one needs the other. The alternating narratives thus allow readers to share the longing of the back-broken hero and the shattered, abandoned angel. In many ways they remain foreign to each other—he is the frightening, beaten figure that comes back to her door late at night, she the desperate woman full of desire for him, more fragile than anyone he has seen. Yet, meeting her empowers Richard to leave Betty. He will be the nurturer to the little girl who is not his own through blood but through love and a common experience of abandonment and vulnerability. He will try to find a new home and make a new start; he thinks, "I had Myra's number in my pocket and I thought I might call her when we got to where we were going. I thought I might wish her some luck" (157). Breaking that barrier—the illusion that the rich are other—and going inside the home and seeing this lonely, desperate woman, offers him the onset of healing. Myra is not an obstacle swept aside in a male narrative but an empowering final image, the subject of Richard's last thought in the story.

The female images in *Facing the Music* prove central to uncovering its revolutionary focus, and that is no accident. The collection came out the same year that Frederick Barthelme's article "On Being Wrong: Convicted Minimalist Spills Bean" appeared in the *New York Times Book Review* and signaled the end of postmodernism as writers again realized that human beings are more compelling than language. There was no going back, however. How empty was realism. How "full of lies, falsifications of experience for the sake of drama—which was paradoxical since it purported to be representation" (26). What writers like Brown became interested in was using a little of both, of representation and realism, to create an intimate sense of experience. Brown's writing is no accident. His precise and careful use of language works like "people rolling down windows to get a whiff of what's out there." He gives us no "made-simple versions of political and moral issues that bad writers and good TV journalists are so fond of[;] you've got to use the language carefully, so that you get more than just language. It's hard, but when it works it blows you away, not because you have *the* world on the page but because you have *a* world, palpable, compelling, frightening" (26). In both his life and his writing Larry Brown was a revolutionary. He entered into the dialectic conversation and changed the dominant narrative, showed us how education and art belong to us all. Brown takes us beneath the spectacle and reveals what really is "out there." It may be a gender-bound activity of looking and being looked upon, but as Brown's men and women step out of the places the dominant culture designates for them, they change the nature of both the gothic hero and the angel in the house and blur class lines as well.

Works Cited

Barthelme, Frederick. "On Being Wrong: Convicted Minimalist Spills Bean." *New York Times Book Review* 3 Apr. 1988: 1.

Bonetti, Kay. *Larry Brown: A Conversation with Kay Bonetti*. American Audio Prose Library, 1995.

Brown, Larry. *Facing the Music*. Chapel Hill: Algonquin, 1988.

Eagleton, Terry. *Ideology: An Introduction*. London: Verso, 1991.

Rev. of *Facing the Music*, by Larry Brown. *Antioch Review* 47.1 (1989): 115.

Rev. of *Facing the Music*, by Larry Brown. *Publishers Weekly* 8 July 1988: 40.

Ketchin, Susan. "Larry Brown: Interview." *The Christ-Haunted Landscape: Faith and Doubt in Southern Fiction*. Ed. Ketchin. Jackson: UP of Mississippi, 1994. 126–39.

Sigal, Clancy. "Looking for Love in All the Wrong Places." Rev. of *Big Bad Love*, by Larry Brown. *Washington Post Book World* 23 Dec. 1990: 11.

Walters, Barry. "Down on the Farm." Rev. of *Facing the Music*, by Larry Brown. *Village Voice* 22 Nov. 1989: 56.

Williams, Tennessee. "The World I Live In: Tennessee Williams Interviews Himself." *Where I Live: Selected Essays*. Ed. Christine R. Day and Bob Woods. New York: New Directions, 1978. 88–92.

Implicating the Reader

Dirty Work and the Burdens of Southern History

ROBERT DONAHOO

In *After Southern Modernism: Fiction of the Contemporary South*, Matthew
Guinn takes note of the problem that Larry Brown's fiction poses for traditional Southern literary critics nurtured on the techniques and ideologies
of such figures as Cleanth Brooks. For Guinn, Brown's "particular attention
to the oppressive hierarchies of [the Southern] community is something
new that cannot be assimilated into orthodox reading strategies" (36). Addressing Brown's connection to the lower-class Southern experience, Guinn
writes, "Brown does not fit the old paradigms by which critics have defined
Southern Renascence literature. One may indeed find in Brown's work the
conventional motifs of loyalty to place, attention to dialect and local color,
elaborate codes of honor, and the dominance of tradition, but these are all
altered or inverted by the author's familiarity with the poor southerner's
experience—a perspective not incorporated into the codified, modernist
checklist of a work's 'southernness'" (37). For Guinn, the best response to
this problem is to read Brown's fiction in terms of a "New Naturalism."
However, it's difficult to envision such a move as a significant break with
the more orthodox reading strategies he criticizes. Without question, when
he discusses Brown's first novel, *Dirty Work* (1989), his reading of its ending differs little from what one would expect from practitioners of New
Criticism. He refers to Walter James as "the nominal murderer" and writes,
"Walter kills as he has done in the past but this time with an entirely different motivation" (45). Such a reading echoes Suzanne Jones's compara-
tive study of interracial relationships in *Dirty Work* and Madison Smartt
Bell's *Soldier's Joy* (1989), in which she states, bluntly, that "Before Walter
is discharged from the hospital, he fulfills Braiden's wish and helps him
die" (109). Owen W. Gilman, in *Vietnam and the Southern Imagination*,
concurs: "Walter starts to strangle his brother," he writes, and "the act of
supreme mercy goes forward" (114). Even the theological perspective that

William H. Becker applies in his review of the novel implies the same reading, for after describing Walter's refusal to kill Braiden, he claims, "Walter
changes his mind" (215).

The uniformity of these perspectives suggests that, even despite their
minute differences, they share an ultimately orthodox reading strategy—
the type Guinn dismisses as inadequate for reading Brown—and turning to
Dirty Work itself only strengthens this conclusion. After a complex narrative related primarily through chapters that alternate between Braiden's and
Walter's first-person points of view, the novel climaxes with Walter's discovery that his head injuries have precipitated a blackout that has caused him,
unknowingly, to kill Beth, a woman who had accepted him as a lover even
despite his disfigurement. Armed with this knowledge, Walter, in the last
chapter, thinks about Braiden, a fellow Vietnam veteran who has spent the
last twenty-two years in a hospital after losing his arms and legs in the war.
The novel concludes with the following passage, conveyed from Walter's
point of view: "I stood over him for a long moment. He opened his eyes
and looked at me when I closed my hands around his throat. He said Jesus
loves you. I shut my eyes because I knew better than that shit. I knew that
somewhere Jesus wept" (236). There is no explicit killing here, no definitive
fulfillment of Braiden's wish, no act of supreme mercy, not even clear evidence that Walter has carried through on his change of mind. At its most
literal level, all the novel claims is that Walter has "closed" his hands around
Braiden's throat. The outcome of this closing is never revealed; the novel,
in short, ends. Any killing, murder, or mercy that subsequently transpires
does so outside the novel and only in the mind of the reader. If Walter kills
Braiden, it is because the reader writes it, forces it to happen, not because either the novel or its author does so.

To propose such a reading of the novel's final passage is not to claim that
Brown wanted readers to close the cover of *Dirty Work* believing Braiden
alive and well. Rather, it instead suggests that the act of applying a truly
unorthodox reading strategy—as Guinn recommends when dealing with
Brown's fiction—may well require rejecting the notion of certainty about
what happens in the text and focusing instead on what Wolfgang Iser calls
its "esthetic" or "virtual dimension" (274, 279).

I apply Iser's work, his publications from the 1970s and '80s in particular,
with no little trepidation. Some of academe's most revered intellects have
attacked and dismissed as fossils his early theories on the role of the reader,
and Iser himself has since seemingly redirected his work (see Thomas).

Iser's focus on the novel as a form for questioning the validity of "social and historical norms" (xii), however, resonates well with *Dirty Work*'s use of Vietnam as a backdrop, its awareness of the struggles of lower-class Southerners, its debate over the morality of euthanasia. As Brook Thomas has argued, "Rather than put us in touch with reality, works of literature, in Iser's model, can force readers to confront the inadequacy of existing constructions of reality. That confrontation has the potential to prod readers into imagining new ways of constructing the world" (22). Such a view, in short, spares us the need to impose on *Dirty Work* or any other work of fiction a sense of what it tries to make us think—its philosophical component—and allows us instead to focus on how the novel involves readers in the struggle to resolve historical dilemmas. If, then, we can recognize that the openness of *Dirty Work*'s final page acts as a call for reader involvement in social and ethical questioning, the problems that demand critical attention become those that ask how the novel encourages that involvement and what we might accomplish by achieving it. After all, the uniformity of critical perspectives on the novel's ending argues persuasively that readers are likely to conclude the novel by acting as an agent in resolving its plot—killing Braiden themselves, in effect—though, given the fictional nature of the text, they may wonder why it matters. The answer to such a question is that *Dirty Work*, in fact, lays out a pattern of morally authorized involvement that demands Braiden's murder as its most logical culmination and that, in doing so, it confronts the reader with one of the central issues of Southern history.

"This the trip I took that day, day they brought Walter in" (1). With these words, Brown sends readers on a journey that, as we have seen, will climax with Walter's closing hands and desperate prayer. Iser, famously, uses the journey metaphor to describe the reader's experience of novels (see, for example, *The Implied Reader* 277), and *Dirty Work* self-consciously begins with one. It also begins by defining the context for the journey as Walter's arrival—"that day"—signaling to the reader that Braiden's story occupies a position subordinate to Walter's and, more subtly, the crucial importance that placement holds in the novel. This importance builds until Diva gives it a powerful voice when she tells Walter near the end of the novel, "Put yourself in his place" (223), thereby setting Walter—and readers—on a mental track that ends with hands around Braiden's throat. Between these two points, the novel repeatedly stages scenes that involve imagining places, beginning with the trip Braiden refers to in the opening sentence.

That trip involves a number of intriguing characteristics for the reader. It begins with the reader ignorant of Braiden's physical condition, his race, his twenty-two years in the Veterans facility, even his name; the reader knows him only as a voice creating an alternate history for himself and an imagined son in Africa. The focus of that history is initiation: the voice leading, goading, ordering his "Boy" to ambush lions that have been "eating too much of my meat" (1, 2). It's a voice that works through dialogue, not monologue, for Braiden imagines not only what he tells his son but what his son tells him, the child's resistance to the father's desires. Though the reader might be tempted to identify with the son—who, after all, would want to face a lion with only a rusty spear?—the blending of the father's and the narrator's voices makes such an identification difficult, and the father ends his instruction with a promise/threat: "How you think you gonna be the king one of these days? How you gonna give orders if you ain't never had to take none?" (5). Such a promise/threat, of course, stresses again the idea of imagining places since it figures the son's replacement of the father, the initiate's replacement of the initiator. In addition, the chapter ends not with the imagined trip but with Walter's real one as Braiden first describes the man who has been brought into his room, then emphasizes Walter's being placed there: "Old boys that brought him said Brought you some company, Braiden" (6)—a statement that, in telling us Braiden's name, places him into the text.

Such play on the idea of place and placement, subtly underscoring Brown's own assertions about the importance of race and class issues in his work (see Bonetti 95, 100), surfaces in all the novel's major episodes—both in Braiden's imagined African journeys and in the stories Walter tells of his past, beginning with what Guinn calls the "miniepic" of "the evil Matt Monroe" (54). For Guinn, this material is valuable for its similarities to such naturalist works as Stephen Crane's *Maggie: A Girl of the Streets* (1893) and Frank Norris's *McTeague* (1899). However, of even greater importance are the imaginative acts of placement performed in and by the telling of the story. The chapter containing it begins with the merest mention of Thomas Gandy, Matt Monroe's first victim, and establishes the time of the story as "right after they sent my daddy to the pen" (27). After three short sentences, a new paragraph begins: "You ever tried to remember the earliest thing you could remember? I mean when you were little and what you were doing? I have" (27). Though the reader may have expected this second paragraph to unfold a story of Thomas Gandy, it does not: seven paragraphs pass before Walter mentions Gandy again. But like the famous "you" in the opening paragraphs of Robert Penn Warren's *All the King's Men* (1946; see Vauthier), this use of the second-person places the reader in the text as surely as Walter's father has been placed in the—note the pun—"pen." More specifically, it locates the reader in Braiden's place since, in the context of the hospital room dialogue, Braiden is the implied referent of "you" even as that pronoun seems to address simultaneously any reader of the text—an act made particularly interesting by Braiden's use of "you" in the previous chapter to refer to himself: "Ain't no need in having a war lessen they just bomb the hell out of *you* like Pearl Harbor or something" (23–24; emphasis added); "What *you* got to do is stay up late at night and check *your TV Guide* for this good stuff" (25; emphasis added). While, at a minimum, these "you"s draw the reader into the violence of the lower-class social milieu, they more importantly place the reader into the connection between Braiden and Walter, superimposing the reader over Braiden and at the same time allowing the reader to see the pattern that undergirds the story Walter relates: putting oneself in another's place.

As Iser's ideas about reader expectations could have predicted (278), the Matt Monroe material does not initially suggest such a complex outcome. Walter merely observes Matt's bullying of Thomas Gandy, an archetypal weakling described as "a little bitty kid with glasses and a crew cut" (29). When Matt discovers that their teacher has stepped out momentarily, Matt corners Thomas, pulls off his glasses, and forces him to eat a dried cow patty. Walter notes that his entire class—himself included—watched "like a bunch of little ghouls" (30), but, he admits, "I'd be lying if I said I didn't enjoy watching Thomas eat the cowturd. . . . But part of me also *hated* watching Thomas eat the cowturd. Because I knew that it could very easily have been *me* eating the cowturd" (39–40; emphasis in original). Indeed, the young Walter does become Matt's victim when Matt discovers him carrying home a box of tampons for his mother. Robbed and humiliated, Walter states, "I went to bed that night and thought about it. I thought about watching Thomas Gandy and wondering about how he felt when Matt Monroe got him down on the ground and shoved that shit in his mouth. And I knew then that he'd felt just like I did right then. Awful" (42).

As if to make this emerging pattern unmistakable, Walter then imagines himself in more than just Thomas Gandy's place. When he describes to his mother Matt's assault, he receives not sympathy but a tongue-lashing for letting him "run over" him, and she orders Walter to "teach him right now that he can't" (42), even if it means picking up a stick to compensate for Matt's greater size. Walter infers from her reaction that he is "[n]ot my father's son" (41), and when Matt abuses him for having a father who is a murderer, Walter reacts as his father might, stabbing Monroe with a knife "that was all I had of my daddy" (47). Clearly, the novel suggests that three factors are working on Walter: the experience of finding himself in Thomas's place, his mother's moral direction, and his own desire to link himself to his father. As a result of these factors, he imagines himself in his father's place and, on the basis of that imagining alone, acts just as his father would.

Even when it digresses from the action in this episode, the novel further emphasizes the idea of imagining places. At one point, Walter interrupts his tale of Matt Monroe to allow for one of Brown's distinctive riffs expressing a first-hand understanding of poverty. The digression begins after Walter tells of laughing when the teacher, after Thomas tells her of Monroe's abuse, beats Matt with a lightcord. Walter begins, "People don't know what it's like to be poor" (33), and for seven paragraphs he describes the poverty of his childhood, creating a clear picture of absent sympathy, a refusal to imagine oneself in another's place: "I know people who say, well, I wouldn't be on welfare and take food stamps or handouts, I've got too much pride. That's fine. Pride is a fine thing to have. The only thing is, *you* can't eat pride. But *you* can eat commodity eggs and flour and rice and cheese and butter and powdered milk, and *your* babies can eat commodity cereal and drink commodity formula and fruit juice and live without pride. Pride ain't worth a damn to a hungry kid who wants something to eat, and if a man says he wouldn't take welfare food when his kids didn't have anything to eat, if he said that, he's lying, and I'd tell him so. I know" (33–34; emphasis added). It's worth noting here not only that Walter condemns the failure to place oneself in the position of another, but that his frequent use of "you" again forges a bond between reader and narrator. After all, if the "you" refers only to Braiden, there would be little need for the digression since Braiden's race and physical conditions would suggest to Walter his knowledge of poverty. Moreover, this narrator-reader bond appears again toward the end of the digression: "In the summertime it would be dusty, and the dust [vehicles] raised would settle on us and *you* could smell it in *your* nose like something old and sour" (35; emphasis added). In short, even as the digression's subject matter makes a case against the failure to connect imaginatively with others, its word choice forms just such a connection between Walter and the reader.

Walter's second digression may be less noticeable than his first, but it nonetheless alludes to the novel's last paragraph by its reference, no matter how figuratively, to the idea of mercy killing. Near the end of Walter's story of Matt's assault on Thomas, Brown inserts this sentence: "I think *you*'ll agree with me when I say that Matt Monroe's mother should have put him in a towsack and drowned him when he was little" (32; emphasis added). Coming, as it does, relatively early in the Monroe material, the statement affects the reader only minimally: who, after all, would endorse or abet the murder of a child? His verbalizing the idea, however, plants a seed in the reader's mind, offers an option that, as Matt's violence and inhumanity are increasingly detailed, becomes less and less unimaginable. As a result, when the Monroe material ends with the young Walter stabbing him and the narrator Walter stating, "Everybody in London Hill was real surprised" (48), a new sense of how few other options are available to Walter is likely to lessen the reader's own surprise. In other words, Brown is prodding the reader to adopt young Walter's position and the violence it entails because his action is the only solution to the problem of Matt Monroe that the novel has made available, that parental authority—the mother's words, the father's actions—has sanctioned, that the extremity of Matt's behavior has justified.

With the pattern so forcefully laid out in the Matt Monroe material, Brown, like a jazz musician, repeats and plays variations on it in subsequent episodes. When Walter describes his family situation to Braiden, for instance, he does so in ways that suggest their failure to imagine themselves in his place. Of his mother, he says, "Hell, I know it hurts her to not see me, but it hurts her to see me, too" (81)—implying that she focuses only on her own situation and feelings. But when he describes meeting Beth, Walter suggests a different response. He tells of going to a convenience store to buy two six-packs of beer after the hour when it can legally be sold. Beth, alone in the store and working the register, initially refuses to complete the sale; Walter explains, though, that "she just changed all of a sudden," and he remembers her saying, "I'm sorry for looking at you. For staring at you" (88). Within a few paragraphs, Beth moves from fearing Walter and refusing to sell him the six-packs to sharing a beer and cigarette with him and then later driving him home. She eventually characterizes her initial reaction to him as the fear of being caught with the marijuana she has stashed under the counter—but when the reader learns of Beth's own scars, the results of a dog attack, it becomes more logical to read her change as a recognition of her similarity to Walter. In short, she becomes able to picture herself in his place.

Braiden first proposes that Walter kill him shortly after Walter tells him this story of meeting Beth. His suggestion, however, elicits shock and outrage, for Walter, clearly, is not yet ready to imagine himself in Braiden's position. Equally important, though, is the fact that Braiden fails to frame the request in precisely those terms. He broaches the subject by way of the 1958 Edward Dmytryk film *The Young Lions*, in which a Nazi lieutenant played by Marlon Brando grows increasingly disenchanted with World War II. Braiden summarizes the discussion as follows: "I asked him did he remember what happened to that German officer in that movie. About old Marlon going to see him and him asking Marlon to bring him something. He looked like he was thinking about something a long way off. He nodded his head real slow. And everything slowed down when he looked at me. Said it was a bayonet, and I said, yeah, that was right" (104). This attempt fails to persuade Walter to imagine Braiden's perspective precisely because of the strategy of its presentation. In selecting as his model a Nazi officer, Braiden has given Walter an unacceptable position in which to imagine himself. During the second half of the twentieth century, Nazism maintained its close connection to the Holocaust—an attempt at genocide, not euthanasia. In short, Braiden has selected a role that, to echo the text, is "something a long way off," something too foreign to help facilitate an imagined link. This foreignness is further accentuated by Braiden's stressing the actor, Marlon Brando, who, in the novel's 1980s, would likely be identified with the role of Mafia don Vito Corleone from Francis Ford Coppola's *The Godfather* (1972)—another "place" lacking the moral authority to encourage imaginative placement. Braiden fails to stress, as he will in later attempts, the element from *The Young Lions* with which Walter might be tempted to identify: the name of Brando's character, Christian. Nevertheless, the failure of Braiden's attempt to force Walter to imagine himself in another's place leads not to a moral triumph but to a moment that is both profane and dehumanizing. Walter's response, repeated for emphasis, is "you son of a bitch" (104, 105).

Positive examples of imagined changes of place return when Walter relates incidents in which sympathy for another requires crossing lines of gender and race. The former appears in the story Walter tells of Mary Barry, a girl he describes as "kind of plain, you know? But she had this great body. And I think she'd had a hard life, she'd been through a divorce with her mama and daddy, and she was sweet" (194–95). When the school's rich boy brags about having sex with her, a claim Walter soon discovers is accurate, his description of his response—first, "it made me sick to my stomach" (195); later, "It just liked to killed me" (196)—echoes his description of Mary as she realizes that she has become the talk of her school: "And I saw her going down the hall, crying, bent over, like she was toting some weight" (195–96). As when Matt Monroe had insulted him, Walter takes physical revenge on the boy. Unconsciously, he has put himself in Mary's place and responded as if he, not she, were the one humiliated.

Though the novel rushes past this scene, it acts, as Iser might explain, both to leave our expectations unfulfilled and to "impose" a consistency upon the text (280, 285). The reader might expect Walter to enjoy the lascivious details of Mary's sexual behavior, sharing them with Braiden in stereotypical locker-room fashion as a way of cementing their friendship, but he instead enforces the pattern of imaginatively taking another's place. As a result, rather than emphasizing the strength of bonds based solely on gender, Brown suggests that the ability to forge an imagined sharing of places depends on commonalities of economic status and experience. For the reader, this stress is important because of what Iser calls "identification": "Often the term 'identification' is used as if it were an explanation, whereas in actual fact it is nothing more than description. What is normally meant by 'identification' is the establishment of affinities between oneself and someone outside oneself—a familiar ground on which we are able to experience the unfamiliar. The author's aim, though, is to convey the experience and, above all, *an attitude toward that experience*. Consequently, 'identification' is not an end in itself, but a stratagem by means of which the author stimulates attitudes in the reader" (291; emphasis added). In short, more than merely sharing Walter's identification with Mary, the passage encourages readers to ignore gender lines and to make again the imaginative move into the place of others.

The importance of such identification grows still more apparent when the imaginative changes of place involve the crossing of racial lines. Conventionally, the relationship between lower-class whites and African-Americans has been seen as one of virulent hatred and fear. That's certainly the idea that lies behind Flannery O'Connor's depiction in "Revelation" of a "white-trash" woman who declares, "Two thangs I ain't going to do: love no niggers or scoot down no hog with no hose" (199). It's also the image frequently depicted in Richard Wright's Southern stories and in his essay "The Ethics of Living Jim Crow," in which a young Wright is victimized by two workers in a lens-grinding factory who don't want to see him rise above his "place" and theirs. In John Shelton Reed's view, the "redneck's essential characteristic is *meanness*"—an image, he says, that "was well-established before the civil-rights era" and "polished and reinforced by the murders and brutality of that period" (40; emphasis in original). Nevertheless, Brown depicts a situation much closer to that described by historian Pete Daniel, who, writing about the South in the years immediately following the *Brown v. Board of Education* ruling, explains that middle-class whites, especially those new to the middle class, dominated the drive to preserve segregation (179). Indeed, Walter and his far-below-middle-class family, despite their frequent use of racist language, consistently demonstrate their awareness of the fact that they share the socioeconomic status of poor African-Americans, thus enabling them to cross racial boundaries, to imagine themselves in the place of black rather than white Southerners.

The novel takes passing glances at such crossings of racial boundaries in the stories in which Walter's father kills a mule that kills "his friend" Hugh Jean (125) and in the mention of "this little short nigger man" who rescues Beth from a dog that attacks her (155). However, Brown develops this idea more completely in Walter's story of Louis Champion, who alongside his family joins Walter and his father, Randall James, in picking cotton for a man named Norris. Though Norris and Randall are "about the same age" (202), Randall neither seeks nor develops any tie to Norris beyond that of employee to employer. Instead, he bonds with the black Champion family because of their shared place near the bottom of the economic ladder: both have to pick cotton to survive. After a day of their working together, the bond strengthens when Randall suggests sharing his family's blackberry pie with the Champions. This leads to interaction between the two families, and Walter tells Braiden, "I don't know. [Mr. Champion] didn't seem bitter. He knew a better day was coming sometime. He just wished it was here now. Then. He wanted his kids to go to college. Get educations. Not have to pick cotton the rest of their lives. I'd never heard a black man talk like that. . . . They were good people" (207). Thus the dawning of Walter's ability to imagine the Champions' place—and it is again the moral authority of a parent that helps reinforce this change. When Randall concludes that Norris is cheating the Champions out of the full value of the cotton they pick, he tells Norris, "If you've cheated [Champion] then you've cheated me too. Me and my boy." Champion and Norris both try to discourage this view, Champion telling Randall "to just leave it alone," Norris telling him, "Now Randall I ain't got no quarrel with you. Said I'm gonna pay you what I owe you" (210). But when Walter's father persists in seeing the two causes as one, eventually even resorts to violence, the episode concludes as follows: "[Walter's father] got me to go call the law and an ambulance and all. He got Champion and them to leave while I was gone. We never heard anything out of them again. Daddy just sat there and waited for the law to come get him. He knew it wouldn't do any good to run. But he gave them the chance to run and they took it" (211). What's striking here is that Randall does not expect this ability to put oneself in the place of another to run two ways. He neither looks for nor appears to want support from the Champions. He merely acts as he imagines they would like to if the racial tensions of the mid-twentieth-century South had not rendered unwise such actions by African-Americans. Nevertheless, if this is his only racial consideration—and it appears from the text that it is—the novel is creating a pattern of sympathetic action in which traditional race-based prejudice is not a viable reason to avoid imagining oneself in another's place. Shared situations and common humanity instead help forge such a link.

Recognizing that the novel privileges imaginative links over traditional Southern racial views not only underscores the pattern of identification created for the reader but calls into question the perspectives of critics who see the novel, largely because of its paired back and white narrators, as race-centered. When Jones claims that Brown "shies away from a real dialogue between [Walter and Braiden] about racial issues" (110), she fails to see that, as in Braiden's imagined journey at the opening of the novel, all of Walter's chapters are essentially internal dialogues, parts of an ongoing, inner debate preparing himself for possible action should he be able to imagine himself in Braiden's position. Similarly, when Gilman describes the novel as "a poignant consideration of what brotherhood means" and claims that "[e]ven the structure of *Dirty Work* highlights the idea of equality" (108, 109), he, too, is overlooking that intense sense of identification with Walter that Brown creates for the reader. Moreover, in that the opening of the novel allows Walter's arrival to establish the context, the chapters that follow create a structural flaw in that equality. It is with Walter, therefore, that the reader identifies.

Braiden, however, does complement Walter. Having identified with Walter, readers discover in Braiden the person in whose place they must imagine themselves, a kind of ultimate test of their ability to forge an empathetic bond. Braiden describes himself in the opening chapter as "Misery" (6)—an apt representation, given the wounds that have robbed him of everything but his hope of death. Nevertheless, the second chapter defines him even further as the helpless victim of popular culture, trapped in front of "that television they leave on all day and night, talking about they detergent and *douche* bags and I don't know what all else" (11–12; emphasis in original). In another sense, he becomes the incarnation of the question and answer he interjects at the conclusion of his second chapter: "Whole world's a puzzle to me, though. Why it's got to be the way it is. I don't think the Lord meant for it be like this originally. I think things just got out of hand" (12).

Such qualities seem to leave Braiden in an imaginative location where few would want to place themselves. He is an other that one could have sympathy for, but he is not one whose place one would want to take. Certainly, Walter makes several references to his desire to leave Braiden and never see him again; however, Brown makes it clear that Braiden is more than his suffering. Throughout, he is a good listener and a man generous with his beer, and in the chapters in which he describes his experience before and during his wounding in Vietnam, something more important becomes clear: he has already made his imaginative connection with an unacceptable other, none other than the man who wounded him. Braiden offers a detailed account of the ambush that cost him his arms and legs, describing the bullets "punching holes in me." However, he adds, "I would have done it to him if he'd give me the opportunity. I remember the first one I killed" (161). Missing here are the bitterness and blame a reader might expect; instead, there is the clear sense of seeing from the other's eyes and, therefore, a consequent acceptance not of what the other does, but of the other's humanity notwithstanding.

Braiden's attitude suggests that he has already begun and possibly even completed the process that Walter and the reader undergo in the novel—that of imagining oneself in another's place—and thereby still further reinforces the identification with the process. Phrased another way, Braiden's is a static position, an end the reader can only move toward or away from, and the passages concerning his conversations with Jesus only strengthen this view. In a chapter just before his first request that Walter kill him,

Braiden states, "I wanted to have a dream about Jesus and I had it. Had part of it and made up part of it." Clearly, such a description prevents the reader from seeing what follows as purely supernatural revelation. Rather, in both dreaming of and fabricating Jesus, Braiden imaginatively puts himself in what he describes as "gold dust[ed] . . . sandals" (91), resulting in a depiction of Jesus as rather earthy: he smokes cigarettes, speaks in a plain, modern dialect, and is willing to engage Braiden's questions about, and accept his anger because of, his condition. Jesus, nevertheless, performs his traditional function of providing if not salvation, then the hope of it, at least, when he tells Braiden, "It won't be much longer"—a statement that soon precipitates Braiden's linking Walter to Jesus: "Then He was gone. I opened my eyes. My savior was looking at me. I think he was wanting another beer" (95). Such linkage generates two significant outcomes: it emphasizes the importance of human participation in salvation, and it validates the identification process as somehow Christ-like and therefore right and good. Though such a reaction is not completely logical and is certainly culture-dependent, it is difficult to rebut given Brown's statements about Christianity (see Ketchin 99–101) and its prominence in the South.

The novel, moreover, continues to stress the connection in both minor and major ways. At one point, when Walter thinks Braiden is asleep, he relates this passage: "I looked over at Braiden. Jesus, his arms. His legs. And twenty-two years on a bed. The shit just comes down and sometimes it lands on you. Or the guy next to you. If you're lucky, the guy next to you" (148). Though the syntax here equates Braiden and Jesus, the fact of Braiden's disability—his missing arms and legs—emphasizes the skewed nature of such reasoning. In addition, the end of the passage shows Walter's failure to imagine himself as the "guy next to you" and in so doing reinforces the need for such imagination even as the mention of Jesus keeps active as a force in the novel the value system Jesus represents.

When the two men engage in their lengthiest discussion about Braiden's request that Walter kill him, we not only see Walter making small steps toward imagining himself in Braiden's place—"I knew he was tired" (172), he says at one point—but we find them focusing on the nature of Jesus's morality. Walter insists on a rigid, absolute view. "Jesus don't condone that kind of stuff" (175), he tells Braiden, but Braiden emphasizes Jesus's compassion, which arises, as he sees it, from shared experiences: "He knows what murder is. He was murdered Himself. He done been through a murder.

He knows about suffering. He done been through that, too" (174). In his longest speech in the novel, Braiden rejects the idea that suffering results from a divine will: "Listen, Walter. God don't cause no shit like that to happen" (177). Instead, he stresses human freedom: "Man does all this stuff to himself" (178). In addition, this oft-cited scene challenges Walter's ability to imagine himself in the place of another even as it reproduces the pattern of doing so. The challenge comes when Braiden tells Walter, "Man, you don't know what it was like. To be so damn poor. And have to live on welfare" (179). Nevertheless, Braiden himself reenacts the pattern when he concludes, "I'm sorry, man. I have to cry. I have to cry for all them wasted lives, man, all them boys I loaded up just like they loaded me up. I couldn't believe it, man. I couldn't believe it had happened to me. I laid on my back and I said it loud. I said Oh Lord, they have shot me all to pieces" (180).

As the novel nears its end, Brown brings two final forces into play to prepare for its conclusion. First, Diva, like a selfless, ministering black angel, delivers to Walter the paraphrase of the Golden Rule quoted earlier: "Put yourself in his place" (223). By invoking the value system of Jesus, she links her words and her request for Walter to act with divine parental authority. Walter responds by at least beginning to imagine himself in Braiden's place, acknowledging, "I couldn't take it either" (223). He does not act, however, until he learns that his dreams of going home and finding happiness with Beth are as much in vain as Braiden's dreams of living in Africa. When his circumstances, in their hopelessness, approximate Braiden's, he is ready to accept the fact that he, not Jesus, must act. When he states, as the last line of the novel, "I knew that somewhere Jesus wept" (236), he signals both his appreciation for the mercy that Jesus represents and his awareness of the irony of all human struggles to practice that value. Like Walter, the reader cannot hope for a fairy tale ending here either. Accepting misery or taking action are the only possibilities that remain. Influenced by the pattern of imagining themselves in another's place, readers act by writing Walter's final actions, creating the virtual text that lives just beyond the novel's pages. As Iser observes, "Once the reader is entangled, his own preconceptions are continually overtaken, so that the text becomes his 'present' while his own ideas fade into the 'past'" (290). No matter what beliefs about the Southern lower classes, Vietnam, or euthanasia readers hold when they begin the text, the esthetic experience of reading it forms a new set of complex, guilt-laden beliefs that are active for the world and the time of the novel. It is a sign of the power of such experience that it can lead readers to give Braiden his release and his death.

In his often-anthologized final essay from *The Implied Reader*, Iser concludes by claiming that "[t]he production of meaning in literary texts . . . does not merely entail the discovery of the unformulated, which can then be taken over by the active imagination of the reader; it also entails the possibility that we may formulate ourselves and so discover what had previously seemed to elude our consciousness" (294). Applying this idea to the experience of reading *Dirty Work*, it becomes clear that, however we define what the novel attempts to bring to consciousness, that reading will focus on the sense of becoming involved, being implicated in the complex emotions of sympathy and guilt that are part of the reader's esthetic experience in moving to the point of killing Braiden. But to make sense of those emotions, to understand why an author would want to generate such an experience, we must first recognize the irony of that murder. For the reality is that, despite Braiden's request that Walter kill him, despite the mercy such an act may entail, it painfully reenacts the South's long and familiar history of violence by whites against blacks—violence often ostensibly justified in paternalistic terms. For all the language of brotherhood that permeates the novel (see Gilman 110), Jones is correct in arguing that Braiden and Walter do not become friends (110); what she neglects to note, however, is that they reenact the chattel/master relationship, as Braiden unconsciously implies when he attempts to convince Walter to kill him by comparing himself to a horse with a broken leg and by describing his life and suffering as having "*paid* my price" (179; emphasis in original).

Brown's readers are not likely to remember chattel slavery in the American South. Many can have only the faintest recollections—if that—of the South before the Civil Rights era. Such readers—especially whites—are therefore likely to feel little connection to the region's bloody and oppressive past, even if today they benefit socioeconomically from its legacy. Reading *Dirty Work*, however, leaves them with little choice but to reenact that past: they become trapped in its moral confusion, no matter how much they may otherwise condemn, if not unequivocally reject that past.

Is killing Braiden, then, the wrong thing to do? To pose the question is to require the novel to state an idea rather than create an experience. Moreover, if the novel posits that there is a moral or immoral response to Braiden's suffering, then Guinn is correct in contending that Brown's work rejects the

Dirty Work *and the Burdens of Southern History*

"old paradigms" that "defined Southern Renascence literature" (37). In such a case, though, it would have more in common with Soviet realism than the work of the Agrarians, Faulkner, and Warren. Applying Iser's arguments to *Dirty Work* shows us that Guinn is mistaken. For whatever other vestiges of the Renascence Brown's novel ignores or contradicts, recognizing that its meaning is the discovery and formation of a complex experience places it well within at least one of those paradigms best defined by C. Vann's Woodward's 1952 essay "The Irony of Southern History":

> The South has had its full share of illusions, fantasies, and pretensions, and it has continued to cling to some of them with an astonishing tenacity that defies explanation. But the illusion that 'history is something unpleasant that happens to other people' is certainly not one of them—not in the face of accumulated evidence and memory to the contrary.... For the inescapable facts of history were that the South has repeatedly met with frustration and failure. It had learned what it was to be faced with economic, social, and political problems that refused to yield to all the ingenuity, patience, and intelligence that a people could bring to bear upon them. It had learned to accommodate itself to conditions that it swore it would never accept, and it learned the taste left in the mouth by the swallowing of one's own words. It had learned to live for long decades in quite un-American poverty, and it had learned the equally un-American lesson of submission.... Nothing about this history was conducive to the theory that the South was the darling of divine providence. (190–91)

Woodward's 1956 essay "The Historical Dimension" points specifically to this awareness in Renascence writers, quoting both Allen Tate's well-known claim that a "backward glance gave us the Southern renascence, a literature conscious of the past in the present" and Katherine Anne Porter's statement, "I had blood knowledge of what life can be in a defeated country on the bare bones of privation" (32, 33). *Dirty Work* recreates that experience of complexity for its readers, giving to generations raised in the Sun Belt's prosperity and the post-Civil Rights era's racial progress a sense of history's burden. The setting has changed: instead of the Civil War or Reconstruction, *Dirty Work* confronts the legacy of Vietnam, but as Woodward himself notes in his 1968 essay "A Second Look at the Theme of Irony," Vietnam raised many of the questions of history that the South had to confront after its own war. Woodward, however, worried that the Vietnam War might fail

33

ROBERT DONAHOO

to force on the nation the sense of irony that the Civil War forced on the South. "The characteristic American adjustment," he writes, "to the current foreign and domestic enigmas that confound our national myths has not been to abandon the myths [of inevitable success and of innocence] but to reaffirm them" (218). However historians judge the degree to which Woodward's fears were realized in the outcome of the Vietnam War, his essay makes clear his view that, to the degree that the South remembers its defeat, the South's "un-American and ironic experience . . . with history" has much to teach the nation (233).

Dirty Work acts to corroborate that idea even as Walter's final claim to know "better than that shit" and his replacement of a loving, benevolent deity for one wounded by human ethical dilemmas and plights imply a oneness with the South's historical sense of desolation and defeat. There is no correct action for Walter to take, no painless escape from the situation in which his environment and actions have placed him. There are only the requirement and the freedom to act—the same circumstances the novel's readers discover in the process of reading. Closing its covers does not end the book. Readers are called to act, and to act in a way that most would hesitate to choose, if not reject out of hand. In finding themselves euthanizing a helpless war victim, are they neo-Nazi eugenicists or angels of mercy? Are they reviving the racial paternalism and violence of the Old South or forging a New South that practices a non-Calvinistic religion of mercy and identification with suffering? Or are they doing both? The burden to decide and to judge themselves is ultimately handed to each of them.

By offering readers an experience of complexity and frustration virtually equivalent to that of the South, Brown's novel guides them to imagine themselves into Southern history. They join the long gray line of those for whom issues of race, class, and religion are, to echo Faulkner, neither dead nor past. They are offered an experience equivalent, if not identical to the one Lewis P. Simpson sees as central to the great Southern writers of the twentieth century: "In summary the education southern writers gained from such masters [as Proust, Mann, Joyce, Yeats, and Eliot] consisted in learning that modern culture is a historical phenomenon. Far from being bardic or epic, or in any sense collective in expression, it takes its character from an isolation—an internalization—of history in the individual consciousness" (212). In other words, instead of rejecting the traditional paradigms of Southern literature, *Dirty Work* broadens the spectrum of Southern society included within them. Readers, as a result—whether Southerners or others, day laborers or aristocrats, black or white—come to know and share the burden of the South's ironic past. They are prodded to feel themselves a part of history that limits and demands their action, and in so doing thereby validate Braiden's words after first seeing Walter: "Everybody toting something" (6).

Works Cited

Becker, William. Rev. of *Dirty Work*, by Larry Brown, and *The Acquittal of God: A Theology for Vietnam Veterans*, by Uwe Siemon-Netto. *Theology Today* 47 (1990): 212–15.

Bonetti, Kay. "An Interview with Larry Brown." *Missouri Review* 18.3 (1995): 79–107.

Brown, Larry. *Dirty Work*. Chapel Hill: Algonquin, 1989.

Daniel, Pete. *Lost Revolutions: The South in the 1950s*. Chapel Hill: U of North Carolina P, 2000.

Gilman, Owen W. *Vietnam and the Southern Imagination*. Jackson: UP of Mississippi, 1992.

Guinn, Matthew. *After Southern Modernism: Fiction of the Contemporary South*. Jackson: UP of Mississippi, 2000.

Iser, Wolfgang. *The Implied Reader: Patterns of Communication in Prose Fiction from Bunyan to Beckett*. Baltimore: Johns Hopkins UP, 1974.

Jones, Suzanne. "Refighting Old Wars: Race Relations and Masculine Conventions in Fiction by Larry Brown and Madison Smartt Bell." *The Southern State of Mind*. Ed. Jan Nordby Gretlund. Columbia: U of South Carolina P, 1999. 107–20.

Ketchin, Susan. "An Interview with Larry Brown." *Southern Quarterly* 32.2 (1994): 95–109.

O'Connor, Flannery. "Revelation." *Everything That Rises Must Converge*. New York: Farrar, Straus and Giroux, 1965. 191–218.

Reed, John Shelton. *Southern Folk Plain and Fancy: Native White Social Types*. Athens: U of Georgia P, 1986.

Simpson, Lewis P. "The Southern Aesthetic of Memory." *Tulane Studies in English* 23 (1978): 207–27.

Thomas, Brook. "Restaging the Reception of Iser's Early Work, or Sides Not Taken in Discussions of the Aesthetic." *New Literary History* 31 (2000): 13–43.

Vauthier, Simone. "The Case of the Vanishing Narratee: An Inquiry into *All the King's Men*." *Southern Literary Journal* 6.2 (1974): 42–69.

Woodward, C. Vann. *The Burden of Southern History*. Rev. ed. Baton Rouge: Louisiana State UP, 1968.

Saving Them from Their Lives

Storytelling and Self-Fulfillment in *Big Bad Love*

JEAN W. CASH

Larry Brown's second volume of short stories is in some respects a continuation of his first, *Facing the Music* (1988). Both focus on what Brown knew best, the working-class denizens of rural Mississippi, men (for the most part) whose lives, though often rife with sordid adventure, are seldom fulfilling. A new focus—and obvious autobiographical emphasis—in *Big Bad Love* (1990), however, falls on certain members of the working class who, by aspiring to become writers, find greater fulfillment than those with nothing to cling to, no Holy Grail to pursue, as Brown once characterized his own desire for literary success (Pettus 1C). The stories in *Big Bad Love* are both imaginatively conceived and creatively executed and feature a variety of devices that influence voice, tone, and content. Using a variety of approaches, Brown continues to explore the lives of working-class characters who try to add meaning to their lives in mundane ways—but their drinking, carousing, and womanizing simply do not satisfy. Only those who turn to writing, like Brown himself, achieve a more complete existence.

When the collection first appeared, it drew more negative reviews than either *Facing the Music* or *Dirty Work* (1989) had. An anonymous reviewer for the *Virginia Quarterly Review*, for instance, wrote that Brown's "minimalist techniques lead to a superficial treatment of intense emotions, a pandering to prurient interests. The stories do not entertain or enlighten; they disappoint" (94). Generally, though, positive reviews outweighed the negative. Clancy Sigal praised the collection in *Washington Post Book World*, suggesting a connection between Brown's popularity and his depiction of the Southern working class: "In a sense," Sigal wrote, "he's the beneficiary of an uneasy feeling among critics and editors that attenuating middle-class angst, the keynote of so much recent fiction, is simply not enough. Larry Brown, poet of the southern white underclass, was there when we needed him" (11). Sigal and others also pointed to the collection's central theme, the despair Brown's working-class male characters suffer when the love they seek as a means to fulfillment goes awry. Don O'Briant, writing in the *Atlanta Journal-Constitution*, asserts that these characters "have been looking for love in all the wrong places and don't know what to do with it once they find it" (N8). Neely Tucker, writing in the *Detroit Free Press*, contended that though such love is "a mean, pitiless thing," it is "ultimately the emotion that makes life worth living or at least worth living well" (7G). Early reviewers, in other words, explored what they saw as Brown's central focus, but they did not find in the often autobiographical stories any real relief for the characters' failed searches for love.

Several reviewers also analyzed Brown's style and diction. O'Briant wrote that he "drives home his message with deceptively simple sentences that carry the wallop of sledgehammer blows" (N8). Tucker asserted that Brown's style, content, and attitude are "much more akin to [those of] modern writers like Barry Hannah and Richard Ford" than those of William Faulkner (7G). Ann H. Fisher, reviewing the collection for *Library Journal*, termed its stories "rich" and "moody" and predicted that "Brown . . . might just become another powerhouse Southern writer" (139). The most notable and laudatory of reviews, though, came from Harry Crews, writing in the *Los Angeles Times Book Review*, where he began with his reaction to reading *Facing the Music* some two years earlier: "In 25 years of writing, it was the first time I picked up the phone and tried to call the author" (3). Crews had not been able to reach Brown at the time (celebrity had already forced the younger author to secure an unlisted number), but his failure to speak with him did not lessen his admiration. The stories in *Big Bad Love*, Crews wrote, "are all rather like some perfect object one has come across in the wilderness like a perfectly shaped stone. Or a piece of hard wood that over the years has been weathered to a natural and unique state" (3). Crews concluded with a statement of absolute approval: "I send Mr. Brown my congratulations and my hope that he will be one of the most prolific writers we have. My hope that he will write a lot is entirely selfish, because whatever he writes, I will read" (8).

Brown and his editor Shannon Ravenel arranged the collection's ten stories into three sections. Eight comprise Part I; all feature male narrators, most of whom are involved in troubled, if not failed relationships with women. Each narrator—heavy drinking, sex-obsessed, and in serious need of focus—typifies Brown's Southern, working-class male. Unlike their creator, none of them turn to writing as a possible release from their frustration, though some of them are good storytellers. As something of an inside joke, Brown gives many of them names or initials that look much like his own: Lonnie narrates "The Apprentice," Leroy narrates "Big Bad Love," Leo narrates "Old Soldiers," and Louis narrates "Sleep." Mr. Lawrence narrates "Discipline" (the single work in Part II), while Leon Barlow, a name derived from Brown's mother's, Leona Barlow Brown, narrates "92 Days" (the single work in Part III). When asked about these names, Brown replied, "That was kind of, I don't know, something I did for fun, I guess. So many of those stories in *Big Bad Love* have . . . however large or small . . . autobiographical elements and when I was writing these stories, I didn't really have it in my head that there was ever going to be a collection put together. But I just got to giving these characters my initials. I don't know why. But Lewis, Leroy, Leon—I know I call that one Leon 'cause my mama's name is Leona and I've always liked that name" (LaRue 51). He doesn't admit it, but Brown's use of names similar to his own may well be his way of implying identification with his characters, a means of showing his similarity—as a one-time member of the working class himself—to these men whose lives are so much less fulfilling than that he would live as a successful writer. He seems to know that, without his writing, he could easily have remained one of them himself.

Though grouped together, the eight stories in the first section vary in content and focus. "Falling Out of Love" and "Wild Thing," for instance, feature congenitally malcontent young men, while "Sleep" and "Old Soldiers" take up older characters with different problems. Despite such differences, their narrative voices often seem so personal that it's tempting to speculate that Brown was writing about his own experience. The degree to which his trouble-seekers are truly autobiographical, however, remains debatable—even though Brown too did his share of drinking in bars, smoking marijuana, and chasing women—but the most pointedly autobiographical of the stories are unquestionably those that involve writers and writing, as well as "Old Soldiers," which he surely based on his experiences listening to war stories growing up and living in Tula, Mississippi. All except "Discipline" are set in the rural northwest corner of the state, the region Brown knew and loved. The stories in *Big Bad Love* thus reveal considerable variety within the people of Mississippi—members of its working class in particular—people whom Brown knew intimately.

As if continuing the two collections without an interlude, the first story in *Big Bad Love*, "Falling Out of Love," features the same nameless narrator as the last story in *Facing the Music*, "The End of Romance." He has since moved on from Miss Sheila to Sheena Baby, but this new relationship is also foundering: she "didn't hurt for me like I did for her. I knew it. I'd thought about shooting her first and me second, but that wouldn't have done either one of us any good" (3). The passage illustrates the wry humor that infuses nearly every story in the collection. As Robert Beuka has written in his essay on Brown for the *Dictionary of Literary Biography*, "Brown uses humor to explore . . . the troubled side of romantic relationships" (61)—and yet this humor masks the narrator's sense of loss. When policemen approach Sheena Baby's crippled car at the end of the story, the narrator thinks, "I saw with a sick feeling in my heart that our happy ending was about to take a turn for the worse" (13). The narrator's failure to form a permanent relationship is the result of his inability to be much more than he is—a drunken, sex-starved aficionado of classic rock-and-roll who lives just one step ahead of the law. As Thomas J. Richardson writes in *Contemporary Fiction Writers of the South*, "love with Sheena Baby has come to two flat tires on an empty road" (62). The ending of the story mirrors that of all those in *Big Bad Love* that tell of relationships between men and women; they often end humorously, but they always end badly. The narrator here is obviously pursuing a losing quest, and though he seems to aspire to little more, that fact does not seem to bother him.

Another unsatisfied male narrates "Wild Thing," the second story in the collection. At its center is the working-class bar where the narrator and a young woman first meet. The narrator is married and has children, but his marriage is unfulfilling: "I'd been out of things for a while. I was having trouble with my wife. One of the things that was wrong was that I was spending too many nights away from home, and it was causing fights that were hard for me to win. It's hard to win when you don't have right on your side. It's hard to win when you know that your own fucking up is causing the problem" (31–32). Despite such self-awareness, the narrator continues to frequent bars, drink heavily, and look for a woman who will pay more attention to him. And, of course, he finds her, a young married woman—with sex and intrigue on *her* mind as well—who turns out to be more than he can handle. Despite problems with both her husband and the law, though, he can't stay away from her; parked with her in an isolated rural area that local police constantly monitor, he knows "it wouldn't be but a little bit before those headlights, somebody's, would ease around the curve" (45). Beuka, again, asserts, "This protagonist's reckless, relentless pursuit of cold beer and loose women makes him something of a representative figure in the collection" (61). The unhappy young narrator is proof again of how little meaning rampant sexuality adds to the life of Brown's undereducated working man. Without a more transcendent escape, he is doomed to endless and meaningless repetition.

Brown begins "Big Bad Love" with a motif familiar to much of his writing, both fiction and nonfiction: dogs often dead or abandoned, a particular feature of the rural landscape. A dog lover from his early years, Brown owned and lost a number of dogs and evinced a particular sympathy for characters who lose them themselves. Sentence one of "Big Bad Love," complete with italics to fully emphasize his middle-aged narrator's despondency, is "My *dog* died" (47). Subconsciously, at least, Leroy sees the dead dog as a metaphor for his dead marriage, and he finds it difficult to bury either. His wife Mildred is "sexually frustrated because of her overlarge organ and it just wore me out trying to apply enough friction to that thing for her to achieve internal orgasm" (52). Loving the way she looked in a swimsuit, he had married her without knowledge of her hidden problem. Dually troubled, then, Leroy, like Brown's other unsatisfied males, drinks, drives, and avoids both his dog's corpse and that of his marriage. He says, "I did not know what I was going to do with Mildred or how I was ever going to be able to come to a life of harmonious tranquility where matrimonial happiness was a constant joy" (59). The platitudinous language helps lead to the ironic denouement of Leroy's plight: when he finally does go home, his wife, having found a lover big enough to satisfy her needs, has left him—and he now must bury both of those corpses. Truly realizing his loss for the first time in the story, he says, "Right about then I started missing her, and the loneliness I have been speaking of really started to set in" (61). Failed marital relationships characterize the lives of many such members of the Southern working class; people enter relationships with the hope that "matrimonial happiness" will compensate for other failures, but often—as is the case with Leroy—there is no "harmonious tranquility," much less "constant joy." For Brown, it seems, life had to have more meaning than that a conventional marriage could provide.

The narrator of "Gold Nuggets," the fourth story in the collection, is both more degenerate and more pathetic than the narrators who precede him. In the midst of a trip to the Mississippi Gulf Coast to pick up shrimp to take back to the state's northwest corner, he confides that he "didn't even like" the wealthier acquaintances who had sent him there (67). One of them, Ed, is a "son of a bitch" who had taken a similar trip without offering to bring him back any shrimp (68), and a second, Ted, had never invited him to his private lake "when they were jerking those ten-pound lunkers out of there" (69). In spite of his mission, this narrator, much like many of Brown's others, is tempted and ultimately brought down by tawdry excitement. He visits a strip joint and quickly becomes the victim of women whose job it is to fleece naïve male customers. Even after being beaten and robbed of much of his shrimp money, though, he remains clueless, little concerned about the loss of either money or fundamental dignity. "I knew all this was just a temporary setback," he says. "It didn't mean that I couldn't ever be saved from my life, or that I'd never find the boat I was looking for. Somewhere, somewhere there, was a connection I could make, and I knew that all I had to do was stay out there until I found it" (77). Showing us how easily his narrator falls victim to negative forces in his environment, Brown clearly implies that—even though alcohol and class envy have blinded his narrator to his own culpability—few gold nuggets will reward such hapless seeking.

The fifth of these stories of aimless, working-class males is "Waiting for the Ladies." Again, the narrator is a middle-aged loser, one this time who, having left a steady job after sixteen years, has too little to occupy his time. When his wife tells him that a man has exposed himself to her at the local dump, he sets out to track him down, casting himself as a grudging knight in not-so-shining armor. At the same time, because he suspects that his wife is having an affair with her boss, he partially identifies with the flasher as well, for he too has to seek sexual gratification outside socially acceptable avenues. Somehow, though, the narrator feels that tracking down and punishing this public nuisance will restore his lost masculinity, a quest whose outright silliness becomes apparent when he visits the sheriff's office only to learn that local officers are well aware of the man's existence but have declared him less harmless than other public menaces. Assuming, then, the role of a lone avenger, the narrator tracks the deviant, pursuing him on a long road chase that ends at the man's home. Instead of the perhaps anticipated showdown, though, the last section of the story reveals the avenger's vulnerability:

> The door was open, and the knob turned under my hand. The barrel of
> the gun slanted down from under my arm, and I tracked their mud on their
> floor. He didn't have his cap on, and his hair wasn't what I'd imagined. It was
> gray, but neatly combed, and his mother was sobbing silently on the couch
> and feeding a pillow into her mouth.

He said one thing, quietly: 'Are you fixing to kill us?'
Their eyes got me.
I sat down, asking first if I could. That's when I started telling both of them what my life then was like. (89)

As his words illustrate, what this narrator needs—more than revenge—is somebody to listen to the story of his increasingly woeful life. His storytelling becomes his release, and in creating this narrator and situating his story where he does in the collection, Brown begins moving toward his ultimate conclusion that narrative art can offer rare and hard-to-find fulfillment—can save such a man from what otherwise had been his life, to paraphrase the narrator of "Gold Nuggets." The revelation is a significant one, one so many of his predecessors in the collection not only fail to make, but don't begin to consider.

Though still set in rural Lafayette County, Mississippi, three stories in *Big Bad Love*'s first section stand apart from the drinking/driving/womanizing sagas of the other five. "Old Soldiers" features a young narrator named Leo who, though a veteran of the military himself, straddles the chasm between the story's older veterans and its non-vets, many of whom differ little from the bar-hopping narrators of previous stories in the collection. Leo hangs out in bars, too, but Brown has granted him qualities more sympathetic than those of many other protagonists. Leo describes himself as "between women" and looking (96)—unsuccessfully—for comfort in the bars he frequents: "I always think I'm going to find something when I go out at night, I don't know why. I always think that, and I never do. I always think I'll find a woman. But if you go out in sadness, that's all you're going to find" (98–99). What he finds instead is a basic humanity that surpasses his sexual needs. Writing of rural veterans of WWI, WWII, and the Korean War, Brown incorporates obviously autobiographical material. On the subject of his own experience with old soldiers, he once said in an interview that he remembered talking about World War I with an array of veterans in and around Tula: "They tell such great stories" (qtd. in Rankin 94), he added. Leo's own interactions with such men, his heartfelt conversations with two disabled vets in particular, show him what the ravages of war can do to men forced to fight: Aaron and Squirrel are so physically and psychologically impaired that they have never married—they seem to have known that, had they done so, they would have been like Leo's father, so damaged that they would have failed as both husbands and parents. These veterans have only each other to depend on, but Leo's own time in the service makes him empathize with their suffering, internalize the war stories they tell him—stories about looking on helplessly as fifty fellow soldiers are "cut . . . all to pieces with machine guns" (101), stories about spending three weeks on the front lines and then "l[ying] down and cr[ying] all night long" (102). Storytelling thus becomes a focus in "Old Soldiers" as well as Leo absorbs the tales of the older men and, by retelling them himself, gives permanence to their often tragic content.

The story that follows, "Sleep," is the anomaly in the collection, a story whose narrator does not share Brown's age, social status, or search for fulfillment through storytelling.[1] The second story and last two selections in *Big Bad Love*, though, all deal directly with aspiring writers from working-class backgrounds: an obsessed beginner in the short story "The Apprentice," an unskillful plagiarist in the satirical colloquy "Discipline," and a writer on the cusp of success in the novella "92 Days." Though not grouped together in the collection itself, they belong together first because they are clearly autobiographical; they even seem partly self-satirical, may even have something of an implied swagger to them, for by the time Brown published them, he had moved from an unfruitful obsession with, to genuine success at writing. All three also further the collection's focus on characters who try to save themselves from dead-end lives by telling stories. More significantly, though, they also illustrate a fact that the narrators of "Waiting for the Ladies" and "Old Soldiers" never—perhaps luckily—discover: that telling stories is one thing, but getting them published is another, an altogether different undertaking fraught with complications of its own.

"The Apprentice," like its companion stories in Part I, features a male narrator, but this one is the would-be sensitive husband of a wife so obsessed with publishing her fiction that she no longer has a life outside her imagination. Lonnie begins the story in frustration, for when he married Judy he had expected her to be an average, lower-middle-class wife. Instead, she does nothing but "Writewritewritewritewrite" (15). On the rare occasions she isn't writing, she denies him sex until he has read and praised what she has recently written. In many aspects—all of them comically familiar to those who know Brown's biography—Judy is a female version of the unpublished-but-increasingly-obsessed Larry Brown: she turns their shared bedroom into a writing room, writes a novel about a man-eating grizzly bear in Yellowstone National Park, sends story after story to magazine after magazine only to receive rejection letters in return. But she does not stop writing, and, eventually—again like Brown himself—she improves enough to begin publishing the occasional story. In the end, Lonnie comes to see the unwelcome changes to their marriage as the results of her drive to express herself, something of an implicit admission by Brown that his own marriage experienced its share of problems as *he* became obsessed with writing. Here, then, Brown creates an obverse mirror of what happens to a working-class family when one of its members sets out to break the cultural bindings inherent in such a life by aspiring to a life of art; to the writer, though, the creation of that art becomes fundamental to existence, is indeed a means to a certain fulfillment that no other outlet can provide. And yet it does not come without its price: but even if that price is the absolute disruption of the domestic scene, from living arrangements all the way to the marital relationship of the couple at their center, it is no less necessary—at least for the writer, that is.

"Discipline," the most experimental story in *Big Bad Love*, continues—but satirically, this time—Brown's focus on the problems inherent in making a career of writing. Its main character is Doyle Huey Lawrence (his name an obvious play on D. H. Lawrence as well as Larry Brown himself), a recidivistic plagiarist serving a five-year sentence in what one character calls "hacks' prison" (123). During the parole hearing that constitutes the story's action, Lawrence argues that, because of what he considers cruel and unusual punishment—he and another prisoner had allegedly been forced to have sex with tattooed, toothless, obese women—his fourth year of imprisonment should be his last. His captors disagree, arguing that as he has recently been caught "copying Faulkner, at *night*, under the covers, with a flashlight" (131), he has not even begun to reform. The story thus combines the obscene, the phantasmagoric, and, of course, the comic—Edgar Allan Poe at his humorous best. Trying to force Lawrence to testify against a fellow inmate convicted of plagiarizing Flannery O'Connor and Cormac McCarthy, the prosecutor demands, "You don't think it's bad to steal from a dead woman? Pilfer words from a sick, dying writer, who barely had the strength to work three hours a day? Who had more guts and talent in one little finger than you and your buddy Varrick have in your whole bodies?" (123). In the end, under the heavy barrage of questioning, Lawrence eventually breaks down and confesses all. Perhaps surprising, though, given his tortured embarrassment throughout the hearing, is his reaction upon being forced to read before the court some of "his" most recent work. He begins unwillingly, the stage directions showing that he moves from "*unbelievable horror*" to "[*b*]*itter resignation*" (136). After Lawrence reads a page of what sounds like Faulkner at his most florid, though, the prosecutor has to try several times to cut him off, has to call several times both to the judge and for bailiffs, who finally have to rush in and restrain him. He stops only when "Discipline" itself does, his final words "Wait! There's more! Do you hear me? Just listen!" (138). "Discipline" thus shows a writer struggling not only with what Harold Bloom called the anxiety of influence, struggling not only with overzealous fans—the tattooed, toothless, obese woman is a member of a book club and poetry society who had been told that Lawrence is a famous writer—but, most significantly, struggling to have his most recent work read, even when he knows it is patently derivative. Sharing it with an audience apparently brings such fulfillment that the drive to do so can hardly be restrained.

"92 Days," the novella that concludes the collection, is clearly the most autobiographical work of fiction that Brown ever wrote. His widow Mary Annie Brown declared its portrait of narrator Leon Barlow's failed marriage "close" to the Browns' own, which, though it never ended in divorce, was "pretty negative at times." Brown's own drive to publish "caused more problems than anything in our marriage," she admitted. "We got to the point where we [she and her three young children] were second to anything and everything. I raised the children and he wrote and that's just the way it was" (Brown, Mary Annie). In an interview with Kay Bonetti, Brown implied the accuracy of his wife's comments by focusing on an altogether different aspect of the novella: "There's more than a little autobiography in that story, mainly a lot of frustration that I felt, not so much in the early days . . .[b]ut later when they were admitting at magazines that yes, this story is good, but we're not going to touch it. . . . That's hard to come to grips with and you begin to say, 'Man, am I ever going to make it? I've done everything I'm supposed to do. I've paid the dues. I've got all these rejection slips. Now what do I do? Do I keep beating my head on the wall some more?' And you say, 'Yeah. You keep beating your head on the wall some more until you get your first book out'" (audio). Brown elaborated on this frustration in an interview with Dorie LaRue, saying that, after 1985, he "was writing what I considered some of my best stories, 'Facing the Music,' 'The Samaritans,' 'Old Frank and Jesus,' 'The Rich'—things like that. And they were still being turned down. And it was not that it was the quality of the work. They had no quibbles with that . . . but 'it was too brutal, my boss is not going to like it.'. . . . And I began to see that even after you get to the point where you were writing publishable work, that there could still be obstacles in your way to keep you from getting published" (50–51).

Leon Barlow, the working-class narrator of "92 Days," has reached the same point. Instead of the semi-comic depiction of such obsession in "The Apprentice," though, the monologue emphasizes the abject depression, alcoholic misery, and all around self-destructiveness that can attend such continued failure. The story's surrogate Brown has sacrificed everything—wife, children, steady job—to his drive to write, and yet he receives in return only grief from friends and family, rejection letters from editors. Most exasperating of all, as Brown told Bonetti and LaRue, one particular editor tells Barlow that, though a novel in which he has invested two years is publishable— "is hilarious in many places and extremely well-written with a good plot, real characters, refreshing dialogue, beautiful descriptions"—the market "is not amenable to novels about drunk pulpwood haulers and rednecks and deer hunting" (143). The situation is more trying than any other in the story, more stressful than his wife's lawyer's frequent threats, than even the two jail sentences he serves for public intoxication: "I tried to write all I could. I tried to put balls and heart and blood into it like a good writer had once told me to do. Sometimes it wasted me, just laid me out. I knew that at least some of what I was writing was good, but I just hadn't found anybody to share my vision yet. Nobody with any power. Nobody who could say yes or no to publication. I knew about the pecking order, and jealousy, and interdepartmental office memos and the little notes that were jotted with a quick hand. They didn't know about the careers they were advancing or retarding with their little papers, the numbers of us who lived and died with a stroke of their pens. They didn't have any idea of the power they wielded" (192–93). "It seemed almost hopeless sometimes," Leon concludes, "but I knew I had to keep going on. I had chosen my own path. Nothing could turn me from it" (193).

As these last lines indicate, "92 Days" is also story of hope and determination. Leon says that his dream seems "*almost* hopeless *sometimes*," after all. He has his low points—in one he sees himself almost as desperate as Breece D'J Pancake and John Kennedy Toole, while in another he says he "wanted to go out into the forest and live like a madman with leaves for clothes and live in a hole in the ground and throw rocks at anyone who came near" (211)—but hope arrives twice during the story in the form of letters from an editor named Betti DeLoreo. Hers too are rejection letters, but she closes her first with the lines, "Please keep writing. Don't let this [rejection] be disappointing to you. You have great talent, and with material like this you will need great stamina" (156). She closes her second in much the same way: "You're too good a writer to remain unknown forever. . . . Please don't give up" (220–21). In the end, Leon's stamina, his refusal to give up—not the realization of his long-held dream to see his work in print—becomes the subject of the novella, for even by its conclusion he has still not published a single word. Nevertheless, he heeds DeLoreo's advice and keeps writing. "92 Days" thus builds on the early obsession with writing glimpsed in "The Apprentice," taking it to the point at which the writer is good but still cannot get published, the point at which Brown himself, as he told Bonetti, realized that "even after you . . . were writing publishable work, that there could still be obstacles in your way to keep you from getting published." "92 Days" is therefore less about fulfillment than staying on the road to fulfillment, even if it sometimes seems endless, even it if comes with nearly debilitating personal, financial, and psychological costs.

In *Big Bad Love*, then, Brown moves beyond the content of *Facing the Music* to combine his stories of the working class with a more clearly autobiographical and artistic focus. His narrators are all dissatisfied with the lives they lead, working day to day in fairly meaningless jobs, anesthetizing their frustrations by drinking, carousing, and womanizing, ultimately finding themselves still more lost as these palliatives fail. Only those who turn to writing achieve focus and a sense of achievement—but even the collection's burgeoning artists never attain a perfect sense of accomplishment. Like Brown himself, they suffer through apprenticeships, are haunted by the notion that their work is derivative, and become so obsessed with publishing that they often lose contact with the world around them. And even when their work finally shows true merit, they still do not see it published. The dream and the movement toward its realization, it seems, mean as much as—if not more than—success itself.

Note

1. Louis, its narrator, is married to a woman who repeatedly hears noises in the night and fearfully—pointlessly—demands that he get out of bed to assure her of their harmlessness. Brown does a superior job in the story of contrasting the warmth Louis feels under the covers with the cold that he knows will assault him upon again crawling out from under them. Despite growing frustration with his nightly expeditions, he remains firmly tied to the joys of physical existence: episodes

of exposure to freezing that he recalls from his earlier life make him appreciate the warmth of his home, the good food and coffee that he will enjoy when morning comes—even if, as he says toward the end of the story, "I don't know what to do with her [his wife] any more" (110).

Works Cited

Beuka, Robert A. "Larry Brown." *Dictionary of Literary Biography*. Vol. 234, *American Short Story Writers Since World War II*. Ed. Patrick Meanor and Richard E. Lee. New York: Gale, 2001. 57–63.

Rev. of *Big Bad Love*, by Larry Brown. *Virginia Quarterly Review* 67.3 (Summer 1991): 94.

Bonetti, Kay. *Larry Brown: A Conversation with Kay Bonetti*. American Audio Prose Library, 1995.

———. "Larry Brown." *Conversations with American Novelists*. Ed. Bonetti, et al. Columbia: U Missouri P, 1997: 234–53.

Brown, Larry. *Big Bad Love*. Chapel Hill: Algonquin, 1990.

Brown, Mary Annie. Personal interview. 12 July 2005.

Crews, Harry. "Perfectly Shaped Stones." Rev. of *Big Bad Love*, by Larry Brown. *Los Angeles Times Book Review* 21 Oct. 1990: 3.

Fisher, Ann H. Rev. of *Big Bad Love*, by Larry Brown. *Library Journal* 1 Aug. 1990: 139.

LaRue, Dorie. "Interview with Larry Brown: Breadloaf '92." *Chattahoochee Review* 13.3 (Spring 1993): 39–56.

O'Briant, Don. "'Love': It's big, bad and wonderful." Rev. of *Big Bad Love*, by Larry Brown. *Atlanta Journal-Constitution* 9 Sept. 1990: N8.

Pettus, Gary. "Writing his way to the Holy Grail." *Jackson Clarion-Ledger* 23 Aug. 1988: 1C+.

Rankin, Tom. "On the Home Front: Larry Brown's Narrative Landscapes." *Reckon: The Magazine of Southern Culture* 1 (Fall 1995): 90–101.

Richardson, Thomas J. "Larry Brown." *Contemporary Fiction Writers of the South*. Ed. Joseph Flora and Robert Bain. Westport: Greenwood, 1994: 55–66.

Sigal, Clancy. "Looking for Love in All the Wrong Places." Rev. of *Big Bad Love*, by Larry Brown. *Washington Post Book World* 23 Dec. 1990: 11.

Tucker, Neely. "A weaving of love's sorrow and pity." Rev. of *Big Bad Love*, by Larry Brown. *Detroit Free Press* 19 Aug. 1990: 7G.

Economics of the Cracker Landscape

Poverty as an Environmental Issue in Larry Brown's *Joe*

JAY WATSON

American ecocriticism suffers from its own peculiar version of the old "West versus the rest" problem, a regional bias that assigns iconic status to the American West as seedbed and Ground Zero of American nature writing, landscape photography, and ecopolitics, relegating other regional landscapes and ecosystems—with the possible exceptions of Thoreau's New England and Aldo Leopold's Wisconsin—to supporting roles. I therefore want to lobby in this essay for the value of more fully and actively incorporating Southern texts, landscapes, and perspectives into the ongoing project of American environmental studies. More specifically, I want to concentrate on a Southern problematic that should be of particular interest to American ecocritics: the way the region's long, highly visible history of poverty and its rich and troubled history of land use intertwine to foreground poverty itself as an environmental issue. My discussion will draw on Larry Brown's 1991 novel *Joe*, a book that takes up the lives of poor whites struggling to survive amid a northwest Mississippi savaged by an extractive timber industry. I am interested in how conditions of economic stress and deprivation work not only to inhibit environmental awareness in Brown's novel but also, perhaps surprisingly, to create it. *Joe* demonstrates that the Southern environment demands a thoroughgoing socioeconomic analysis: because natural history in the South so pointedly *is* social history—and vice versa—any responsible account of what Georgia writer Janisse Ray has called the "ecology of a Cracker childhood"[1] must be accompanied by an economics of the Cracker landscape. To approach *Joe* in particular in this way is to uncover unsuspected ambiguities in what might otherwise seem a straightforward poor-white fable of surrogate fatherhood and sonhood.

Joe features a pair of protagonists whose lives become progressively entangled. The title character, Joe Ransom, is a hard-living independent contractor and ex-convict who, when the novel opens, works for the timber giant Weyerhaeuser, clearing second-growth hardwood from vast tracts of corporately owned land and replanting them in more profitable pine. The work brings Joe plenty of money but little satisfaction: his marriage has recently ended, he is alienated from his grown children and new grandchild, and, despite his relative wealth, he still seems thoroughly inscribed in a poor-white social dynamic of drinking heavily, driving the backroads, and engaging in fits of sudden, restless violence. The other protagonist is fifteen-year-old Gary Jones. Mired in abject poverty, Gary and his family have drifted through Texas, Tennessee, Georgia, and Florida as migrant laborers before arriving in the pine hills of Mississippi to squat in a rundown log cabin and scavenge as best they can off the rural landscape. The father, Wade, who apparently hails from the area, is an amoral, alcoholic monster who abuses his children and their mother, steals from them to buy liquor and cigarettes, murders a wino for food stamps and booze, and later proves capable of even worse crimes. The mother, unhinged by grief for a lost son whose absence remains a mystery for much of the novel, wanders in and out of reality, barely able to care for Gary and his sisters Dorothy and Fay. Explicit associations with trash emphasize the family's status as social flotsam: Gary is forced by his father to root around in dumpsters for aluminum to recycle; the father is later thrown out of a whorehouse to lie shaking on the ground among broken beer bottles and scraps of metal; Gary's brother Tom is killed in Florida when, like one of the novel's ubiquitous beer cans, he falls off a truck and is crushed by a trailing vehicle; and various Joneses spend large parts of the narrative drifting up and down the Mississippi roadsides like so much human litter. Gary is honest, hard-working, and responsible but seems caught with his family in a vicious cycle of hunger, violence, dependency, rootlessness, and shame.

As Gary attempts to lift himself and his loved ones out of the pathology of poverty, the text begins to foreground his interaction with the nonhuman environments of north Mississippi. This focus acquires a startling intensity in what is arguably *Joe*'s most important scene, that in which the two protagonists first meet and the novel's parallel plots finally make contact. Just before this scene, Wade and Gary have weathered a tense encounter in a cypress swamp with Willie Russell, a character whose drunken violence and festering rage hint at the dark path down which the elder Jones is leading his son. One morning not long afterwards, Gary slips out of the cabin to roam the nearby woods alone, and the narrative follows his wandering for three pages of dense, descriptive prose. If the landscape appears unremarkable, even impoverished at first—pine woods and "sparse" (110), fire-scarred second-growth forest, hardly the stuff of Sierra Club calendars—the narrative lingers to register its effect on Gary, as this child of privation and violence encounters a world of sensory and spiritual density, of mystery and solace. The shell of a box turtle "flicker[s]" with "patterns of yellow sunbursts" like "the imprint of a kaleidoscope" (109). Water "course[s] musically over the shattered stones" of a creekbed (108) or sings to the boy in "a low and throaty warble" from a nearby spring, whose "soft undulation . . . ripple[s] the surface gently and ke[eps] grains of sand in motion, ceaselessly turning and resettling on the clean bottom" (109). So marginalized and isolated elsewhere, Gary finds intimacy, even a kind of recognition, in the woods. An "abundance of squirrels" greets him with "black eyes bright and hypnotic" (108), and when he bends to drink from the spring, he participates in the landscape "the way some foraging animal might." The water is "sweet with a faint taste of iron and so cold it made his teeth ache" (109). Here, then, a half-starved youth can finally find a kind of nourishment. Here also we see the same annealing process that is at work in the wilderness landscapes of Faulkner's *Go Down, Moses* (1942); as Gary wanders the edge of a bluff, he stops "to run his hands over the old knife scars of names and dates healed almost unreadable in the bark of a giant beech riddled with squirrel dens and half toppling out over the void below. A hollow tree, it was once burned on the inside by squirrel hunters, the flames from the bed of leaves running up it like fire within a flue. He looked up into the top branches. A fat coon stared down at him from a fork, then put its hands over its eyes and turned away, an obscure lump of fur residing most peacefully this fine spring morning" (111). The sheltering function of the burned-out tree would not be lost on a boy who has known both migrancy and vagrancy firsthand. Moreover, in contrast to the pinched and vulnerable spaces of the log house, as devoid of privacy as any Erskine Caldwell cabin, the woods hold out a promise of secrecy, of room to maneuver; Gary will later hide money from his father beneath these rocks and trees.

As his ramble in the woods takes a sudden and disturbing turn, though, Gary's response to the landscape proves somewhat bipolar.

They emerged slowly in the distance through the slanted trunks and matted tangles of briers, slashing doggedly at the trees and the nets of vegetation hung like the giant webs of spiders across their paths. Faint cries could be heard. They were a group of seven or eight black men, with their shirts tied around their waists, some with flashing silver tubes in their hands and some with bright orange, all of them spread out arms' width apart and traveling slowly to the trees, then around and around them, stabbing and slashing. . . .When they were almost abreast of him, he could see that there was one who moved among them holding plastic jugs in his hands, attending to them when they called out. They were shouting back and forth to one another things he couldn't make out, only a word now and then. (111)

The men, of course, work for Joe Ransom, "deadening" a stand of timber by injecting individual trees with poison. In a week or so the trees will start to die. In six months the land will be replanted in pine seedlings. And within a few years the dead trees will be on the ground, completing this triumph of monocrop silviculture. But Gary doesn't know any of this yet. He is not quite sure what the men are doing in the woods—"There seemed to be no logical purpose to their work"—but he immediately registers the strangeness and violence: the indecipherable language, almost a foreign tongue, the furious stabbing and slashing, the noise and chaos "disturb[ing] greatly the solitude of the woods" with which the boy appears to identify. This antagonism toward the landscape is compounded by fear; when the men stumble across a snake, they go wild with "hysterical abandon," hacking at the animal with sticks, screams, and curses, "frantic in their fear of whatever lay so helpless in the face of this ferocious attack" (112). Only a few moments have elapsed, only a single page of text, but we seem to be in a completely different world from that in which the coon in the beech tree had stared down at Gary.

I linger on this scene to emphasize Gary's alertness to the contrast between the work crew's hostile and purely instrumental attitude to the woods and his own reverent sense of the landscape as numinous, sheltering space. This makes it all the more incongruous when, on meeting Joe and having the deadening work explained to him, Gary instantly and uncritically accepts the older man's offer to hire on with the crew: in response to Gary's question about whether the men work for him, Joe asks, "You don't want to work, do you?" Gary, immediately taking "three anxious steps forward," answers, "Yessir, I need a job. My daddy needs one, too." Joe's account of the work all but domesticates the poisoning of the landscape: "[T]his ain't good enough timber to log it. It's just scrub stuff, so all they want to do is get rid of what's on it so they can put pines on it" (115). It is also likely that Gary's estrangement from his father and Joe's from his daughter and son inform both the man's offer and the boy's answer; indeed, one way to read the remainder of the novel is in terms of Joe's increasingly paternal relationship with Gary, his attempts to rescue the boy from Wade's influence. Still, Gary makes his decision only after seeing its destructive consequences firsthand; he knowingly enters into a zero-sum game in which self-reliance and self-esteem will come at the expense of nonhuman nature.

Gary's poverty takes an environmental toll here. The boy's life is so bleak and deprived, his material need to "get by," to assuage his family's hunger, so urgent that no amount of spiritual value or consolation can substitute for the raw economic opportunity he now senses in the forest landscape. His desire to escape or ameliorate the human violence that surrounds him makes violence against the woods seem acceptable. Moreover, to one in Gary's predicament, self-extension into nature may represent a much more tangible and immediate—and *American*—way to counter the crippling effects of poverty on identity than either self-abandonment in nature or intimacy with it. Gary starts work that very morning, racing to Joe's truck for a poison gun of his own. It is a brutal equation: his quickening equals nature's deadening.

For all its ostensible celebration of the deepening bond between Gary and Joe, the novel never quite loses sight of this mournful irony. As Gary slowly climbs the economic ladder and is initiated into the simple pleasures of rural white life by Joe, the shadow of their complicity against the land remains to darken and undercut the central symbols of his economic progress and personal growth. Perhaps the most obvious of these symbols is the pickup truck Gary buys from Joe for two hundred precious dollars saved out of his deadening wages. The truck has seen better days, but to Gary it offers the pleasure and privileges of self-extension in at least two ways: through physical movement and through conspicuous consumption. Gary has long dreamed of such freedoms, but two chilling scenes late in the novel completely discredit the automobile as an emancipatory or empowering force, linking it instead with the abuse and enslavement of children. In the first scene, Wade pimps his youngest daughter to Willie Russell and an equally degenerate companion—out of the back of Gary's truck, the same truck, of course, in which Joe once carried his deadening crews out to despoil the forest. (Dorothy's mysterious muteness, alluded to several times throughout the novel, is thus finally explained.) Immediately following this scene is a long flashback in which Wade barters away his son Calvin to a wealthy but childless couple for a Lincoln automobile. (We thus learn the origins of the mother's shattering grief.) With the help of the pickup and the Lincoln, Wade in effect commodifies his own blood in scenes that underscore how the same breaches of sexual and familial ethics that once plagued the plantation world of Faulkner's fiction continue to hold sway in the pine plantation economy of contemporary Mississippi.

On another occasion Joe takes Gary out drinking. The evening, which ends in a brothel, is a blue-collar initiation into Southern manhood, but by this point in the novel the reader has witnessed so much alcohol-induced cruelty, violence, and crime that the drunken camaraderie between Gary and Joe seems strained, more than a little suspect. The human damage wreaked by alcohol is everywhere in *Joe*, reaching into nearly every home, worksite, motor vehicle, and place of recreation. Beer cans so litter the landscape as to form an alternative landscape of their own, piling up in front of houses like little mountains or, at one point, filling a fourteen-foot aluminum boat; even the spring that sings to Gary holds two six-packs that Wade has put there to keep cold. Bearing in mind Joe's preferred method of deforestation, we might say that alcohol leaves the novel's human landscape as poisoned and deadened as Joe's chemicals leave the forest landscape. The analogy is entirely unaccidental: at one point Wade passes out after a drunken spree, "toppl[ing] over slowly, a bit at a time like a rotten tree giving way, until the whiskey lay spilling between his legs" (43). It is hard to celebrate Joe and Gary's beer-fueled revels once we see that they are simply doing to themselves what they do to the woods. And could well do to others: the emotional "deadening" of Gary's sister and mother, after all, can be directly traced to the drunken outrages of the father.

Finally, a curious scene late in the novel appears to undercut the middle-class lifestyle toward which Gary's and Joe's economic aspirations implicitly point. Joe heads off to Tupelo for a night of carousing and awakens the next morning in a strange bed. Wandering the halls of the house, he discovers it to be a tastefully decorated showcase: paneled walls, parquet floors, satin sheets, and, outside, a gas grill and a swimming pool. His lover is tan and trim, and the day unfolds as a kind of middle-class idyll: lots of swimming and sunning, steaks on the grill, great sex, and, of course, plenty of beer. We are caught off guard, then, when Joe falls asleep in his lover's arms and begins to dream . . . of prison, "of clearing the roadside grass with sickles," of "enduring it all, watching the days tick off the calendar one by one," "of the heavy wire mesh fences that fenced in the inmates" (327), and "of the smoky lights that loomed in the darkness outside the camps, where in the black towers the unseen guards with their rifles sat watching for movement in the packed dirt beside the buildings" (327–28). Before dawn he slips out of the house and drives away without so much as a backward glance, "reaching down for the last lukewarm beer in the cooler, eyeing the whiskey that was still on the seat" (328), once again choosing his poison. If middle-class existence is tantamount to a prison sentence, if economic advancement leads only to desperate entrapment, then what kind of bargain have Joe and Gary really struck in trading away the woods for the means of access to this genteel world? How different is this bargain, finally, from trading a boy away for an automobile?

Reflecting on Gary's and Joe's destructive attitudes toward the woods, we might ask whether their gender plays a role in the way they look at nature. Feminist studies by Nancy Chodorow, Dorothy Dinnerstein, Carol Gilligan, and others who approach gender identity through the framework of object relations indicate that masculine selfhood is often defined against the world of other people and things, in competition with it or conquest over it, whereas feminine selfhood is more often defined in connection with the world, in an openness and a sense of responsibility toward otherness.[2] Boys are taught to fear dependency, girls to accept their own dependency on mothers, fathers and, later, husbands, and to provide care in turn for others who depend on them. This, in turn, has led ecofeminist Marti Kheel to suggest that "women's self-identity" may be less "bound up" than men's "with the urge to negate one's dependence on the natural world" (137). Suggestively, then, Brown ends his book with a two-hundred-word portrait of a mother, a child, and the Southern pine woods, a coda whose tone, mood, and emphasis seem especially forbidding:

> That winter the trees stood nearly barren of their leaves and the cold seemed to settle into the old log house deep in the woods. The old woman felt it seep into her bones. Each morning the floors seemed colder, each day it was harder to crank the truck. The boy piled wood for colder days to come. At odd times of the day they'd hear the faint honking, and they'd hurry out into the yard to see overhead, and far beyond the range of men's guns the geese spread out over the sky in a distant brotherhood, the birds screaming to each other in happy voices for the bad weather they were leaving behind, the southlands always ahead of their wings, warm marshes and green plants beckoning them to their ancient primeval nesting lands.
>
> They'd stand looking up until the geese diminished and fled crying out

over the heavens and away into the smoking clouds, their voices dying slowly, one last note the only sound and proof of their passing, that and the final wink of motion that swallowed them up into the sky and the earth that met it and the pine trees already green and constant against the great blue wildness that lay forever beyond. (345)

The wintry austerity of this passage contrasts sharply with the springtime accents of Gary's early rambles in the woods. The sense of absence is palpable, unnerving. Neither Wade Jones nor Joe Ransom, for instance, is anywhere to be found. Joe has most likely fled the area or wound up back in prison after catching Willie Russell with Dorothy Jones and presumably killing him. Wade is last seen slinking away into the forest thickets during the same scene, ironically concealed by the nonhuman world he seems so indifferent to elsewhere. Neither, for that matter, is Dorothy mentioned in the epilogue. Perhaps she simply remains inside the cabin, keeping warm, but it is just as likely that she, too, has joined Fay, Tom, and Calvin in the ranks of lost Jones siblings. Nor is the sense of privation limited to loss of kin. The mother is damaged, the boy no doubt overmatched by the challenges of getting by as the Mississippi winter descends. Joe's absence means that Gary will not, as planned, spend the season planting pine seedlings; has he managed to find work elsewhere? The log house is inadequate shelter against the cold; the truck is unreliable. We sense the terrible evanescence of Gary's brief forays up the class ladder in earlier chapters; as the novel closes, the Joneses' situation seems more precarious than ever.

Which is perhaps why the passage shifts its attention away from the economics of the wintry landscape to linger on its natural beauty. For all their poverty, the implication seems to be, the Joneses still "have" nature, still exist in proximity to, perhaps even share in, its abiding wealth: the thrilling call of the geese, the "blue wildness" of the sky, the enduring pines. I, for one, though, find the swelling lyricism of that final paragraph a little too good to be true, perhaps even deliberately forced. Those "constant" pines, for instance, strike a particularly false note: we know good and well that they are grist for Weyerhaeuser's mills, no more constant or secure in their grip on the land than the Joneses themselves. That leaves the great blue flyway above, as remote and inaccessible to Gary and his mother as the parquet floors and swimming pools of Tupelo. The geese drifting through Brown's scene only mock the entrapment of the Joneses, who began the novel as fellow migrants but now, set down in Wade's "nesting land" and then abandoned there, find themselves looking *up*—with longing?—at migration. The geese, we know, will be back with spring—but the Joneses? Brown preaches a homely, hard truth: that all too often the rootedness of the poor only underscores their vulnerability. Brown's conclusion aches with longing, a longing utterly conditioned by the unrelieved poverty of the characters. We see a final time how economic exigencies work to shape Southern responses to the environment.

Brown's account of a poor-white childhood in the Deep South suggests that the relationship between human poverty and the nonhuman environment may be more complex, and less monolithically antagonistic, than it might appear at first glance. He also suggests that any environmental ethos worthy of the name in the South must include the pursuit of economic justice for the many casualties of the region's extractive industries and exploitive labor arrangements. The economics of the Cracker landscape demand no less.

Notes

Originally published, in different form, in *Mississippi Quarterly* (Fall 2002); included here with permission of the *Quarterly* and its editor, Noel Polk.

1. See Ray's *Ecology of a Cracker Childhood* (Minneapolis: Milkweed Editions, 1999).
2. See Nancy Chodorow's *The Reproduction of Mothering: Psychoanalysis and the Sociology of Gender* (Berkeley: U of California P, 1978), Dorothy Dinnerstein's *The Mermaid and the Minotaur: Sexual Arrangements and Human Malaise* (New York: Harper and Row, 1977), and Carol Gilligan's *In a Different Voice: Psychological Theory and Women's Development* (Cambridge: Harvard UP, 1982).

Works Cited

Brown, Larry. *Joe*. Chapel Hill: Algonquin, 1991.

Kheel, Marti. "Ecofeminism and Deep Ecology: Reflections on Identity and Difference." *Reweaving the World: The Emergence of Ecofeminism*. Ed. Irene Diamond and Gloria Feman Orenstein. San Francisco: Sierra Club, 1990.

The White Trash Cowboys of *Father and Son*

THOMAS ÆRVOLD BJERRE

In *West of Everything: The Inner Life of Westerns*, Jane Tompkins asserts that the aesthetics of the pulp and cinematic Western have saturated twentieth-century American culture. The well-known archetypes of the genre—the cowboy, his horse, the gunfight, the good-hearted saloon girl, the immense and indomitable landscape—have inspired, pervaded, even overpowered an entire culture, often without our awareness (5–6). Southern novels have proven no less susceptible to their influence: Cormac McCarthy, Barry Hannah, William Gay, Chris Offutt, Ron Rash, and Larry Brown have all written fiction that bears the imprint of the Western. *Joe* (1991), Brown's second novel, for instance, tells the tale of a young boy who falls in with an adult hero facing tough moral decisions against a violent backdrop— as does *Shane* (1953), the George Stevens Western that Brown once cited as one of his favorites (Algonquin Books of Chapel Hill). Even as critics continue to characterize him as a latter-day heir to the Southern literary tradition—bestowing upon him, in effect, the mantle of William Faulkner but not Zane Grey, Flannery O'Connor but not John Ford—Brown has at the same time borrowed from, and in one particular novel added to, the legacy of the American Western.

In his introduction to *Westerns: Making the Man in Fiction and Film*, Lee Clark Mitchell characterizes the Western as an endlessly recurring set of problems, among them problems of honor and justice "enacted in a conflict of vengeance and social control; the problem of violence, in acknowledging its value yet honoring occasions when it can be controlled; and subsuming all, the problem of what it means to be a man" (3). This is the same set of problems central to *Father and Son* (1996), Brown's third novel, also a story of honor, justice, violence, and "what it means to be a man." In *Father and Son*, Brown creates a story of almost mythic proportions by reducing his subject matter to the bare essentials—to love and hate, forgiveness and revenge, good and evil—and the result is a morality play set in the South of the late 1960s. It is the story of Glen Davis, an ex-convict who returns to his Mississippi hometown bent on revenge. His half-brother, Sheriff Bobby Blanchard, had arrested him three years earlier, and both men are now in love with the same girl, Jewel Coleman. The plotlines and characters create exactly the sets of problems at the heart of numerous Westerns, making *Father and Son* Brown's most formulaic novel by far. As will become clear, though, Brown also subverts classic Western conventions to fit his own purposes.

The lines of regional influence originally ran in the opposite direction, of course, not West to South, but South to West. Georgia was the westernmost of the original thirteen British colonies, and for years after the 1783 Treaty of Paris, the Mississippi River marked the westernmost border of the fledgling United States. The South, in other words, *was* the West—or, rather, the frontier the West would later represent—a fact embodied in the title of the James Kirke Paulding novel *Westward, Ho!* (1832), which follows a group of Virginians into Kentucky. At the heart of the myth that grew out of this earlier frontier, though, was a hero in many ways different from he who would emerge as the country pushed farther west. Richard Slotkin explains that the hero of the Southern frontier was "the military aristocrat... a chevalier, a conquistador, subduing and subordinating the masses of a savage race, the conscious agent not of individual ambition alone, but of corporate will" (141)—and yet, as Robert Rebein notes, the hero of the Western frontier, different though he would be, would not be without his Southern characteristics, most apparent his "embodiment of the medieval chivalry southerners picked up from reading too much Sir Walter Scott" (115). Southerners, moreover, figure prominently in some of the century's most celebrated Westerns. The title character of Owen Wister's *The Virginian* (1902) is a Southerner, and as Edward Buscombe notes, Western film is "full" of "discontented" Southerners: Stonewall Torrey in *Shane*, Ben Allison in Raoul Walsh's *The Tall Men* (1955), Ethan Edwards in John Ford's *The Searchers* (1956), Benjamin Tyreen in Sam Peckinpah's *Major Dundee* (1965), and Josey Wales in Clint Eastwood's *The Outlaw Josey Wales* (1976) (9). In drawing more from the Western than the Southern variant of the frontier myth, then, Brown and his contemporaries essentially reverse the original lines of influence. In that their heroes, though far from military aristocrats, often bear the mark of Scott's and Wister's chivalric characters, though—are plain folk but gentlemen at the same time—they also retain something of the Southern frontier hero as well.

One of the most crucial elements of the frontier is the land itself, and though there are obvious differences between Western and Southern geographies, Brown uses *Father and Son*'s Southern landscape in accordance with the Western formula. The Western has often infused the land with rejuvenative powers; as Mitchell notes, "landscape is not only a model but a medicine" (104). The same is true of *Father and Son*: in a scene in which nature cures even the villainous Glen of his vices, he fishes with one of his few friends and is content for the only time in the novel: "Glen didn't say anything," Brown writes; "the old familiar pleasure came back into him like those distant mornings on the river with his old man. He smiled now" (222). The landscape surrounding him is of almost Edenic beauty, and the descriptions read like those in a Zane Grey novel: "He saw the trees above the water and the way the wind was moving through the branches. He looked at the dark water and the small ripples that lapped at the bank. He looked at a hawk soaring lazily by the cypresses on the other side of the lake, the beds of water lilies floating in their mats of stems" (223). When Glen catches a ten-pound fish, he decides to turn it loose because, as he says, "He never done nothin to me" (224). The land, even if only fleetingly, thus offers Glen a rare oasis of peace amid an otherwise troubled existence.

Nature is almost larger than life in both West and South. Tompkins describes nature as "the one transcendent thing, the one thing larger than man ... the ideal toward which human nature strives" (72). In *Father and Son*, descriptions of man and nature mirror those of the Western, as when Brown writes of Glen's father Virgil walking "beneath the sky and on top of the land, a tiny figure moving like an ant" (65). But nature is also violent and has been since James Fenimore Cooper's influential Leatherstocking Tales (1823–1841), Wister's *The Virginian*, and Grey's *Riders of the Purple Sage* (1912). Brown uses the outdoor world almost naturalistically, as a way to test his characters, to burden them still further. As he had in *Joe*, he charges nature in *Father and Son* with man-crushing powers: when Bobby, burrowing into the heart of human depravity, is digging up the bodies of two children killed by their parents, he closes his eyes for a second as "[a] thunderbolt barked far off. A dry rumbling cracking that seemed to be heading his way with one purpose and that to split the heavens open and devour him and everything in the world that was under it. He could hear it forming up in the distance and thunder building on thunder and it began to rain.... The lightning moved in and it began to arc down to the land. He heard a bolt explode nearby. He felt that he was about to be struck and ... dove to the ground" (277–78). What's interesting here, especially when compared to *Joe*, is that in the first half of the passage nature sets Bobby's mood. In its second half, nature unleashes its destructive forces and threatens to destroy him as well. Having his characters battle the natural elements is one way Brown tests his characters for moral and physical strength, a technique, as Tompkins points out, borrowed from numerous writers of Westerns: "The qualities needed to survive on the land are the qualities the land itself possesses—bleakness, mercilessness. . . . To be a man in the Western is to seem to grow out of the environment, which means to be hard, to be tough, to be unforgiving" (73).

It is not only because of the landscape, however, that the novel's cast of characters would be almost as much at home a century earlier and a thousand miles west. The novel takes place in the mid-twentieth-century South instead of the mid-nineteenth-century West, but both regions are populated, by and large, by working-class heroes and villains. The terms "white trash" and "cowboys" employed in the title of this essay are thus used loosely, refer not to either sharecroppers or cattle wranglers specifically but to blue-collar workers, plain folks in general. Ultimately, though, both terms imply more cohesion than they can deliver. Just as not every male character in *Father and Son* completely fits the stereotype of the poor white Southerner, not every Western hero is a cowboy: many, more accurately, are gunslingers, cavalry officers, even sheriffs. Brown from the beginning of his career unflinchingly depicts the lives of hard-living, working-class whites, and in *Father and Son* he combines these archetypes, conjoins the blue-collar hero and the cowboy hero. This fusion of the working-class narrative and the Western aesthetic is apparent even on the dust jacket of the novel's first American edition, which shows a black-and-white close-up of a man's waist, complete with an oversized belt buckle, jeans, a coarse shirt, and a rough-hewn left hand, its fingernails grimy with grease or dirt, clutching a smoldering cigarette. He could be the average blue-collar worker on a break, or he could just as easily be a lone cowboy relaxing as he gazes over the prairie. In many ways, the figures are essentially the same.

John G. Cawelti pointed out more than thirty years ago that one of the enduring strengths of the Western formula is that it "lingers on." Even though it evolves and changes with the times, it remains "basically recognizable" ("Prolegomena" 66). *Father and Son* is a clear case in point, for in it Brown adheres to the fundamental dictates of this formula, one of the most essential being that "clearly opposing players form basic moral reference points" (67). The novel's first twenty pages set up several paired conflicts, among them those between Glen and Bobby, between Glen and Jewel, and between Glen and his father Virgil. In each case, Glen stands out as the morally inferior character against those who, in one way or another, embody decency and communal values. Cawelti also explains that "there must be a series of acts of violence to set the three-sided game in operation and to provoke and justify final destruction of the villain in such a way as to benefit the good group" (68). Again, this pattern clearly fits the novel. By killing a bartender and his innocent assistant, raping a young girl, and threatening and repudiating his son and father—all within forty-eight hours of his release— Glen Davis supplies the "acts of violence to set the three-sided game in operation," and the consequent showdown is soon to follow.

Serving as counterpoint to Glen and his violent actions are the novel's more positive characters. According to Brown himself, Bobby Blanchard, the sheriff and hero of *Father and Son*, is "a really good man. He's [the] voice of reason in the book" (Bonetti 247). Throughout the novel, Bobby is the embodiment of kindness and decency, a fleshed-out version of the peripheral but kindly sheriff Earl in *Joe*, who tries to talk sense into the title character, and a predecessor of the highway patrolman Sam Harris in Brown's subsequent novel *Fay* (2000), all three of them lawmen who do their best to be loyal to their job and to themselves. But Bobby is not just an almost archetypically righteous Brown hero; he is also, in many ways, the image of the traditional Western hero, that forged by Wister in *The Virginian* and subsequently tempered by a century of literary and cinematic practitioners. As Richard Etulain explains, the nameless hero of *The Virginian* replicates "the courage of intrepid men like Daniel Boone and Kit Carson" and resembles Cooper's Natty Bumppo "in his willingness to confront dangerous foes and dutifully carry out difficult tasks assigned to him." Furthermore, his courageous actions mirror those of the heroes of Buffalo Bill's Wild West Show (68). Lacking aristocratic background, distinguished family lineage, and an education, the Virginian nonetheless "proves himself a man among men" through both physical power and "common sense" (70). As will become clear below, Bobby Blanchard embodies many of the traits that made the Virginian the quintessential Western hero. Throughout the novel he is placed in situations that test his courage, authority, and loyalty to his profession.

The characteristic that Etulain calls "common sense" is what Michael Blake refers to as "a code of honor" in his discussion of Will Kane, the upright sheriff of Fred Zinneman's *High Noon* (1952). Blake argues that "the men of the West who wore a badge were a breed unto themselves.... all had a code of honor." In today's "more pessimistic society," he continues, "the cowboy's code of honor is seen as something facile or primitive" (49). In a postmodern age in which tradition and authority are constantly called into question, blind loyalty to a specific doctrine is rarely considered a positive trait. It smacks of anachronistic conservatism and lack of an independent mentality. But Will Kane, Blake stresses, "understood what it meant to wear a badge and the responsibility it invoked. He also had his own personal code of honor, which went hand in hand with that of a lawman. Despite the cost, he had to stand up for what he believed was the right thing to do" (51). Blake also distinguishes Kane from the more shallow heroes of B-movie Westerns. Unlike, for instance, infallible cowboys from Tom Mix and Gene Autry to Roy Rogers, Kane "has real feelings; he is afraid, nervous and worried that he will die" (52). Much the same can be said of Bobby Blanchard: he too embodies "common sense" and "a code of honor." His gentlemanly behavior and self-restraint qualify him for the group of revered lawmen that legendary Dodge City sheriff Bat Masterson described as "just plain ordinary men who could shoot straight and had the most utter courage and perfect nerve—and, for the most part, a keen sense of right and wrong" (qtd. in Blake 49). This same quality points to the Western hero's moral superiority, a trait that is almost always taken for granted in the Western and that helps define the hero as exactly that. These characteristics will later prove crucial to the life-or-death decisions Bobby will face, and, together with his indispensable self-restraint, will still further characterize him as a Mississippi version of the traditional Western hero.

Jewel Coleman has just as much in common with the traditional Western heroine. Glen's former mistress, she has become the object of Bobby's affection since Glen's incarceration. Jewel is a young woman who cuts her grass "on weekends in her swimming suit, barefooted, dust coating her red toenails" (91)—a male fantasy come to life, in other words. To Bobby she is pure and chaste, Grace Kelley's Quaker grade-school teacher from *High Noon*, while to Glen she is anything but, Claire Trevor's prostitute—without the obvious possibility of redemption—from Ford's *Stagecoach* (1939). Furthermore, as in the traditional Western, Brown transforms Jewel from an independent woman capable of taking care of herself and her son into a woman ready to assume a more subservient role. As the novel progresses, she comes to rely more and more on Bobby, and at its end she has joined a traditional family. As Cawelti concludes in his analysis of women in the Westerns of Wister, Grey, and William S. Hart, the ultimate result of the hero's confrontation with "wild nature and violent men" is "an affirmation of such traditional American values as monogamous love, the settled family, the basic separation of masculine and feminine roles" (*Adventure* 240). With the exception of Bobby's mother Mary (to whom we shall return), *Father and Son* seems to advocate exactly these traditional values. After Glen's final acts of violence—he rapes Bobby's mother and then is himself killed—Brown offers, on the last pages of *Father and Son*, an almost Edenic image of family bliss. As "the last sinking tip of the sun sends light up" (346), Glen's father Virgil rocks his sleeping grandson in his lap on the porch. He has apparently kicked his alcoholism and has formed a relationship with Mary, who has just arrived with Bobby and Jewel. As Virgil holds his grandson "close to him as if to protect him from any harm" (347), the sun literally sets on the happy new family. Any trace of the trauma everyone has just experienced has seemingly evaporated along with the "scattered clouds" in the sky (346).

Before this idyllic conclusion, though, Bobby must first win Jewel, which means facing Glen's wrath—but, of course, he must do so according to codes both legal and moral. The Western code enumerates a set of rules specifying which actions are legitimate and which are not, and, as Cawelti points out, "one of the most important . . . is that the hero cannot use violence without certain justifications" ("Prolegomena" 68). Whenever Bobby is tempted to use violence, he manages to restrain himself, thus upholding the Western code. Even though he often comes close to breaking it, reason and restraint finally keep him on solid ground. Early in the novel, during his first angry clash with Glen, Bobby offers to make peace with him: "Now if you want to," he tells him, "we'll shake hands like grown men. Put all this behind us" (14). He then offers Glen his hand, but, as he stands there in the empty silence waiting for a response, his half-brother spits, then snarls, "You take that badge off for five minutes and I'll stomp your ass in the ground." Instead of acting out of anger, however, or with the righteous indignation of a lawman taunted by an ex-convict, Bobby withdraws his hand, says, "You wouldn't win" (15), and walks back to his cruiser. The issue is not whether Bobby lacks the desire or courage to respond to such threats. Several passages reveal that, if it were not for his badge, he would already have engaged Glen: "Maybe Glen would stay out of the way and leave Jewel alone. And if he wouldn't he could always take his badge off for that five minutes. Five minutes. You could hurt somebody real bad in five minutes. But he hoped it wouldn't come to that. All he wanted was for Glen to leave Jewel alone" (310). Bobby must show restraint in other situations as well. When an abusive husband and father, a man who has murdered his own child and buried it behind his trailer, tries to kill him, his restraint stretches to its breaking point. Bobby points his gun at the man and, for a few seconds, at least, debates whether to kill him. Finally, though, he checks himself, deciding to arrest the man instead—but "[i]n that tiny second when he decided not to kill him he became very sad" (279).

Bobby thus offers us still further examples of an honored attribute that goes all the way back to Cooper's Natty Bumppo. Such exhibitions of manly restraint are crucial to the Western, Mitchell points out (155), adding that they help distinguish the hero from other men: "indeed, it requires the distinction of others whose lack of restraint provides a foil to the true man's achieved coherence" (166). Mitchell also points out the obvious paradox that restraint can be understood only upon contrast with surrounding chaos; it "can only be demonstrated through narratives of excess." Without scenes of such excess, scenes in which "this supposedly masculine virtue" is roused and tested and "strained to the breaking point," the "blankness of the hero's countenance expresses only blankness, not the deliberateness of prudent intention or the saving power of self-control" (167). Glen's violent spree and aggressive behavior, in other words, also serve to enhance the reader's positive impressions of Bobby. His self-restraint becomes all the more impressive when faced with tough moral decisions, such as how he will choose to react to the child-killer and to Glen.

This dynamic, then, explains much of the violence in *Father and Son*. As in much of Brown's fiction, violence serves as a moral testing ground for his hero or heroine. Young Gary in *Joe* is surrounded by violence, but he ultimately survives it. Likewise, the eponymous protagonist of *Fay* must struggle through all kinds of abuse and violence before she can claim her freedom. As Brown himself explained, all his characters face "some kind of struggle" that forces "a resolution or an ending." He called it "sandbagging": making "things as hard on them as I can so . . . I'll see how they're going to react and what's going to happen and what the story's going to be about" (Manley 125). Without the surrounding chaos of violence, including the destructive powers of nature mentioned above, Brown's characters would not be able to prove their moral worth; Bobby would not prove his ability to shoulder any burden. Brown, in short, is interested in seeing how humans react when pushed to their limits. Their violent reactions not only propel them through the plot but offer insights into the cruelty of mankind for both readers and characters. For Bobby, "[t]he things that people did to each other didn't surprise him anymore, ever since he'd learned they were capable of doing any thing you could imagine and some things you couldn't" (51). He becomes a wiser man than most, a morally superior character, a mid-twentieth-century Mississippi version of the classic Western hero.

The stock Western traits with which Brown endowed his characters parallel certain traits of the Southern, if not broadly American, working class as well. Despite Bobby's position as a middle-class sheriff, he can be seen as a working-class hero, a purer version of other Brown heroes like Joe Ransom and Sam Harris in that he does not possess the kinds of human flaws that make these characters more credible. In John Shelton Reed's terms, the values Brown bestowed upon Bobby—honesty and courage in particular—position him as an "authentic, indigenous working-class hero," a "good old boy," a young Southerner who is "positive, independent, competent, and strong" (35). Granted, he is not the antebellum yeoman that Reed sees as the foundation of the working-class hero, but Bobby's predominantly optimistic and morally flawless behavior does qualify him for Reed's term. And yet, even though Bobby rises above all others as the moral center of the novel, he does cut loose from time to time, as seen by way of his wish to put his badge down briefly and do things his own way. Indeed, though he never exhibits any actual malice, there is "an element of rowdiness about him," a quality that Reed detects in good old boys in general (38).

Yet *Father and Son* also features a cast of lower-class types, many of whom have far more rowdiness about them. As Reed would have it, they range from the "redneck" Glen to the "poor white trash" embodied by Glen's brother Puppy. Bobby's half-brother Glen is what Reed terms a "redneck villain," for he has "an outlaw quality that the good old boys lack" (38). Glen's violent strain and his indifferent attitude to the world around him clearly make him an outlaw, and the contrast between him and his sheriff half-brother could hardly be more distinct. Reed explains that the redneck's "essential characteristic" is "*meanness.*" He "fights because he wants to *hurt* somebody, often somebody helpless." The violent redneck, Reed argues, even to a certain extent created the dominant American perception of the white, working-class, Southern male, and not least because of his regular appearance in popular culture (40). Watching Glen as he violently engages in rape and murder, we perhaps find it difficult to distinguish admirable traits—and yet, in Larry Brown's fiction, all such figures possess at least some degree of dignity. Digging below the stereotypical surface, Brown explains Glen's life of violence by writing of his tragic upbringing. As a child, he had accidentally shot his younger brother and, ever since, has had to live not only with the consequent guilt, but with anger at his father for keeping the gun loaded. He has also endured a quasi-incestuous relationship with his mother, Emma, the most obvious indications of which come as he rapes Bobby's mother Mary. He wants her to pay "for what she had caused between him and his mother" (323). "She was almost as beautiful as his mother," Brown writes, "and he began to undress slowly, quietly, taking a great pleasure in it, thinking of how it was going to be, how fine to finally join with that flesh" (324). Glen had never had the best relationship with his father, either, who earlier had had a relationship with Bobby's mother, shortly thereafter producing the future sheriff. Glen's uncertainty and frustration have simmered since childhood, and they finally boil up into uncontrollable wrath that, from Brown's perspective, can assume no form other than violence.

Glen, though, doesn't embody just the distinctly Southern socioeconomic traits of Reed's redneck. In that he clearly belongs to a group of men who find action speaking louder than words, he also embodies further traits inherent in the Western aesthetic. Peter Schwenger points out that "it is by talking that one opens up to another person and becomes vulnerable. It is by putting words to an emotion that it becomes feminized. As long as the emotion is restrained, held back, it hardly matters what the emotion itself is; it will retain a male integrity" (44). As Tompkins implies, Schwenger's analysis neatly coincides with the masculine code of the Western: "Language is gratuitous at best; at worst it is deceptive. It takes the place of things, screens them from view, creates a shadow world where anything can be made to look like anything else" (52). Westerns are full of relatively silent, or at least tough-talking men; best known, perhaps, is Clint Eastwood's antihero from Sergio Leone's *A Fistful of Dollars* (1964), *For a Few Dollars More* (1965), and *The Good, the Bad, and the Ugly* (1966). This tacit belief that silence equals machismo becomes evident even within the first five pages of Brown's novel. When Jewel first sees Glen after his three years in jail and offers condolences for his mother's death, he "didn't say anything. He pulled out a cigarette and lit it, plucked a bit of tobacco off his tongue" (5). After his first confrontation with Bobby—during which, Brown writes, Glen "didn't trust his voice" (14)—Glen tells his brother Puppy only to drive him somewhere that he "can get a beer and shut up" (15). In Glen's world, talking does not solve problems; it reveals weakness. Even when he does talk, it is in the tough, spare language of countless figures from the Western, among them Jack Palance's Jack Wilson, the villainous gunslinger from *Shane*; John Wayne's Ethan Edwards, the antiheroic Confederate veteran from *The Searchers*; and Marlon Brando's Rio, the vengeful escaped convict from Brando's own *One-Eyed Jacks* (1961).

Much of what emotion there is in the novel derives from Glen and Bobby's contention over Jewel. Despite his obsession with her, Glen does not really love her, nor is he comfortable with her version of their future. "I know what she wants," he complains to his father at one point, "Same thing ever woman wants. Get married" (58). He not only does not want to play father to his own son; he does not even "like looking at him" (108). And when Jewel questions him as to his whereabouts, she only threatens his masculinity by trying to impose her rules on his way of life. Eager to tip the balance of power back into his favor, Glen resorts to physical violence, reasoning that abusing Jewel is his right as a man. He resorts to sex as well, which becomes a way for him—not Bobby, significantly—to "possess" her. As Brown thereby prepares us for a battle between men over a woman, that woman becomes the motive behind the violence to ensue. The same, of course, is true of many classic Westerns: "women are the motive for male activity (it's women who are being avenged, it's a woman the men are trying to rescue) at the same time as what women stand for—love and forgiveness in place of vengeance—is precisely what that activity denies" (Tompkins 41). Men, after all, avenge women in Eastwood's *High Plains Drifter* (1973) and *Unforgiven* (1992); men rescue women in *The Searchers*, Richard Brooks's *The Professionals* (1966), and Leone's *Once Upon a Time in the West* (1968). With Jewel as the motive for male action, *Father and Son* is as male-driven a novel as these films are male-driven Westerns.

Such a tight focus on the men, moreover, often reduces the women in these works to either saints or whores, domesticated or wild animals. For Glen, the only virtuous woman is his dead mother, whom he sees as a Madonna-like martyr who has sacrificed herself for her family, especially her son: "Never spoke of her hurts, was always cheerful for him. She'd sent cookies, cakes, at Christmas little packages of gifts, small wrapped presents, the fried apple pies he'd always loved" (110–11). Since his mother is the only Madonna, all other women are inevitably "whores." Jewel "ain't nothing but a goddamn whore" (284), he bellows at one point, and he finds the same true of other women. He thinks of Bobby's mother Mary as another "whore," one who "need[s] her ass whipped too. Or worse" (160). Women are also described in animal terms. Ashamed of her sexual longing for Bobby, Jewel tells herself, "You're worse than a damn cat in heat" (242), and when Glen recalls having sex with her, he remembers "the whimpers she made and the soft animal sounds that had no description to them, so natural and pure they were" (163). The young girl Glen rapes is described as "a little demon of flashing eyes" who has "the quickness of something raised in the woods"; her eyes are "wild like a trapped animal," and she has "flashing white teeth" (114). To Glen, clearly, women beyond his mother are some wild other that he must find some way to tame.

His attempt to tame Mary Blanchard, though, brings about his early death—a murder that, significantly, does not come about according to Western conventions. Tompkins stresses that the hero, as we may expect, is to be the avenger, and that he is to resist the urge to retaliate until he has been pushed "too far." When the hero finally retaliates violently, the reader wants it to happen, for this is the point at which "retaliatory violence becomes not simply justifiable but imperative" (228). The late scene in *Father and Son* in which Glen rapes Mary Blanchard is a good example of the point at which this justifiable imperative arrives; the reader expects Bobby to rescue his mother at the last minute, for Brown has been building up to a violent confrontation between hero and villain from the earliest chapters of the novel. Bobby never does so, however. As the rape occurs he is asleep in his boyhood room in his mother's house, unaware of the atrocities occurring outside in the barn—a fact that points toward a significant subversion of his role as hero. Despite all his masculine traits, he, like Glen, suffers from a dominant mother bond. He still lives in his boyhood room, and his mother still wakes him up every morning and makes him breakfast. Both are aware of the unusual situation, as his mother teasingly asks him, "When you gonna find you a nice girl and get married? You can't live with your mama your whole life" (99). Even though Bobby does show some sign of a mature individuality in his occasional wish to leave his boyhood home and his mother, the depiction of him napping in his bed as she is being raped debunks the heroic image that Brown has been building from the beginning of *Father and Son*.

The classic showdown between hero and villain, then, does not occur. Instead, while Glen rapes Bobby's mother, *she* kills him. Brown thus deflates the sheriff's formerly traditional heroism and in the process distances his story from the "heroic code" that, as Tompkins puts it, "imprisons the Western" (5). But does this deviation from the code come because Brown is reluctant to taint Bobby's goodness, or is he merely debunking the reader's expectations, as he does in the short story "Falling Out of Love"?[1] Brown faces a dilemma here. If he places Bobby at the scene of his mother's rape, Bobby has sufficient reason to kill Glen; doing so, though, would taint Bobby's innocence. By keeping him away from the scene, Brown is able to preserve Bobby's innocence and thereby protect his position as the novel's only truly moral character, its voice of reason. Brown, then, does not debunk the myth of violent resolve as much as subvert the role of the male hero and reinforce the role of the woman, who manages in this case to kill the villain. Inherent in the act is a startling reversal of the Western's traditional positioning of gender and power. Rather than remain a passive victim reliant on male power to save her, Mary emerges as a resourceful, even heroic agent. One might even argue that she looks forward to the much more developed heroine of Brown's next novel, *Fay*. However, despite this significant shift in the traditional structure of gender and power, we should also note that the physical and psychological power granted Mary comes very much at her own expense. She is raped and almost killed before she can assert that power and kill Glen.

In line with this deflating of the Western code at novel's end, Brown also mitigates Glen's evil by having him apologize to Mary just before he dies. Brown kills off his villain, but before Glen dies he confesses his sins: "I'm sorry," he tells Mary— "and she believe[s] him" (341). Brown thus redeems Glen at the moment before his death, thereby turning him into a tragic character, one worthy of the reader's sympathy, and it is this tragic dimension that finally removes the story from the pattern of the morality play. As James Gilligan argues, "morality plays reduce the question to that of 'innocence' versus 'guilt' (the 'good guys' vs. 'the bad guys')" (8). The same argument applies to the traditional Western, whose "clearly opposing players . . . form basic moral reference points" (Cawelti, "Prolegomena" 67). But Brown's empathy and compassion for his characters, even his murderers, finally produce a complexity that is more typical of the anti-Western, the anti-heroes of which began appearing on-screen in Eastwood and Leone's so-called spaghetti Westerns and whose literary equivalents reached a terrifying zenith in Cormac McCarthy's *Blood Meridian* (1985). What remains of the traditional Western and the morality play is the good and innocent sheriff, Bobby, who remains untouched by the violence of the final showdown.

Just as Westerns are ultimately about the construction of manhood, *Father and Son* sets up conflicts between men who behave badly and men who make decisions in accordance with moral guidelines. The male characters in *Father and Son* incorporate from the traditional Western both working-class codes and stock traits. The hero protects himself and those around him, especially the women, but he does so according to a clear set of moral guidelines. What Brown ultimately creates by mining the Western formula for his novel are a recognizable landscape that is both real and symbolic—for it both tests and rejuvenates his characters—a clearly driven plot, and, finally, a distinct set of moral codes that match his characters, both good and bad. The novel is both a formulaic page-turner and a statement of hope and humanity in a context of violence and despair. Brown presents Bobby as the ideal man, a yardstick character whose common sense and moral strength and virtues are further emphasized by the violent excess around him. His half-brother Glen embodies most of this violence: he repudiates his family and lashes out in blind anger against anyone who threatens him. He is Bobby's opposing player and, at first sight, an almost quintessential Western villain. But in Brown's world, even the most morally degenerate character possesses a sort of stoic dignity, forcing us again to recognize the value of the lives of the overlooked "white trash" of America. This sympathy, again, sets the novel apart from the traditional Western, but Brown's insistence on Bobby's everlasting purity leaves that one foot in the West. *Father and Son* is thus the work of a contemporary Southern writer who not only echoes the overshadowing tradition of Faulkner and his followers, but who has also been shaped by a less respectable but more influential tradition—the American Western. Even though rattletrap pickup trucks have replaced more storied horses, a clear line runs from the American Western to Larry Brown's violent South.

Note

1. The title of the story is finally a jocosely literal reference to the fact that, on the last page of the story, its central characters fall out of a car while making love.

Works Cited

Algonquin Books of Chapel Hill. "Larry Recommends: His Top Ten." *Algonquin Books of Chapel Hill*. 4 Oct. 2000. http://www.algonquin.com/larrybrown/larry2.html.

Blake, Michael F. *Code of Honor: The Making of Three Great American Westerns*. New York: Taylor, 2003.

Bonetti, Kay. "Larry Brown (1995)." *Conversations with American Novelists: The Best Interviews from the Missouri Review and the American Audio Prose Library*. Ed. Bonetti, et al. Columbia: U of Missouri P, 1997. 234–53.

Brown, Larry. *Father and Son*. 1996. New York: Holt, 1996.

Edward Buscombe. *The Searchers*. BFI Film Classics. London: BFI, 2000.

Cawelti, John G. *Adventure, Mystery and Romance: Formula Stories as Art and Popular Culture*. Chicago: U of Chicago P, 1976.

——. "Prolegomena to the Western." *Critical Essays on the Western Novel*. Ed. William T. Pilkington. Boston: Hall, 1980. 61–71.

Etulain, Richard W. *Telling Western Stories: From Buffalo Bill to Larry McMurtry*. Albuquerque: U of New Mexico P, 1999.

Gilligan, James. *Violence: Reflections on a National Epidemic*. New York: Vintage, 1997.

Manley, Michael. "Telling Stories: An Interview with Larry Brown." *Delicious Imaginations: Conversations with Contemporary Writers*. Ed. Sarah Griffiths and Kevin J. Kehrwald. West Lafayette: NotaBell Books, 1998.

Mitchell, Lee Clark. *Westerns: Making the Man in Fiction and Film*. Chicago: U of Chicago P, 1996.

Rebein, Robert. *Hicks, Tribes, and Dirty Realists: American Fiction after Postmodernism*. Lexington: UP of Kentucky, 2001.

Reed, John Shelton. *Southern Folk, Plain & Fancy: Native White Social Types*. Athens: U of Georgia P, 1986.

Schwenger, Peter. *Phallic Critiques*. Boston: Routledge & Kegan Paul, 1984.

Slotkin, Richard. *The Fatal Environment: The Myth of the Frontier in the Age of Industrialization, 1800–1890*. Middletown: Wesleyan UP, 1985.

Tompkins, Jane. *West of Everything: The Inner Life of Westerns*. New York: Oxford UP, 1992.

Hard Traveling

Fay's Deep-South Landscape of Violence

ROBERT BEUKA

Larry Brown begins his 2000 novel *Fay*, the gripping and violent tale of a young woman's experiences upon escaping an abusive home life and traveling alone through Mississippi, with the following imagistic paragraph: "She came down out of the hills that were growing black with night, and in the dusty road her feet found small broken stones that made her wince. Alone for the first time in the world and full dark coming quickly. House lights winked through the trees as she walked and swung her purse from her hand. She could hear cars passing down the asphalt but she was still a long way from that" (9). The reader immediately notices Brown's subtle attention to what seem small details: the physical pain Fay feels as she walks the rocky road in worn-out tennis shoes, the darkness enshrouding the north Mississippi landscape, the distant hum of cars cruising the distant highways. As the narrative progresses, it becomes clear that Brown's tightly constructed opening paragraph actually foreshadows his treatment of Fay's journey and her violent coming-of-age. As he does throughout the novel, he here depicts his naïve protagonist struggling to prevail, alone, in a hostile environment. The Mississippi setting Brown presents in *Fay* might best be described as a landscape of violence, a brutal place where love, hope, even life itself seem prone to random termination at any moment. Epitomized by the fatal car crashes that recur throughout the narrative, the extreme violence of Brown's Mississippi becomes the defining feature of Fay Jones's journey.

The violent atmosphere of *Fay* would hardly surprise readers familiar with Brown's earlier work. By the time of its publication, Brown had already built a reputation as a chronicler of hard-living, working-class Mississippians persisting in an uncaring and often hostile Deep South. Along with such kindred spirits as Harry Crews—to whom Brown dedicated *Fay*, describing him as "my uncle in all ways but blood"—and Barry Hannah, Brown helped develop a school of rough-edged, modern Southern realism characterized by starkness and violence. Sometimes referred to as Grit Lit, Brown's style of contemporary Southern fiction borrows from the Southern Gothic tradition to create a dark vision of the Deep South landscape. In *Fay*, as in much of his work, Brown creates a contemporary South suffused with the "climate of violence" that Louise Gossett has identified as one of the more defining characteristics of the Southern literary tradition (4).

The road, the central symbol of the novel, best embodies this aura of violence. While the open road has represented American freedom and mobility throughout our national literature, Brown's novel inverts this image. Though Fay Jones, an uneducated, seventeen-year-old runaway, takes to the open road to escape the horrors of her family life, what she finds in her travels is only more of the same. The road in *Fay* quickly becomes associated with danger, violence, and gruesome death. State Trooper Sam Harris, Fay's initial love interest, spends much of the novel sorting out fatal car wrecks and supervising the carting away of corpses, two of which are those of his own daughter and wife. Brown spares few details in his grisly depictions of these accidents and their victims, including one who begs Sam to shoot him in the head to put him out of his misery. For Fay herself, the road poses altogether different kinds of danger. Early in the novel a young man picks her up and gives her a ride only to try to force her to perform oral sex on him. A subsequent one-night male acquaintance gets her drunk and rapes her while she lies unconscious in the back of his van. And this pervasive violence is not limited to the road alone: gun violence and death shatter the tranquil calm of Sam's home on Lake Sardis, and the novel's Gulf Coast is utterly suffused with violence, from the nightly brawls at the strip club Fay frequents to the physical and sexual abuse of her female acquaintances to the bloodbath in Pass Christian that closes the novel.

One may fairly wonder what message Brown is trying to convey through such a violent environment. An immediate result of his strategy—whether intentional or not—is the exoticizing, the othering of both the Deep South and its inhabitants. Reviewers including Clancy Sigal, writing in *Washington Post Book World*, have noted Brown's tendency to depict back-roads Mississippi as a kind of "Third World America" (11), and Bill Nichols expresses a similar sentiment on the front of the 2001 Scribner paperback of the novel: "Brown will show you another America—his America—and dare you to try to forget it exists." Observations such as these, though accurate in their own fashion, raise difficult questions about the nature of Brown's depiction of the Deep South. If, as Fred Hobson has argued, the

Southern writer has felt compelled to answer the injunction of William Faulkner's Shreve McCannon to "Tell about the South," has "felt he *had* something to explain, to justify, to defend, or to affirm" regarding his region (3), one might ask just what it is that Brown is "tell[ing] about the South" in this novel. In his hard-luck characters mired in a world of extreme violence, are we to find evidence of a clear-eyed realism or a lurid sensationalism? Critics have noted both tendencies, and surely Scribner's choice of cover blurb suggests a willingness to use sensationalism to sell books. At the same time, however, a careful examination of the novel reveals that its violence is not merely a device for generating lurid appeal, nor is it random and pointless. Instead, Brown saturates *Fay* with violence to illustrate his characters' vulnerability and powerlessness. Paradoxically, by situating his characters in such a brutal environment, Brown is able to imbue even the worst of them with sympathetic characteristics and a sense of dignity.

In his handling of this dark environment and its effect on his characters, Brown recalls not only the Southern Gothicism of Faulkner and Flannery O'Connor but, perhaps more importantly, the school of literary naturalism. As Matthew Guinn argues in his entry on blue-collar fiction in *The Companion to Southern Literature*, Brown uses "the conventions of naturalism to chronicle a segment of Southern culture seldom afforded full representation" (109). While the classic naturalism of Theodore Dreiser and Stephen Crane created indelible impressions of the teeming inner city as the dark, suffocating world of the lower class, the mostly rural settings of *Fay* present an entirely different realm of deprivation, but one that presents a similarly deterministic trap. At the same time, though, the empathy Brown creates for his characters runs counter to stereotypical depictions of the Southern poor white, "one of America's oldest and most enduring folk figures" (Cook ix). For if, as Duane Carr argues in *A Question of Class: The Redneck Stereotype in Southern Fiction*, poor whites "have long been degraded in Southern literature," have long been portrayed as "simple-minded, shiftless, lazy, and violent—a subspecies to be detested and ridiculed" (3), then Brown by contrast affirms the humanity of his characters—despite, or even because of, the aura of violence that surrounds them. Each of his main characters is driven by a futile quest for an idyllic environment apart from the grim world in which he or she lives: Fay, derided by a rival as a "[w]hite trash piece of shit" and haunted by her childhood of itinerant labor and parental abuse (92), seeks only for a sense of belonging and "a place nobody could run you off from" (266); Sam Harris, outwardly the most comfortable of the main characters, builds a lakeside home intended as a peaceful retreat from the harrowing world of highway crashes he oversees as a state trooper but ends up shattered by the deaths of those closest to him; Aaron Forrest, who divides his time between the incongruous locales of the seedy Biloxi strip club world and his mother's pre-Civil War mansion in stately Pass Christian, lives a life of drug-dealing, small-time pimping, and perpetual violence while dreaming (right up to the moment of his early death) of the long-lost, simple pleasures of a youth spent working on his father's shrimp boat. Adrift and isolated in an unforgiving contemporary South, all the characters are, in a sense—to borrow O'Connor's World War II-era title phrase—"displaced persons."

Nowhere is this more clear than in the case of Fay Jones, whose blind travels around the state in search of anything other than her former way of life lack direction both literally and figuratively. From the outset of the novel, Fay is at the mercy of her environment, and precisely because she has no understanding of it, no real idea of where she is. In this sense, one might consider the irony of her name: a fay is a fairy, elf, or sprite, an ethereal being who transcends the everyday world. Fay Jones, on the other hand, is anything but transcendent, continually fails—as a result of the crushing ignorance brought on by the deprivation that has characterized her seventeen years—to understand her environment in anything but the most basic and immediate terms. As she traverses the hills of north Mississippi at the beginning of her journey, she reflects on her past in a manner that underscores the degree to which her extreme poverty goes hand-in-hand with her dissociation from her surroundings:

> The long muscles in her legs said they would be sore in the morning from pulling the hills. But she seemed to be nearing the last one. Off to the north lay a low glow among the trees nestled at the top of the world and she knew it had to be a town. She thought it might be Oxford. She had heard her father mention that place. She thought that was where he went to get his whiskey, but she'd never been there. They had come in from the southeast, through Georgia and Alabama, the two-lane roads, the sleepy towns off the interstates where they spent the nights in the parks rolled in quilts or just stretched out on the grass. And back before he'd lost the truck, in the cab and the bed of it. But she was used to walking, a road in front of her. This one no different from any other in that they all led somewhere. (15)

For Fay, the road behind and the road ahead are equally unknown and unknowable, and in this sense her solitary walking becomes a metaphor for the lostness that each of her fellow characters faces. As Paul Lyons argues in an essay on Brown's *Joe* (1991), "Brown portrays a generation of dirt poor Southerners whose 'culture' is that of not knowing.... Lacking a sense of place-history, they lack a sense of future direction" (112).

Brown carefully constructs the scene of Fay's first stop to emphasize the perils her directionless roaming will later bring. Here, religious imagery stands in stark contrast to the dark world Fay will eventually inhabit. Discovering a roadside church, she literally (though not figuratively) sees the light, but she is drawn in by the hope of physical, rather than spiritual, relief and renewal: "She walked past a building set well back from the road and saw a dark cross set into the wood high up near the gable. She stopped. There was a light somewhere inside, a yellow beam that shone through stained glass windows. She wondered if there might be a water tap in the yard or on the side of the house" (10). Ultimately Fay enters only to escape a growling dog, a symbol of the troubles to come: "The dog seemed propped on its legs and a bit of drool swung from its jaw. The canines were bared in a bloody muzzle and its eyes were sick. Another ragged growl escaped it and it seemed hard-pressed to draw each breath. The foot that was caught in the rusty trap was nearly severed and the dog tried to hold it aloft as it came toward her, half whining, maybe for help" (11). The two images Brown juxtaposes here, one of holy sanctuary and one of abject pain and misery, suggest the extremes of Fay's travels to come. Though she will seek—and temporarily find—shelter from the pain of her past, the wounded animal stands as the more fitting symbol not only of Fay, but of those she meets along her journey. Her reaction to the church, "A room like none she'd ever been in" (11), suggests her ignorance of organized religion as well as her more general naïveté. Brown handles the scene in a manner reflecting Fay's essential innocence and goodness: after fixing herself a dinner of leftovers she finds in the church kitchen, she leaves behind a dollar—half of her bankroll—as an offering. Though only a brief moment at the beginning of Fay's journey and the only time religion factors explicitly into the narrative, this solitary stop at the church suggests a latent yearning in the novel for something beyond the desultory secular world of highways and back roads, trailer parks and strip clubs.

Certainly a primary yearning in the novel is for a sense of family. While

Fay begins her journey as a means of escaping her unbearably abusive family situation, she also spends much of her time on the road searching for the sense of safety and belonging that a family structure ideally would bring. The abusive nature of Fay's father, which Brown chronicled in *Joe*, is a potent, silent force in this narrative. Though Fay makes only occasional reference to him, it is clear that the damage he inflicted on her and her family has been severe. Shortly after meeting Sam, she explains the reason that she left home, describing "the two times her father had crept up on her in the dark, how he'd ripped her clothes and put his hand around her throat and tried to choke her down, and of how she'd fought . . . until she was able to get away from him almost naked and run into the woods to hide" (46). We later learn of the father's abuse of Fay's mother and siblings, of his trading Fay's little brother for a car. Fay's abusive and dirt-poor upbringing has the psychological effect of making her vulnerable to anyone who, like the troubled and violent Aaron Forrest, is willing to provide her temporary comfort and shelter. By contrast, Sam and Amy Harris offer her genuine shelter and the closest she will come to a functioning and supportive family. That the section of the novel transpiring at the Harris home in Sardis ends in death and utter despair seems Brown's strongest comment throughout on his characters' predetermined fate.

Nevertheless, for a time it seems that Fay will escape the troubles she faces not only at home, but also on the roads after her escape. After running away from home, Fay's first adventure, with a trio of roughneck young men and the older woman who puts them up in her double-wide trailer, reveals a family structure not altogether different from the one she had left behind, characterized as it is by drug and alcohol abuse and aggressive sexuality. Fay at one point watches in horror as the woman's baby, unnoticed by its mother, falls out of its crib. She picks the child up and cradles it protectively, and Brown portrays Fay's maternal instinct alongside a symbolic foreshadowing of the pain to follow: "'Wouldn't let nothin happen to you,' she said in a whisper. Out there beyond the pine trees there was nothing but the night" (27). Much as darkness enshrouds this ad-hoc "family," the darkness that follows Fay will overshadow her dreams of a family of her own. She escapes this misadventure in much the same way that she had once fled her father's abuse, by fleeing alone into the woods under cover of night.

The dramatic contrast between family structures in the hill country and at Sam's home parallels the contrast between the two physical environments. When Sam first discovers Fay walking by the side of the highway the next day, she is dehydrated, baking in the sun, the potential prey of a buzzard circling overhead. Fay remains defiant in the face of her troubles—she says aloud to the vulture, "You gonna have to wait a while if you waitin on me" (40)—but Brown's stark symbolism here speaks for itself. (Later Brown again uses circling buzzards to foretell Amy Harris's fatal car crash, emphasizing the inevitability of her demise.) In a classic naturalistic gesture, Brown depicts Fay here as being totally at the mercy of her environment until Sam discovers her and rescues her. As she enters his air-conditioned police cruiser, dramatic changes in both her environment and her perception are clear: "She sat down and was enveloped in a waft of cold air. . . . The glass was tinted and now the outside world was not bright and hot like it had been" (42). The sensation of having entered a new, better world is heightened as Sam takes her for a drive in the cruiser: "they were running down the hill in the cool air and the world was softened and diffused and she felt that they were floating on a cushion of air, rushing headlong toward those distant hills and the green line of trees slightly shimmering beneath that awful sun" (44–45). Similarly, life at Sam's peaceful home on the lake in Sardis seems a new world to Fay, who describes it as "the nicest place I've ever seen" (54). Sam and Amy take Fay in and treat her as if their own child, though it soon becomes clear that she is merely standing surrogate for Sam and Amy's daughter, whose death in a car crash has essentially destroyed the family. When alcoholism and despair eventually bring on Amy's death in a drunken-driving crash, Fay becomes Sam's lover and almost immediately becomes pregnant with his child, raising again the specter of illicit sexuality and throwing into chaos the semblance of a family structure briefly established at the Harris home. Fay's subsequent shooting of Sam's lover, Alesandra, permanently shatters the illusion of this setting as a peaceful oasis and forces Fay back on the road again. By this point in the novel, the connections between violence, broken families, and Fay's solitary road journey have become fully defined.

What is less fully defined is the extent of Fay's complicity in these problems. Is she a young innocent at the mercy of the men she encounters, or does she craftily use her sexuality to advance beyond her dirt-poor background? She seduces Sam, after all, just after Amy's funeral, rationalizing, "He was a good man and she wouldn't find one better, so why not be like a wife to him?" (117). After fleeing to Biloxi, Fay quickly latches on to Aaron, realizing that he may be the only person there who can save her from the local horrors of the trailer park and strip club. Though she claims to be thinking "only of Sam" (288), she goes to bed with Aaron shortly after meeting him, thinking, "If there was anything better than this she didn't know what it could be" (289). This decision earns her a permanent move to the house, and we seem to be seeing nothing more, nothing less, than Fay's mercenary nature. However, a dream she has of running off with Sam and having a "whole snowy-headed flock" of children suggests her enduring, girlish innocence (457). Indeed, Fay's contradictions seem to center not only on her sexuality, but also on the issue of children. She has premonitions of her baby's death, and despite her budding maternal instincts, her reckless lifestyle during pregnancy eventually causes a miscarriage, resulting from a drunken fall down the stairs of the Pass Christian house. This fall ends her attachment to Aaron, and the manner in which she summarizes their arrangement is telling: "She didn't owe him anything. Not a damn thing. He'd let her have a place to stay for a while and she'd fucked him for a while so they were square minus one baby" (480). Fay's pathetic, yet all-too-accurate analysis reveals not a social climber but a realist: one of the few lessons Fay seems to learn on her journey is that her sexuality is the only asset she has and can trade on. As a poor, "white trash" girl from the hills, she sees no alternative. Her family and socioeconomic background precede her and have already determined her fate, as she realizes upon considering questions she might need to answer on a job application form: *Well my daddy's a drunk and my mama's a frigging fruitcake and they live in a little rotten cabin up in the woods and the floor's so dirty you can't stand to walk on it barefooted. And you have to be careful inside because the wasps keep building nests. Anything else you want to know?"* (253).

The attention Fay pays in this passage to her former home in the woods is only fitting in a novel so concerned with homes and locales. Brown himself commented on how he constructed the novel, using its settings as a framework: "I got the idea of putting it into three sections: up in the hills, around here [Oxford, Mississippi], and down on the coast when Biloxi was just a little fishing village" (qtd. in Steinberg 44). Clearly, the varied settings and their respective homes carry symbolic meanings, from the dirt-poor hill country that still haunts Fay to the would-be safe haven on Lake Sardis outside Oxford to the decaying mansion in Pass Christian, evocative of lost connections to the Old South. For Fay, who flees the hill country with only two dollars and a half-pack of cigarettes to her name, the journey from one region to the next allows her to discover, more than anything else, how much the odds are stacked against her. Though she initially selects Biloxi as a destination almost randomly, fantasizing that it will provide a carefree life of sun and palm-lined beaches, the life she finds there, defined by still more violence and sexual abuse, only mirrors the one she has attempted to leave behind.

Though she traverses symbolic as well as physical landscapes, much of their significance is lost on Fay—who, with her fifth-grade education and her poor, rural upbringing in near total isolation from the outside world, has no understanding whatever of the South's history or cultural legacy. She first learns of the Civil War while watching a documentary about it at Sam's house on the lake. Later, while residing at Aaron's mother's home in Pass Christian—a mere stone's throw from the Jefferson Davis estate in nearby Biloxi—she senses about her the presence of history but completely lacks the intellectual framework necessary to understand it: "Old photographs of the house she stood in were hung on a wall, the trees out front much younger then, women in long dresses standing on the steps, a horse hooked to a buggy waiting beside a bush. . . . She raised her face to look at the beadboard ceiling, thinking of how old this house must be. She wished she'd gone to school more. Just one more thing she'd missed out on because of her daddy, the chance to learn things, the history of places, old wars that were fought. . . . She wanted to know how old this place was" (243). Brown's fascinating conceit here—of viewing a relic of the antebellum era through the eyes of a *tabula rasa* like Fay—dares to suggest what such an Old South monument may have turned into in the New South: merely a big, nice, weathered old house up the highway a few miles from the action, the convenience stores and strip bars of Biloxi. Brown thus uses Fay's ignorance to suggest a broader cultural disconnect from the past. Though the narrator's language—Fay "wished"; she "wanted"—portrays her hunger for historical knowledge, the novel's thoroughgoing determinism makes clear that these desires will not be fulfilled.

In a broader sense, Fay's inability to understand the history that surrounds her functions as an ironic rejoinder to the theme of the inescapable past that has characterized so much classic Southern literature. In Brown's novel, while the past is still present in the contemporary environment, most characters neither understand nor even recognize it; as Paul Lyons argues, Brown creates in his depiction of the New South neither a flattened postmodern landscape devoid of history nor a modernist Southern landscape redolent of the "over-remembered past" but a "'prepost'-erous Southern time in which a forgotten past . . . saturates the land" (111). This seemingly contradictory notion, which Lyons applies to Brown's *Joe*, describes *Fay*'s atmosphere as well. Fay is far from the only character either ignorant or forgetful of her environment and its history: the Harrises see their Sardis home as a point of retreat from the rest of the world, for example, while Aaron dreams of his own long-lost past as if in reaction to his own brutal environment. By way of such relationships to lived space, Brown suggests the solace offered by imagined, constructed, or remembered retreats from the violent modern environment. Fay, however, is the one character denied such a relationship to place. Having lived her entire life in a world of violence and pain, she also lacks completely the kind of historical and cultural knowledge that might afford her another way of understanding her environment. Thus Brown characterizes Fay as a symbol of the South's forgetting itself, of what happens when the shared traditions of the past fade away and ultimately dissolve into the random, aggressive, valueless contemporary environment.

If the Gulf Coast setting of the novel, with its references to antebellum homes and the Jefferson Davis estate, is the one most closely tied to a landscape of the past, it is also, paradoxically, the setting both most modernized and most fully gripped by violence. Though Brown chose to portray pre-casino-era Biloxi, depicting the town when it was, in his terms, still just "a little fishing village," this setting is clearly a landscape moving away from its antebellum and maritime roots and toward an atmosphere of aggression and consumption. Aaron Forrest's trajectory, from his youth in the family shrimping business to his adult life busting heads in a low-rent strip club, emblematizes the changing values of the region; his constant travel along the Gulf Coast Highway exposes him to the commercial and spiritual wasteland of what is sometimes called the Redneck Riviera: "And then there was the long drive back home, up past . . . the million tiny stores and the places that sold shells or fishing gear or fixed boats and motorcycles and the endless bars and package stores and grocery stores, places to get your palm read, your arm or your chest tattooed, places that sold four-wheelers and all the signs that lined the highway advertising something else for you to buy" (330).

The centerpiece of the novel's aggressive Gulf Coast is the strip club where Aaron works as bouncer and manager. A truly nightmarish place, the club fosters on a nightly basis an atmosphere that encourages violence, prostitution, drug abuse and sexual abuse. Musing on the club's clientele, Aaron seems to display an understanding of the pointless theater of violence he has helped create: "He knew they'd all be drunk eventually. Somebody would get rowdy. Somebody . . . would bump into somebody else who was drunk and had one reason or another to shove back and it was the same old shit over and over. He didn't care which one it was. All he was waiting for was the happening of it" (423). Despite his perceptive understanding of this cyclic violence, Aaron is unable or unwilling to divorce himself from it. And despite his seeming desire to play the old-fashioned, chivalric Southern gentleman to Fay, he inevitably returns to the codes of aggression and violence reinforced nightly at the club. In his failure to break free from this abusive mindset, Aaron seems to conform to a pattern that Richard Gray has noted in contemporary Southern fiction, one in which characters are presented "as belonging to a world, a cultural landscape where there is no norm from which to deviate" (396). The absolute absence of any sort of abiding social code is brought home to the reader when Brown reveals that Aaron—who has already gotten away with a major drug deal and a vicious murder—had also "purchased" Fay, for five-hundred dollars, from the stripper who had taken her in upon her arrival in Biloxi. Epitomizing the amoral universe Brown depicts in the Gulf Coast section of the novel, this financial deal reveals the depths of Aaron's duplicity, Fay's ignorance, and the desperation of them both.

Given the hyper-violent and ill-fated atmosphere of the novel, it comes as little surprise when, at its close, Aaron and Sam engage in a gun battle that leads to both of their deaths. A sort of postmodern, mock-chivalric duel, their bloody shootout caps the cycle of senseless violence in the novel. What does come as a surprise is the brief epilogue that follows the text proper. Here, by way of a vignette of Fay walking through the French Quarter of New Orleans on a summer evening, we learn something of her life following the shootout. Her destination is a strip club where she appears to be something of a local celebrity. As she enters, greeted warmly by the doorman and club patrons, the novel closes on a most curious note; as Albert Mobilio points out in his review of the novel, "It's hard to say whether Brown wants us to count this as her personal triumph or as a metaphor for the commercialized South—from backwoods to Bourbon Street" (18). Indeed, the choice of setting for this scene does seem significant. On her walk, as

Fay traverses historic Jackson Square, Brown takes one final opportunity to underscore the sense of a Southern landscape in transition. Passing through, Fay "looked at old coins and Civil War muskets or mummies in shop windows and she smiled as she walked" (491). Here Southern history is reduced to mere artifacts, commodities to be perused, perhaps purchased by passing tourists. In a sense, this is a fitting final destination for Fay, the ignorant runaway from the hill country who has survived her difficult journey by learning to trade on her own commodities. And yet, despite the seemingly upbeat tone of the epilogue, the reader cannot simply ignore the recurring reminders of Fay's destiny being as bleak as it is predetermined—a thought that reemerges as she takes the final steps of her epic journey, right into another strip club.

In *The Dream of Arcady: Place and Time in Southern Literature*, Lucinda MacKethan argues that "the Southern writer today finds perhaps his greatest challenge in involving his characters in quests for a way to live actively and responsibly within a broken world" (217). While MacKethan made this comment some two decades before Brown published *Fay*, it still seems appropriate to this work and its vision of Mississippi. In fashioning a different sort of road narrative, one seen through the eyes of a seventeen-year-old runaway who is both wild and, in her own way, utterly innocent, Brown allows readers to view this Deep South landscape through fresh eyes. The vision he presents is not for the faint of heart. From the physically and emotionally abusive situations in the hill country Fay flees to the pall of despair that finally eats away at the illusion of a happy family life the Harrises construct in Sardis to the ultraviolent world of trash culture in Biloxi, Brown offers a dark vision of the evolving Southern landscape, one that continually tests his characters' will to survive and press on. The novel's brutality—every major character except Fay is killed—leaves readers with the discomfiting task of making so much despair add up to something. Ultimately, through his presentation of Fay's tenacious will to survive, and of Sam and Amy's openhearted devotion to her, Brown makes a case for perseverance and grace in an otherwise heartless world. This latent idealism, this ironic humanism, is what elevates *Fay* from a mere page-turner to a work of art. Without it, the novel's hyper-violent conclusion would lapse into utter nihilism, leaving the reader little choice but to concur with the ferocious yet hapless Aaron Forrest—who, while lying in a pool of his own blood, dying on the floor of his mother's home, can only conclude, "Damn. All that fucking trouble for nothing" (489).

Hard Traveling: Fay's Deep-South Landscape of Violence

Works Cited

Brown, Larry. *Fay*. 2000. New York: Scribner, 2001.

Carr, Duane. *A Question of Class: The Redneck Stereotype in Southern Fiction*. Bowling Green: Bowling Green State UP, 1996.

Cook, Sylvia Jenkins. *From Tobacco Road to Route 66: The Southern Poor White in Fiction*. Chapel Hill: U of North Carolina P, 1976.

Gossett, Louise. *Violence in Recent Southern Fiction*. Durham: Duke UP, 1965.

Guinn, Matthew. "Blue-Collar Literature." *The Companion to Southern Literature: Themes, Genres, Places, People, Movements, and Motifs*. Ed. Joseph M. Flora and Lucinda H. MacKethan. Baton Rouge: Louisiana State UP, 2002. 108–09.

Gray, Richard. *Southern Aberrations: Writers of the American South and the Problems of Regionalism*. Baton Rouge: Louisiana State UP, 2000.

Hobson, Fred. *Tell About the South: The Southern Rage to Explain*. Baton Rouge: Louisiana State UP, 1983.

Lyons, Paul. "Larry Brown's *Joe* and the Uses and Abuses of the 'Region' Concept." *Studies in American Fiction* 25.1 (Spring 1997): 101–24.

MacKethan, Lucinda Hardwick. *The Dream of Arcady: Place and Time in Southern Literature*. Baton Rouge: Louisiana State UP, 1980.

Mobilio, Albert. "Biloxi Bound." Rev. of *Fay*, by Larry Brown. *New York Times Book Review* 16 Apr. 2000: 18.

Sigal, Clancy. "Looking for Love in All the Wrong Places." Rev. of *Big Bad Love*, by Larry Brown. *Washington Post Book World* 23 Dec. 1990: 11.

Steinberg, Sybil. "PW Talks with Larry Brown." *Publishers Weekly* 10 Jan. 2000: 44.

Home and the Open Road

The Nonfiction of Larry Brown

ROBERT G. BARRIER

I've just been out in the gloam with my cousin. We've been riding around drinking a few beers, what my mama used to call 'acting ugly.' If you don't know what the gloam is, you can find out by
reading some James Street. . . . he knew what it felt like when the
sun went down and left about an hour of light before dark. It's the
very best time to ride around and listen to some music. Run over
snakes. We try to do it several times a week in the summer. A man's
got to have a bro to run with sometimes.

If I go to a bar, Ireland's is the bar I go to. On a really lively night
you'll see drunk women falling down, fights and potential fights,
sweet young things and big-butted women, cowboys and construction workers and firefighters. I probably spend more time at Ireland's than I should. I live out in the county, out here in the land
of the Big Sky country. I live at the edge of a river bottom, and the
clouds can go all mushroomy and marshmallowy late in the afternoon and loom up big and white in the sky so that they can capture your attention. We have our own catfish pond, and we feed
our fish. (*OF* 25–26)

This passage, taken from late in Larry Brown's life as a firefighter but relatively early in his life as a published writer, captures specifically and poeti-
cally the place and native types of his nonfiction volumes *On Fire: A Personal Account of Life and Death and Choices* (1994) and *Billy Ray's Farm:
Essays from a Place Called Tula* (2001). It also says much about his now
larger-than-life persona and ultimately implies almost as much about the
content and character of his fiction. Brown is known far more for that fiction, for *Dirty Work* (1989) and *Joe* (1991) and *Father and Son* (1996), for

86

instance, but the expanded journal entries and magazine pieces that constitute his two volumes of nonfiction deserve attention in and of themselves as material distinct from, not just integral to, his novels and short story collections. Both volumes explore the roles of firefighter, family man, and author, document the desire to work, write, enjoy life, and leave something behind for those who follow. *On Fire* interlaces two lives until one wins out, while *Billy Ray's Farm* envisions a dream farm, a creation of craft and imagination no less real than the Thoreauvian cabin Brown begins building toward the end of the book. His good-old-boy ride through the gloam with his cousin parallels this same solitary structure in the wild, for it too embodies a journey to the farthest reaches of home, just close enough for familiarity and yet far enough away for independence. It too metaphorically embodies the themes of male companionship, controlled exuberance, and testing the open road, yet returning home when it's all over.

While *On Fire* bids farewell to almost two decades of Brown's life, much of it spent fighting fire, *Billy Ray's Farm* more thoroughly details his years as a burgeoning writer and somewhat reluctant farmer. Both, though, address his work habits, his fears and desires, his love of family and the land, the inextricable ties between his writing and his way of life. Even despite their autobiographical character, these subjects also appear in Brown's fiction, and each collection has a unity both among its own offerings and with the rest of Brown's oeuvre. Both volumes reflect the enduring theme of Brown's career—his empathy for working-class Southerners—and both have much in common with the overriding atmosphere of his stories and novels: selections center on his empathy for the common worker; on the lives and feelings of animals; on Brown's self-conscious, self-reflective attitude toward himself as a celebrity but his thoroughgoing respect for writing; and on his overall appreciation of craftsmanship, of studied, hard-won expertise.

On Fire engages the day-to-day worklife of ordinary, lower-middle-class Southerners—and realistically, without the quaintness running to perversity of Harry Crews, Brown's friend and mentor. The volume's firemen, townspeople, and victims of catastrophes, though examined from a minimalist perspective, exist in what commentators of an earlier literature would call "the realistic light of common day." *Billy Ray's Farm* focuses on the more personal, on onerous work as well as carousing play, with the so-called simple pleasures and a place of ownership and acceptance as ultimate motivators. As such, these works indeed echo and anticipate Brown's fiction, but mostly as theme, the role of landscape, and productive, law-abiding characters are concerned. Though given to a ride through the gloam, the main character, Brown himself—unlike so many of his less law-abiding fictional characters—always returns home from the open road to his comfortable, loving relationships with companions, mentors, and family.

Reviewers were not entirely kind to *On Fire*. Some, seeming to miss the gritty narrative voices of Brown's fiction, criticized the volume for its casual, at times heartfelt tone. Writing in *Village Voice*, Sally Eckhoff scoffed that "Sentimentality has replaced [Brown's] hell-bent smoke-eater swagger. So do something for him: buy a smoke alarm, but not this idiot-savant shtick" (20). Roger Caitlin of the *Hartford* (Connecticut) *Courant* complained about the volume's length, or rather lack thereof: "Even double-spaced with fat margins and chapters that are always ending early and starting halfway down the page, 'On Fire' doesn't fill many pages, and it has the feel of an overdone pamphlet. Maybe it was presented in bite-size chunks for the guys back at the fire station to read in between bells and S and V on HBO" (G4). More positive reviewers, though, found value in Brown's autobiographical turn: "*On Fire* is partly a fire-department memoir and partly an agglomeration of scraps: exercises in razor observation and storytelling in the plain style," James Donnelly wrote in *Whole Earth Review*. "Not all have the laconic gracefulness of his fiction—it's harder to channel and manipulate reality, I suppose. But it's a pleasure to get to see, piecemeal, the constituents that add up to Larry Brown stories" (106).

Only about half of *On Fire*'s forty-six numbered sections detail scenes of housefires or car wrecks, convey the flavor and atmosphere of Brown's seventeen years as a firefighter: as a whole, the volume's contents are indeed, as Donnelley wrote, "piecemeal." Its other half takes up subjects such as Brown's family, his dog Sam, other animals—raising, hunting, and killing them—and his long apprenticeship before the publication of *Facing the Music* (1988). All, though, are observations of humane sympathy and sardonic self-effacement, written always with an honest, straightforward style. Madison Smartt Bell, in the first and still most complete analysis of the volume, found a unity amid what so many dismissed as disparate selections. Brown's "first work of nonfiction . . . does not resemble any conventional literary memoir, indeed scarcely resembles any sort of memoir at all," Bell wrote. "At first glance it seems to be a grab bag of nearly random observations and anecdotes, but on closer inspection it turns into a work of great thematic integrity that reveals itself as much between the lines as in them" (38). The collection does begin discursively, as Bell points out, with simple enumeration and gathering of materials, details of the firehouse and epi-sodes of death and extrication, glances into his family life—his children, marital difficulties, and the stupidities of his beloved dog Sam. What begins with his last hour of duty at the firehouse ends with his coming back from a *Today Show* interview, leaving his first career to begin his second as a full-time writer, and driving through the gloam one spring night, following the engines to a wreck and becoming, instead of one of the participants, one of the spectators of the "brotherhood of men" that he had given up (181).

On Fire is not strictly a journal, though Brown did begin keeping one the year before he left firefighting; it is rather a four-years' progress of autobiog-raphy: "Usually it was a simple matter of remembering the situations, and that wasn't hard because so many of the things that happened over those sixteen years left an indelible impression on my memory," he wrote in his Author's Note. "You don't forget death and pain, or fear. All the events were there, but I had to try and make some sense out of it." *On Fire* is an "attempt to explore" the way "two totally different careers had to mesh and make room for each other, until one of them finished first." Despite Brown's as-sertion here, it is difficult to see any conflict of careers amid the sequencing of the chapters, and perhaps his effort to "put in only the things the story needs" among the "ton of stuff" that could have been there does omit the details or implications of that conflict (ix).

Any "mesh[ing]" the work itself has thus comes from what Bell called the spider web connections of implication—"In the end," he wrote, "'On Fire' shows itself to be constructed like a spider web; one may touch any fila-ment to discover the delicate interdependence of the whole" (38)—or, bet-ter yet, the rhythm of interrupting short, expository chapters with longer narrative chapters. After five sections of detail about the firehouse, the dan-gers of firefighting, and the brotherhood it creates, for instance, Brown in-serts a narrative about suppressing a fire on the sixth floor of the law school building at Ole Miss, an episode that reveals the necessity of doing "some-thing in your life that is honorable and not cowardly" (20). A listing of sub-sequent sections would reveal similar interplay. Structurally, for the casual reader, the work is a "grab bag," as Bell put it, of firefighting episodes, scenes of home life, and meditations on fate, accident, and courage. Its effect is cu-mulative, ultimately resulting in perhaps our best depiction of the life of the firefighter, a rare and honest look at the ordinary person's everyday work.

In contrast to *On Fire*, *Billy Ray's Farm* exhibits the mark of a studied ar-tistic maturity in that its component parts are closer to familiar essays than random reflections. Comprised primarily of essays Brown published previously in magazines, it does not have *On Fire*'s immediate sense of sequencing. Brown wrote only the Preface and the concluding piece, "Shack," specifically for the collection. Its structure is more obvious than that of *On Fire*, though. It begins with a discussion of how Oxford has changed from what it had been during Faulkner's day. Brown tries to answer the perennial question, "*What is it about Oxford that produces writers?*" (3). His response, nebulous thought it may be, is that for him "'the land sort of creates the characters. . . . I mean I look at the people around me and wonder what their stories are, or I think of some character and put him in a situation and then follow him around for a while, see what happens next'" (4). Writing, then, is a "drawing upon the well of memory and experience and imagination. . . . A writer rolls all that stuff together kind of like a taco and comes up with fiction" (5). Comments of the sort ignore the fact that Brown is introducing a collection of essays, nonfiction works primarily about place and how he lives in his, but they also imply that the essays that follow will focus on various aspects of creation.

In an early response to charges of cruelty and overemphasis on crude, low-life characters (1989's *A Late Start*), Brown pointed out how he wanted to make comfortable readers understand something about the worth and value of even these: "As a writer, it bothers me to be accused of brutality, of cruelty, of hardheartedness, of a lack of compassion" he wrote. "Only a few reviewers of my work have lodged these complaints. But more than a few seem to register a certain uneasy feeling, and I wonder if it is because I make them look a little too deeply into my characters' lives" (2). His novels introduce many such characters, and yet, no matter what else they lack, they all have a bit of humanity. They do not often show up in the nonfiction, though, except in a section from *On Fire* that takes up dumpster diving, materials Brown later would put to use in *Joe*. *On Fire*'s victims, coworkers, and bystanders and *Billy Ray's Farm*'s neighbors and fellow writers constitute the characters in his non-fiction, for these are the people he knows as real, not created. As Brown's widow Mary Annie said in a 1999 interview, "When it's nonfiction like *On Fire*, those stories . . . that's our life, but . . . the novels and the short stories he writes, that's not us" (Watson 157).

Perhaps the best example in *Billy Ray's Farm* of Brown's empathy for lower-middle-class Southern whites is the surrealistic "So Much Fish, So Close to Home," which begins at midnight in a local bar and ends the next afternoon at a fish grab at the just-drained Enid Reservoir. Brown's reverie in response to this bonanza is something of a stylistic *tour de force*:

> there'd been fishblood and fistfights in the midst of a fishgrabbing frenzy. I could imagine stinking heaps of bream and carp, maybe bulletheaded behemoths in torn T-shirts standing in them, bloodied, with fishbillies in their hands, the weeps and near-orgasmical moans of a grandmaw in a cotton housedress, a big buffalo lodged and wiggling dumbly between her thighs, others wading forward to help, clubs raised. I could smell the blood and death of it, could see how the sun would be shining down on the carnage at nine o'clock in the morning. Would the soaring September temperatures rise and would tempers rise within them and incite them to fall upon each other, excited by the orgy of death? Would they be clubbing each other's toes in the bloody water? Lorna said you could get little ones for your pond. I said I wanted big ones for my skillet. She said reckon I wanted to go? I said, Aw shit my damn bull's out, I got to go home to see about him. (102)

The narrative's last, long section involves the difficulties of extracting fish from the reservoir, the hallucinatory sense of misadventure among the multitudes at the fish grab, the hot morning sun beating down on the concrete of the drained concave hole where hundreds of happy fishers shovel dying fish into trash cans, baskets, and containers of all sorts and where Brown decides to go farther down, to the last drainage hole, where there are bigger fish still ungrabbed. Despite his hunger and difficulties in finding bread at an ultra-modern (fake) country store, Brown helps several slower and older participants obtain fish and is angered to see government functionaries dump fish into a pickup truck to take them to soybean fields to whiten in the sun, no longer consumed by the needy but happily used nevertheless by animals: "the flies would come, and then the crows, and the buzzards, and the possums, and then the coons, and I knew that the owls would watch silently from the trees that night while it became a thing a person wouldn't want to look at" (144). And yet despite this eerie reverie, counterpoint to the energetic fish grabbing early that morning, there were still fish frying all over Yalobusha and Grenada counties, and his old truck "probably ran like a son of a bitch. Like a wild-ass ape" as he honked at his friends, if they were awake, to let them know where he was "at that moment in the world" (144): a returning to reality after more than twenty-four hours of surreal moments—the most fiction-like episode of living in the gloom in Brown's entire nonfictional oeuvre.

Such sympathy—for both people and animals—appears throughout both collections. He expresses strong sympathy in *On Fire* for the fathers of children who have died, for mothers whose children have been burned, sympathizes in both *On Fire* and *Billy Ray's Farm* with the dignity and courage of trapped victims: he apologizes for grabbing the "ladyhood" of a woman pinned by the dashboard of a wrecked truck (38), he covers the decapitated remains of a truck driver, he laments putting Billy Ray's cow through the pains of removing a stuck fetus, and he even regrets having to bash a mouse that attacked him. His firefighting episodes blend into later scenes of saving lives (the resuscitation of a dog that had "died" from smoke inhalation) and hunting and harvesting animals, all of which exhibit his sympathy for all living things: even though reviewers ridiculed his feeling "God in my trigger finger" the day he shot his last deer or chided him for apparent callousness toward the poor people raiding dumpsters for food (122; Caitlin G4), he deplores the fact that hawks can be shot by "any sorry son of a bitch" (95), expresses sympathy for cats caught in a moving car, rabbits raised for food, even coyotes who might eat his dog Sam. And animals are not the only targets of such sympathy: he feels sorry for the poor boy he gives a castoff bicycle, for a fellow firefighter who resigns, for yet another who dies, both from the stress of their shared profession. Here, as elsewhere, Brown exhibits his life-long sense of empathy, especially for those often-ignored working-class Southerners and the animals that are their pets or food.

Such empathy plays perhaps its largest role in "Billy Ray's Farm." The fantasy of an ideal farm contrasts sharply with what Brown calls "[t]he fickle finger of cow fate" (79), exemplified by three episodes involving bad luck with livestock: the loss of a calf in birth; the near-death of a prize bull almost killed when fifteen people try to move him from a trailer into his pen; and Brown's attempts to extract a dying calf from a heifer collapsed in the woods at the edge of his farm. This last section details the horrific process of using a "come-along" to pull the calf from its suffering mother, of struggling for several days of false hope as the cow seems to regain her strength but ultimately becomes so weakened that Brown has to give his son a revolver and the bullets to do what is necessary. The vividness, the sheer authenticity of such scenes derives from the way Brown recorded them: "as soon as something happened I'd go home to write it down. I think the day I had to pull that dead calf . . . I came home after all that all day long and wrote about twenty-one pages on it. I was putting it down as fast as it happened. . . . [I]t was just pure emotion . . . like I was transcribing exactly what it felt like" (Rankin 115–16). "Billy Ray's Farm," though, ends happily, for the gray matter Billy Ray had seen protruding from the cow turns out to be the water sack and not a dead calf, and after the author spies with his field glasses the shakily standing, just-born calf, he writes, "Life seemed to have regained its balance. There were no cows suffering anywhere because of me" (84).

Animals, of course, are central to much of Brown's work: he even dedicates *On Fire* to his unnatural and erratic dog Sam. Still more unusual, corresponding somewhat to a certain grotesqueness of action and character in his fiction, is the Immaculate Kid of "Goat Songs," which breeds three kids from his own mother. They were "just about the cutest things I'd ever seen in my life," a surprised Brown wrote. "You could pet them. They weren't deformed. They looked pretty normal." And yet, he continued, "I felt a failure to prevent animal incest nonetheless" (161). Still, Brown expresses reluctant resignation when a "coy-dog" kills them: "He was just an animal, but still he got the best of me. He came, he saw, he ate, he left" (171).

Both *On Fire* and *Billy Ray's Farm* also celebrate Brown's mentors and friends, hunters and writers, surrogate fathers and others who aided him at different stages of his life. "Thicker than Blood," the second essay in the second volume, describes that formative time after his father's death when the older men of Tula educated him in "the fine points of guns and dogs," taking part in a "common act of sharing their hounds and their carbide lanterns and their secret places to hunt" (16). "Harry Crews: Mentor and Friend," which follows "Thicker than Blood," drew praise from many reviewers, among them Jonathan Yardley of the *Washington Post*, as his favorite essay in the collection. Here Brown is elated that someone else "walk[ed] this earth" ahead of him and explored the same subjects in fiction (19): "I'd never read anything like [*A Feast of Snakes* (1976)] and didn't know that such things could be done in a book" (17). The essay is a personal appreciation of a writer who befriended him without introduction and who taught him lessons about combining "hilarity and stark reality and beauty and sadness" and, particularly, about the necessity of "keep[ing] your ass in the chair" (17–18, 20). "Chattanooga Nights," a before-and-after reminiscence of two literary conferences, Brown's first, in 1989, and a 1995 coda, continues this literary autobiography. At the first one, this "greener-than-Mississippi-grass" author is astonished by the writers in attendance and engages in self-effacing humor about his lack of sophistication in their presence (Charbonneau F5). This is essentially the same Brown who playfully told a college audience in 1990, "When Algonquin wrote me, I hadn't even heard of him" (Barrier). Writing about his second visit to Chattanooga, Brown seems confident in his relationships with celebrated Southern writers but is still appreciative and surprised at being accepted among their number. He recalls the easy talk of Madison Jones, who writes "vividly, eloquently" of "streets full of shade trees . . . desolate town squares where yellow lights shine in the gloom of night" (33). He is overwhelmed by the realization that Jones had visited Flannery O'Connor and her peacocks while he, as a twelve-year old, was "rolling on my steel skates up and down the sidewalks of Memphis" (35). He is gratified to be in the company of writers who put themselves into the lives of their characters and into the land that they all loved.

Throughout these sections Brown hints at late-night talks "about our lives, about dogs, about drinking, about women, about everything" (23), but he does not detail specifics about his work, about problems of plot and character, all of which would be material for later essays and an autobiography not to be. A few reviewers of *On Fire* and *Billy Ray's Farm* criticized this reticence, especially in personal matters and situations in which he might have increased our insights into his work. In only one section does he mention any domestic trouble (he tells of taking a .22 rifle away from his wife after a quarrel and then returning four days later, climbing in a window in the dark). He also mentions that, on another occasion, he accidentally flipped Billy Ray out of a toy wagon and onto his head and later dropped firewood on the head of his younger son Shane. Though such scenes do not begin to detail a thirty-year marriage, they do show Brown admitting his shortcomings as a husband and a father. Significantly, the section describing the fight with his wife and the accidents with his sons is also the section that includes his lengthiest description of the joys of driving through the gloam.

"Fishing with Charlie," an essay about the death by drug overdose of Brown's friend, singer Charlie Jacobs, is another case in this point. According to Andy Soloman, writing in the *Boston Globe*, "Brown's tight lips tell us too little of Charlie Jacobs' life to make us sense Brown's grief or to value the life he mourns" (D5). Yet Brown implies that he knows more than he is willing to tell. The two friends fished in an "almost magical" lake, where the water was dark "yet somehow invested with a strange clarity that often lets you see the fish when it strikes" (85), and Jacobs "talked a lot but he didn't *talk loud*" (86; emphasis added). The episodes of fishing at the lake and on his pond, eating ribs, almost getting stuck on a muddy road, and "laughing together the way only good friends can" recover his friend's memory and segue into a journal entry about being informed of his death (87). Brown describes the funeral on the Delta where Jacobs's band members played soft and sweet and low, "their last gig with Charlie" (91), after which he drove home through the soft Delta night. It is all he will say, and it is enough, a reticent and poetic tribute—the last picture he keeps, his friend "finally at peace out on that Indian mound, overlooking his beloved Delta, the land of his blues" (93).

The ultimate and connecting theme of Brown's nonfiction is the desire to find a place where he can be happy as a family man and a writer. That place is, of course, home, and it is gained by control over time and place and by the plot device of going out and coming in from the gloam. *On Fire*, without an apparent or contrived plot, moves toward Brown's decision to leave firefighting to concentrate on writing. The key episode that probably compelled that decision is the one most reviewers cited as the book's best-written passage, Brown's visit to Notre Dame to give a reading. This section not only presents his alienation from the academic world and his dislike of commenting on student work but clearly reveals his desire to be at home, not feeling like "a whore with a high price" (110)—an objective that resurfaces in *Billy Ray's Farm*, which reveals his ultimate aim of getting off this "big old groaning bear" of the book promotion circuit so that "one day it will all be over, and you can return to your unremarkable life, the one where you sit every day at this machine and write your little words, and drink your coffee, and wander out in the yard" (150, 153).

When he receives word of an accident at home and anxiously learns that Mary Annie and Shane are safe but then hears that his dog Sam has died, that desire intensifies: the proportion and emphasis of the last sixteen sections reveal that slowly-arrived-at tension, which shifts to the peacefulness of Tula, anticipation of a book on Miss Lutee's Pond, and a Thoreauvian desire to have a place to confront reality. Moving from room to room, hunting for a place to write, Brown wonders if he will ever sell a manuscript, and even while he works second and third jobs he thinks of characters set in future scenes, such as the one that would open *Joe*. He has "chosen this thing to do," putting "black symbols on a white sheet," and it has both purpose and motive—"I love this thing, even if it does not love back" (155). After the acceptance of *Dirty Work*, he appeared on the *Today Show*; he knew then that he had revealed himself and become vulnerable to the general public. The firehouse no longer provided the sanctuary of work and companionship necessary for his true profession.

In the first essay of *Billy Ray's Farm*, "By the Pond," Brown continues this theme, this time mixing the elemental and the mundane. He clears land and pulls out waterlogged trees to burn them on "cold fall days" in "great leaping fires that lasted into the night" (8), releases "little fish . . . into the dark depths, vanishing into their world" (9), and then plans to "sit and watch the water, and look at the ice-shattered pines, and think of all the work I still have to do, with chain saw and sweat, in July's burning air" (10). The essay ends with his anticipation of building "a little cabin right over there above the pond, up in the deep part of that shade" (11). The cabin of course becomes the subject of the collection's last essay, "Shack," a careful and sardonic detailing of his building the structure.

"Billy Ray's Farm" establishes a fantasy home for his son that "does not yet exist on an earthly plane. It is a vision of his imagination so far, and I have no idea of the form it will ultimately take in real life" (50–51); the writer imagines for his son an Edenic place of tall trees, rolling pastures, and sleek calves, with—lord of it all—a solitary bull "intelligent, omnipotent . . . [with] his swinging bag of registered sperm sway[ing] in a dignified manner as he walks" (51). The barn will be well-lighted, with well-equipped rooms for all the eventualities of cattle raising, and each cow will have an acre of grass, well-fertilized and mowed. "The mud will be kept to a minimum" (52). And Billy Ray himself will exist in a blissful abode described in Biblical terms reminiscent of Job after the suffering is over: "he will be happy, and his life will be fulfilled, and he will know a great peace in his soul such as few men have ever known. God will smile down upon him and his efforts, and the farm will hum like a well-oiled machine." As a crowning pleasure, "There will be dogs, and life will be good" (52). It will be home.

After many turns and riffs, Brown ends at his own writing home, "Shack," an essay that begins with a motion that catches both a fox's eye and that of the builder on the roof as he creates among the diminishing wilderness a place for himself, despite mistakes and accidents. This is a narrative about precision and planning, about reading and annotating the *Tiny Book of Tiny Houses*, about daydreaming and still more planning, the sincerity of which can be seen in its style: "But everything had to be level and square, didn't it? Everything had to be laid out properly, didn't it? You had to kind of know what you were doing, didn't you? It needed not to leak. It needed to be able to be heated in the winter, maybe cooled a little in the summer. Would it have electricity or would it not? Would it matter? It might. If I was going to write over there I'd need my electric typewriter for sure. I'd need some kick-ass music and there wasn't any doubt about that. On a cool evening in October when turned-orange sycamore leaves were drifting down onto the still face of the pond I might want to plug one of the guitars into the amp and turn it up to Scream to celebrate sundown" (178). Throughout its construction Brown refers to Thoreau both directly and indirectly. He talks about his frugality and stresses throughout the essay his individualistic approach to the project. He maneuvers the walls in by himself with the come-along, suffers the interruption of Mary Annie's gallbladder operation, and measures two walls three inches too short. The day before Thanksgiving, with the help of Shane, he nails in the rafters. At essay's end, the cabin stands windowless but roofed, and the builder can say with a great deal of quiet satisfaction, "I go over there all the time. . . . I go and sit in it if I know a rain storm is coming. It does not leak" (205). It was the best of both worlds, the domestic and the gloaming.

In the three years remaining in his life, Brown spent a good deal of time at the cabin, playing his guitar, listening to music, drinking with friends, and writing. He continued to talk of eventually finishing it (O'Briant D1). Just before he died, he did—except for the electrical work. He furnished it with a futon and chairs, and candles to provide lighting. He also added a small generator that allowed him to listen to music while writing. In an unpublished August 2004 letter to Jean W. Cash, he wrote: "I got my shack finished on the inside and moved a little furniture in and I've been enjoying working on the novel in longhand over there, then transcribing it over here onto the computer. There's nothing but crickets and splashing fish and the music I play to hear over there at Tula. It makes a tremendous difference." When he died, he had finished a script for a movie about Hank Williams; he had also nearly completed what would be his final novel, *A Miracle of Catfish*, which even in its unfinished state evokes in its richness of characters and scenes these lifelong themes of sympathy for the everyday person in trouble, of the attraction of the declining landscape, and of the conflict between home and the open road, with all its attendant implications. Reviewers of *Billy Ray's Farm* had called for an autobiography, but the personal content of the essays in both collections is as autobiographical as Brown would become. It reveals where he had arrived in this search, for as he stated in his last published interview, "I don't get out much. I prefer to stay with my growing family and my work and my pond and my little house I built in the woods behind it. That's plenty of life for me" (Day 196). What remains is the body of work itself, the finished cabin, and the two personal memoirs, all with Larry Brown's distinctive voice and presence.

Works Cited

Barrier, Robert G. *Videotape of Larry Brown Presentation.* Kennesaw State College Contemporary Literature Conference. Marietta, GA. 27 Apr. 1990.

Bell, Madison Smartt. "He Could Stand the Heat." Rev. of *On Fire: A Personal Account of Life and Death and Choices,* by Larry Brown. *New York Times Book Review* 6 Feb. 1994: 38.

Brown, Larry. *A Late Start.* Chapel Hill: Algonquin, 1989.

———. *On Fire: A Personal Account of Life and Death and Choices.* Chapel Hill: Algonquin, 1994.

———. *Billy Ray's Farm: Essays from a Place Called Tula.* Chapel Hill: Algonquin, 2001.

Caitlin, Roger. "'On Fire' Burns but with a Feeble Flame." Rev. of *On Fire: A Personal Account of Life and Death and Choices,* by Larry Brown. *Hartford Courant* 13 Mar. 1994: G3.

Charbonneau, Jean. "Essay Collection Isn't Larry Brown at His Best." Rev. of *Billy Ray's Farm: Essays from a Place Called Tula,* by Larry Brown. *Denver Post* 15 Apr. 2001: F5.

Day, Orman. "That Secret Code." Watson 190–96.

Donnelly, James. "On Fire: A Personal Account of Life and Death and Choices by Larry Brown." Rev. of *On Fire: A Personal Account of Life and Death and Choices,* by Larry Brown. *Whole Earth Review* 85 (Spring 1995): 106.

Eckhoff, Sally. "Sinners and Saints." Rev. of *On Fire: A Personal Account of Life and Death and Choices,* by Larry Brown. *Village Voice* 10 May 1994: 20.

O'Briant, Don. "An appreciation: Larry Brown, 1951–2004. Hardscrabble rural South gave novelist his material." *Atlanta Journal-Constitution.* 27 Nov. 2004: D1.

Rankin, Tom. "On the Home Front: Larry Brown's Narrative Landscapes." Watson 99–118.

Soloman, Andy. "Shaped by the Deep South, Shadowed by Its Giants." Rev. of *Billy Ray's Farm: Essays from a Place Called Tula,* by Larry Brown. *Boston Globe* 22 July 2001: D5.

Watson, Jay. *Conversations with Larry Brown.* Jackson: UP of Mississippi, 2007.

Yardley, Jonathan. "Cow Sense." Rev. of *Billy Ray's Farm: Essays from a Place Called Tula,* by Larry Brown. *Washington Post* 29 Mar. 2001: C2.

The Rabbit Factory

Escaping the Isolation of the Cage

RICHARD GAUGHRAN

Reviewers of Larry Brown's *The Rabbit Factory* (2003) tended to stress either its unconventional form or its characters' desperation. Those who emphasized the former noted that the book represents a departure for Brown in that it combines—some would say not very successfully—both the short story and the novel, two genres at which he is certainly accomplished. Some commentators implied that Brown was either confused or indecisive in doing so, as if he did not know whether to write a novel or a collection of stories and therefore balked, producing a perplexing combination of the two. David Finkle's comments in the *New York Times* typify this perspective, characterizing the work as a "book-length take on a Deep South community in what are [*sic*] essentially a series of short stories peopled by loosely interrelated characters" (53)—characters who, as Finkle's fellow reviewers would have it, are either "desperate" (Vice), "down and out" (Scott), or even "churlish" (See). Jeff Kunerth, writing in the *Detroit Free Press*, was even more blunt: "In essence, the book is six short stories chopped into pieces and sewn back together in alternating order." Still other reviewers skirted the issue of form altogether by noting, accurately, that films from Robert Altman's *Nashville* (1975) to Paul Thomas Anderson's *Magnolia* (1999) provide parallels, if not precedents, for *The Rabbit Factory*'s structure (Vice, Stankard). Even though we should not expect a book reviewer to analyze a work exhaustively—one cannot address *everything*, after all, in so few column inches—those charging that Brown had loosely stitched together a group of short stories have missed the point entirely. *The Rabbit Factory*'s structure, in short, is anything but accidental.

Rather than present a dark comedy for its own sake, the novel presupposes but ultimately disproves the argument that contemporary life inevitably and irreversibly reduces the individual to pure commodity. *The Rabbit Factory* expands upon Brown's concern for and ultimate sympathy with characters from the lower strata of society—even, in some cases, characters whom society has all but discarded. Even in its most grotesque images, its most darkly comic passages, moreover, the novel celebrates the basic human desire for connection—even as, at the same time, it acknowledges the profound obstacles that can make such connections, love utmost among them, difficult to achieve, much less maintain.

If, in calling *The Rabbit Factory* a novel, I've just contradicted a good many of the reviewers cited earlier, I'm not alone in doing so. For what it's worth, the dust jacket of the first American edition refers to it as a novel. A work comprised of short chapters or sections with alternating characters and points of view, moreover, is not exactly unique among Brown's oeuvre. He employed a similar structure in *Dirty Work* (1989), in which short chapters present the alternating perspectives of two hospital patients, and although *Fay* (2000) begins with the title character's point of view, it later shifts to that of Sam, her would-be rescuer, and then to that of Aaron, her self-appointed keeper. No earlier Brown novel has as many as six alternating scenarios, but the later chapters of *Fay* nonetheless anticipate the novel that would follow it three years later. (And yet there are, certainly, more than six different points of view in *The Rabbit Factory*. Some characters, however—Frankie Falconey among them—do not live long enough to appear in that many sections; others, such as Mr. Hamburger's dog, do not bring with them a wide enough range of experience or emotion to achieve full significance.)

Almost without exception, these peripheral characters either further *The Rabbit Factory*'s larger action or link its other, more central characters, sometimes without even knowing it. Ken, the bartender at the Peabody Hotel in Memphis, occasionally has sex with Arthur's wife, Helen, and Harv Pressman sometimes provides temporary refuge for the wandering Anjalee. In fact, on only one occasion does a minor character enter the novel without advancing its overall action. About halfway through, in section 45—the novel has exactly one hundred sections—Eric is alone, working at the pet shop, when a small man whom he thinks an "elfin Eskimo" enters, desperately seeking help for Bobby, his beloved and now ailing monkey. Aside from the fact that the incident parallels others in the novel in which characters cling to animals past the peak of health—Eric and his pit bull Jada Pinkett, Merlot and his grotesque dog Candy—the scene's primary function is to announce nothing less than the theme of the novel as a whole. The conversation between them is brief, the man futilely pleading with Eric to buy the monkey or in some way save it from whatever ails it, and before long the distressed man leaves, shuffling up the street with Bobby, seeking help elsewhere. Before he does so, however, the man utters a significant non sequitur: "The loneliness of the cage . . . Your cage, mine. What does it matter whose? Somebody cages us all, don't they?" (137).

Populated as it is by so many animals, there are, of course, plenty of cages in *The Rabbit Factory*. Eric works at a pet shop full of them. Domino delivers meat to caged lions (and will soon become lion food himself). He has lived in what is essentially a human cage—a jail cell—and is determined to stay out of another, though he will soon discover that the trunk of a police cruiser serves much the same purpose. Anjalee is also eager to avoid a jail cell, and when we last see Helen, she herself is in a similar cage, having been arrested again for drunk driving. The novel's title (to which we will return) also refers to a kind of cage or enclosure. Fittingly, moreover, the earliest dialogue in the novel centers on the Havahart trap that Arthur will use to capture the stray kitten that he and Helen have found. The device functions as both trap and cage, the novel's second sentence in fact calling it a "Havahart cage." Most of the novel's first section concerns its operation, and an exasperated Helen at one point asks, "Don't you know anything about trapping?" Arthur replies with what we soon take to be a sarcastic reference to Helen's habit of seeking sexual satisfaction outside their marriage: "No . . . But I bet you do" (2). After Jada Pinkett finally captures the kitten, it too finds itself in a cage, one that Eric provides.

More important than these literal cages, however, are the figurative cages in which various characters find themselves. Arthur is beset by sexual dysfunction, a condition from which he yearns to escape so he can satisfy his much younger wife, who herself paces the cage of a loveless marriage and increasing alcohol consumption. As in Arthur's case, many characters face physical limitations or deformities. Miss Muffett, apparently through no fault of her own, has lost a leg in a boating accident. Her employer, the sinister and domineering Mr. Hamburger, has been mutilated by a posthole digger. Domino, thanks to a prison employee who fired a shotgun too close to his ear, has been rendered partially deaf. Wayne, the sailor with a gift for boxing, suffers from ominous headaches. Merlot, self-conscious about his skinny legs, looks at a photograph of his father and uncle and realizes that they were first theirs, a "hereditary thing you couldn't do anything about. Some people got handed down buck teeth or big ears" (232). Maiming, deformity, and physical deficiencies also afflict the non-human characters of

The Rabbit Factory, and in far more cases than just that of Bobby, the sick monkey. Jada Pinkett, Eric's dog, has been shocked into a new personality by a "near-death experience" in the pit (84). Merlot's dog Candy, now living on what constitutes life-support, is hardly recognizable as a dog. Many of the lions kept on Yocona River Road have only three legs. Wayne's ship collides with a whale, ultimately killing it with its propeller in an incident that parallels Miss Muffett's boating accident as well as Domino's hitting a whitetail deer with his delivery truck.

Brown, of course, has used physical deformities to circumscribe characters before. The main characters of *Dirty Work*, for instance, are both confined to hospital beds. One has no limbs at all, and the other has a severely disfigured face and has evidently sustained a serious brain injury. Braiden Chaney, the amputee, at one point thinks, "in here was like prison. Ain't no bars on the windows, but ain't many ways to leave" (57). And if the backdrop of *Dirty Work*, the Vietnam War, seems to indicate that the cages in which Brown's characters find themselves derive from extreme circumstances, *The Rabbit Factory* suggests that physical and emotional isolation is common among humans, and perhaps among other species as well. As Wayne stands on the deck of his ship after its collision with the whale, he empathizes with its now-orphaned calf: "He hated to think about it out there in the wide open, a baby, swimming along all by itself, looking for a new pod where it could hang" (142). As Miss Muffett bemoans her limited options and, more specifically, the prosthetic leg that Mr. Hamburger's dog has buried in the yard, she asks a question familiar to many Brown characters, and not only in *The Rabbit Factory*: "What if she just walked out the door?" Her fellow characters could supply her answer as well as she does: "She couldn't. She was trapped and she knew she was trapped" (310).

Such traps, of course, imply trappers. Some characters—the confined animals, for instance—find themselves isolated for relatively simple reasons. Arthur, Helen, and Eric place the stray kitten in the cage; Mr. Hamburger confines his dog to the house. Their human counterparts, however, are trapped for reasons more difficult to ascertain. Some simply exert power over others—Domino's older sister had abused him when he was young, for instance, and a military hierarchy restricts Wayne's actions—but simple domination by another does not completely explain these characters' entrapment. The man with the monkey suggests that "Somebody cages us all" (137); pinpointing that somebody, however, is difficult at best. Seemingly insignificant actions can have profound repercussions. Accidents happen.

The aptly named Domino often finds himself thinking of the inscrutable way that chance creates chain reactions for which individuals can hardly prepare. As he lies blindfolded in the trunk of Rico's car, he thinks,

> None of this would have happened if he hadn't hit the whitetail. That was what messed him up. Out of the blue. Complete surprise. Something you couldn't account for or figure into any plans. Which was actually bad timing. Which was the worst thing in the world for somebody who was doing something they weren't supposed to be doing. It was something you couldn't see coming and there was no way to predict it. Ten seconds, hell, five seconds, maybe, sooner or later, he probably wouldn't have hit it. It might have jumped before then or it might have gone the other way. Domino knew that life was sometimes measured in small but critical increments. Looking down from approaching traffic for just one second to light a cigarette. Wiping your ass with the winning lottery ticket because it's the only paper thing you have in your billfold besides money. Getting in a hurry zipping up and catching some pretty tender skin in those little brass teeth, standing there so all alone at the urinal, can't go up or down with it, struggling silently, trying not to scream. (218)

As he assesses the course his life has taken, Domino thinks, "Kind of like a preordained thing or a snowball effect when you considered all the elements over the years" (101). Considering the possibility that he might have taken a straighter path, he concludes, "He wished he'd gone straight. As it turned out, like the flip of a coin, he hadn't, but easily might've" (319).

Literary naturalism, of course, takes up just such notions of restriction and entrapment, and reviewer Brad Vice is at least partially correct in characterizing *The Rabbit Factory* as a latter-day example thereof. Vice writes that, "by reducing the city of Memphis into a mere rabbit hutch of lust and hurt, Brown is evolving into an old-school naturalist like the novel's modernizing masters: Dreiser, Crane and Faulkner." His comparison of Brown to Faulkner is appropriate for yet another reason, though, namely the way that theme and form in *The Rabbit Factory* complement each other much as they do in Faulkner novels that feature multiple points of view, *The Sound and the Fury* (1929), *As I Lay Dying* (1930), and *Absalom, Absalom!* (1936) among them. As are many individual sections in these novels, *As I Lay Dying* in particular, each of Brown's in *The Rabbit Factory* is relatively short. Section 35, in fact, contains a mere twenty-seven words. The one hundred sections, therefore, are in effect one hundred cages, one hundred solitary confinement cells. And if a quick perusal of them seems to leave the impression that, because they contain so many characters, there is considerable interaction among them, just the opposite is actually the case. More than one-third of the sections contain no dialogue, and thirty-seven include interior monologue only, characters spending time with little more than their own thoughts. Other characters are sometimes nearby, as when Domino finds himself in the trunk while Rico is at the wheel, or when Wayne catches a crowded bus to Memphis, but in most such cases the point of view focuses only on the section's central character. Section 72, moreover, never releases Domino—or, in effect, Brown's readers—from his confinement in the trunk.

To underscore such isolation and imprisonment, Brown does something unusual in sections 76 and 77. Merlot and Penelope, having established a genuine connection with one another, have thus far proven an exception to the novel's general rule. Rarely apart since their accidental meeting, they here awaken "as lovers do" in the canopied bed of a roadside guesthouse (232). And yet, even amid such an ostensibly idyllic scenario, the sections' central players are irredeemably trapped. Each section is narrated from the third-person perspective—section 76 derives from Merlot's point of view, section 77 from Penelope's—and the conversation on which each centers concerns the same seemingly innocuous topic, the dream from which Penelope has just awakened. Brown allows readers of section 76, however, to believe what Merlot does, that Penelope has dreamt about picking blackberries with her grandmother, while he reveals in section 77 that Penelope has actually lied to Merlot, that she has in fact dreamed about the baby she had had in her youth and had put up for adoption. Penelope lies not once but twice, in effect, not just not telling Merlot what she had dreamed about but inventing a story calculated to enhance her attractiveness to him, an innocent and bucolic tale about blackberry-picking, while the truth is something altogether different: "she just made up a bunch of bullshit about picking blackberries out in the country with her mamaw, when in reality the itching chigger bites on her private places had always driven her apeshit" (240). In that Merlot, similarly, is still hiding from Penelope the soon-to-be-undeniable existence of his ailing dog Candy, we see that even the novel's two most intimately connected characters, alone in the novel's most intimate setting, remain prisoners of their own thoughts. Each, still, is profoundly alone. And as Brown does throughout *The Rabbit Factory*, he enlists narrative technique, in this case one scene narrated from two different perspectives, to more deeply engage his central concerns.

And yet, even though the one hundred sections of *The Rabbit Factory* function as individual isolation chambers, many do on occasion intersect one another. As noted earlier, coincidences and parallels sometimes steer the reader toward making connections among seemingly unrelated sections, or what we might call spheres of plot. In section 2, for instance, Arthur watches from a coffee shop window as a drunk man in a trench coat lurks outside a barbershop across the street. In section 3, narrated from inside the same barbershop, the drunk man carries out a hit on what will turn out to be the wrong target. Soon thereafter, we learn that the trench-coated killer is Frankie Falconey and that the man who had hired him is Mr. Hamburger, the same character who employs Miss Muffett and Domino, the same character whose crimes will precipitate Merlot and Penelope's initial meeting. Arthur's casual glimpse of this hit man thus eventually connects far more characters than we might at first imagine. Frankie is Anjalee's current "sugar daddy," moreover, and, until Mr. Hamburger kills him, the couple stays together in his room at the Peabody, the same hotel where Ken tends the bar that Arthur's wife Helen frequents. Wayne, the sailor, falls in love with Anjalee upon first seeing her, and this set of connections grows even stronger when his superior officer advises him to spend his time in Memphis at the Peabody Hotel. Just one glance across the street, then, connects all of these characters, as well as their respective stories. Intersections of the sort are numerous in the novel: another involves Miss Muffett's having sex with a one-armed stranger nicknamed Mr. Nub, presumably the same Mr. Nub who had worked with Eric's father at the rabbit factory. Such coincidences may not appreciably advance the novel's action, but they do suggest that these initially distinct spheres of plot—what we have been calling isolation chambers—are not, in the end, entirely inviolable.

Naturalistic determinism is indeed the philosophical bedrock upon which Brown builds *The Rabbit Factory*—and yet, it is also as if the novel only superficially or temporarily accepts a possibility that it only halfheartedly wants to embrace: that its characters will forever be trapped, isolated within their individual cells, with no recourse to a way out. The novel's numerous parallels suggest instead that there are other forces at work here, forces struggling to bend back the bars of each respective cell. The seemingly self-contained cubicles of plot are not static, therefore, but dynamic: they are pulsating and alive, in effect, not locked into predetermined patterns of closure but striving toward potential redefinition. Each scenario contains the possibility of change, yearns for intersection and enlargement. Rather than remaining a series of isolated cells (a collection of short stories?), the cells contain within them the energy for intersection (a novel?).

To be sure, the coincidences listed earlier are an author's creations and in themselves do not constitute an argument for a life force at work; numerous other forces, however, work toward creating interaction. For one thing, *The Rabbit Factory* continues Brown's highlighting of popular culture, particularly popular film and song. It is no exaggeration to say that practically every page of *The Rabbit Factory* contains at least one allusion to a television program, film, or popular musician. The novel's first few pages refer to a TV show called *The Operation*, to Sam Peckinpah's *The Wild Bunch* (1969) and Martin Scorsese's *Goodfellas* (1990), to musicians Ted Nugent, Billy Joel, Eric Clapton, and B.B. King, and this concentration of references only continues. Just before Domino kills constable Elwood "Perk" Perkins, the latter is alone in his car changing CDs. Immersed in the music of Patsy Cline, Jim Reeves, Ray Price, Merle Travis, and Hank Williams, he hopes to soon visit the Grand Ole Opry and Dollywood, where he may be lucky enough to have Dolly Parton herself hear one of his songs. Brown's narrators are precise, moreover, in detailing such references. After he kills Perkins, Domino examines the CDs left on the seat of his cruiser: "He'd picked up Townes Van Zandt's *Rear View Mirror*, Hank Williams's *Rare Demos First to Last*, and The Gourds's *Stadium Blitzer*" (92). Occasionally, the allusions sound as though Brown himself may be promoting a particular artist. After Anjalee at one point asks Harv Pressman, "Who's that you got on the stereo?" he replies, "Patty Griffin . . . It's her new record. Isn't she great?" "She's mighty good," Anjalee responds, "I can't believe I've never heard of her" (247). Characters and narrators alike at times refer to these artists as if on a first-name basis with them. Riding in a car, Merlot and Penelope engage in the following conversation, concluded here with a narrator's comment:

> 'What about Al Green? You got any Al?' Merlot said.
> 'I did have but he got to skipping. Let me see what else I've got.'
> She looked.
> 'I've got Lightnin' Hopkins,' she said.
> 'Stop right there,' Merlot said.
> They'd been listening to mixed Motown and she pushed the button to

eject it. She got Lightnin' out and pushed him into the player. Guitar strokes like bolts of velvet lightning started throbbing up in the Four-Runner. (251)

Such references to popular culture, particularly those to the world of music, appear often in Brown's works; in *Dirty Work*, the hospitalized Walter is forced to listen to whatever shows play on the nurses' TV, insipid commercials interspersed among them. He especially objects to the music being hawked: "Want you to buy a Slim Whitman album. Why don't they sell the Temptations, or Jackie Wilson? Hell, why don't they sell some Otis Redding?" (12).

Allusions of the sort do not always refer to just movies and music, though. When readers are first introduced to Anjalee, she is "sipping on Mountain Dew spiked with Absolut Citron and smoking a Camel filtered" (10). Far from signifying themselves alone—or, worse, sinking to the level of promotion, if not pandering, known as product placement—such brand names in *The Rabbit Factory* imply further spheres of meaning, alternative worlds or systems that the characters who patronize or champion them yearn to enter and explore. For these trapped characters, these realms of meaning suggest that there are, in fact, means by which they might escape their respective cells, ways to enter and intersect with the worlds of others and ultimately forge a connection. True, these new arenas of meaning might simply be new traps, as in the case of Helen's increasingly problematic escape via alcohol, but a recognizable brand or artist's name implies a world that otherwise isolated characters can together enter and share. Just before his fatal encounter with Domino, for instance, Perkins seems to leave his world for another: "he had discovered that if he took his own sandwiches and parked off the road and totally immersed himself in chewing and the songs of people like Hank Williams and Merle Travis, in his mind he could go to another place. He could actually go out of his mind. There was this music playing and they were singing about plowing the last mule on the last row of cotton on a ridge in south Tennessee. It didn't get any better than that. Unless it was Miller time. Then it got better than that" (55). Such a pervasiveness of brand names indicates a desire on the part of many characters, conscious or otherwise, to connect to a world outside the one in which they find themselves trapped. Even as seemingly commonplace an activity as watching a nature program on the Discovery Channel indicates a fundamental urge for characters to move outside their own circumscribed worlds, to shed their isolation and loneliness. And it only makes sense that characters would frequently look to popular music for that passage beyond, for popular songs often take up the topic of making, or failing to make, connections with others. Characters who refer to recording artists by their first names only seek this connectedness still more profoundly. A character who asks "You got any Al?" and a narrator who, referring to Leonard Cohen, imitates the characters by telling us that one is "putting Leonard CDs onto the tray" (301) are insisting, in spite of earlier evidence to the contrary, that another world is indeed their own in an unusually intimate way.[1]

To be sure, however, the language of popular culture can itself become a trap. Miss Muffett's way of expressing her desire is decidedly clichéd: "She knew love was out there for everybody, if they could just find it. Some found it sooner than others. She hoped to find some herself one sweet day." The next sentence then bluntly undercuts her optimism: "It wasn't like she hadn't been looking her whole life already" (231). And various characters' attempts at making connections, at mitigating loneliness, hardly guarantee success. Miss Muffett is no better off at the end of the novel than at the beginning. Merlot and Penelope, who find temporary bliss on the road—assisted by tips from *Southern Living* magazine—are nonetheless doomed by their failure to communicate with one another. Domino follows his impulses in trying to make a connection, but his urges are those of an animal, dominated by such desires as a taste for the meat of whitetail deer. It is fitting that he resorts to eating cat food at one point in his peregrinations and later becomes cat (lion) food himself. Anjalee and Wayne are together when we last see them, but the popular love-at-first-sight cliché, or the whore-with-a-heart-of-gold myth, are questionable foundations upon which to base a lasting connection. And what about Wayne's headaches? In the end, his shared happiness with Anjalee remains little but a projection of his vivid imagination. Arthur tries to reconnect with Helen, even purchasing a pump to correct his sexual dysfunction, but it is too late; he is left "[a]ll pumped up with no place to go" (156). Arthur does, however, make a new connection as surrogate father to Eric. The final section of the novel shows them together with Jada Pinkett and the once-stray kitten, about to watch Sergio Leone's *Once Upon a Time in the West* (1968). They briefly mention new plans, namely to communicate with Eric's biological father, but there is no telling what new patterns of cause and effect this effort will put into motion.

In the end, *The Rabbit Factory* does not celebrate its characters' successes. Reviewer Carolyn See is accurate in remarking of its conclusions, "mainly we live in a precarious made-up land of hope." *The Rabbit Factory* does celebrate an urge for connectedness, however, the impulse or life force behind these characters' desires to escape the isolation of the cage. This impulse surfaces in spite of heredity, karma, bad decisions, physical limitations, the commands of bosses, the dictates of military officials, even unlikely chances for success—and in animals as well as in humans. Even more populated by animals than other Brown novels, *The Rabbit Factory* demonstrates that this life force operates up and down the chain of being. Mr. Hamburger's dog greatly frustrates Miss Muffett, but his mischief derives primarily from an urge to escape the narrow confines of the room in which he is locked. One short comic passage, section 59, briefly describes his having what looks to be a wet dream—nothing more, nothing less, again, than the life force manifesting itself, this time irrespective of its host's conscious desires. In the end, the central character of *The Rabbit Factory* is no single human or animal but this same force, for all the novel's characters, human and otherwise, express it in one form or another. In the final lines of the novel Arthur remarks that Jada Pinkett misses Helen, and the once-hissing kitten then comes walking down the hall, now "mewing softly." The narrator says of the kitten's voice, "it sounded like a question, like somebody looking for friends" (339). The novel's last line thus rephrases the quest that the novel, in both its content and form, celebrates throughout.

In this context, *The Rabbit Factory*'s curious title deserves comment. A rabbit factory is an oxymoron, and as a title for this novel it refers to antithetical ways of imagining the world. A factory is mechanized and linear, a closed system predictable by design: no surprises, certainly no wet dreams. On the other hand, rabbits are commonly understood, even to the point of cliché, to be inveterate reproducers, embodiments of the life force itself. The vigorous energy they exercise and represent can hardly be replicated or controlled in a factory. Likewise, these supposedly powerless characters rebel against their assigned roles, attempting, albeit sometimes in grotesque ways, to vault the barriers that would contain them—or, in other words, to escape the loneliness of the cage.

Notes

1. A preoccupation with the products of popular culture and endless conversations about them characterize several contemporary films, and the effect is similar to what occurs in *The Rabbit*

Factory. I'm thinking, in particular, of Quentin Tarantino's work, especially *Pulp Fiction* (1994), and such spin-offs as Gary Fleder's *Things to Do in Denver When You're Dead* (1995).

Works Cited

Brown, Larry. *Dirty Work.* 1989. New York: Vintage, 1990.

———. *Fay.* 2000. New York: Scribner, 2001.

———. *The Rabbit Factory.* New York: Free Press, 2003.

Finkle, David. "The Disconnections." Rev. of *True Cross*, by T. R. Pearson, and *The Rabbit Factory*, by Larry Brown. *New York Times Book Review* 16 Nov. 2003: 53.

Kunerth, Jeff. "Short Stories Woven into a Neat Novel." Rev. of *The Rabbit Factory*, by Larry Brown. *Detroit Free Press.* 26 June 2004. http://www.freep.com/features/books/other14_20030914.htm.

Scott, Russell E. "Don't Stop Until the Road Ends." Rev. of *The Rabbit Factory*, by Larry Brown. *PopMatters.* 26 June 2004. http://popmatters.com/books/reviews/r/rabbit-factory.shtml.

See, Carolyn. "A Visit to the Land of Character Flaws." Rev. of *The Rabbit Factory*, by Larry Brown. *Washington Post Book World.* 26 June 2004. http://www.washingtonpost.com/ac2/wp-dyn/NewsSearch?st=.

Stankard, Linda. "Passing the Rabbit Test." Rev. of *The Rabbit Factory*, by Larry Brown. *BookPage.* 26 June 2004. http://www.bookpage.com/0309bp/fiction/rabbit_factory.html.

Vice, Brad. "Irony and Pathos Percolate in Memphis." Rev. of *The Rabbit Factory*, by Larry Brown. *San Francisco Chronicle.* 26 June 2004. http://www.sfgate.com/cgi-bin/ff/qr?term=.

A Miracle of Catfish and the Recursions of Art

JOHN A. STAUNTON

Every man is tasked to make his life, even in its details, worthy of
the contemplation of his most elevated and critical hour. (81)
—Henry David Thoreau

I.
Aesthetic Experience and Fishing for the Live Creature

Where everything is already complete, there is no fulfillment. . . .
Because the actual world, that in which we live, is a combination of
movement and culmination, of breaks and re-unions, the experience of a living creature is capable of esthetic quality. (17)
—John Dewey

Early in Larry Brown's posthumously published *A Miracle of Catfish* (2007)
we ride along with one of the principle characters through familiar narrative, descriptive, and thematic territory. The vehicle is a '55 Chevy that the
character—always referred to in the narrative as Jimmy's daddy—has under-
taken as a project to occupy much of his time, money, and mental ener-
gies. We witness both the aesthetic reverie and the frustration of turning
the concrete details of life into an artistic machine, and in the tension between these two states we find a fitting analogue to the critical reception to
Brown's final and forever unfinished work. Emerging from "a shitload of
Bondo" to become something "mighty fine to ride around in . . . after a good
rain" (74), the '55 prompts Jimmy's daddy toward contemplation of the aesthetic pleasures of driving while drinking through the backroads and low
hills of northern Mississippi. But the vehicle's deficiencies call him back to
its tenuous coherence: "It was aggravating not to have third gear. You had to

get up some speed going up hills. . . . He finished the beer in his hand and threw the empty out the window, then reached to the cooler in the floorboard for a fresh one. Popped the top. Took a drink. . . . Turned his parking lamps on and the dash lights didn't come on. What the hell. Son of a bitch. He bumped the dash with his hand and they flickered. Then they came on. Then they went off. He hit it again. They came on. They went off. Son of a bitch. He hit it again and they flickered. He hit it twice and they came on and then went back off. Piece of *shit!*" (74–75). It is tempting to come to a similar assessment of the work itself, one that might identify not a few pleasures singular to the experience of reading a Larry Brown novel, moving us forward carelessly so long as we don't seek too much illumination. Indeed, at least one reviewer has taken that tack, finding the novel "at once rambling, melodramatic, and undisciplined" (Dold). But in this description of the '55 Chevy and Jimmy's daddy, himself undisciplined and forever trying to outpace his responsibilities to self and family, we see more than failure, either of character or narrative. We see the complex rendering of life at the cultural, economic, and spiritual bottom, struggling to rise.

In interview after interview, Brown recounted his own attempt to restore a vehicle just like Jimmy's daddy's. The story acquired a sort of legendary status after years of interviews, and Brown seemed to revel in telling it to establish both the context of his unlikely decision to become a writer and his firm belief that writers are not born with any particular talent but are rather made through an arduous apprenticeship of discipline and regular writing. "One of my last projects before I started writing full-time was disassembling a '55 Chevrolet," he told Jim Dees during a 2000 interview: "Took the sumbitch completely apart, jacked it up with these trailer jacks, jacked the whole damn thing up off the frame, took the whole thing completely apart. Completely dismantled the car and was going to put it back together. I never did get the damn thing back together. It sat out in the yard on them jacks for a couple of years. Somebody finally come hauled it off. So when I told Mary Annie [Brown's wife] I was going to start writing she said okay. But I'm sure she thought it was going to be about like that '55 Chevy" (165). Both encounters with the '55 emerge out of the subjective layering of everyday experience to reveal the promise of something better. Both accounts also, however, betray the simultaneous suspicion that hope itself, especially for the working-class men and women of Brown's real and fictional landscapes, might be just another dead-end.

A Miracle of Catfish *and the Recursions of Art*

Rather than seek out the supposed artistic failings of Brown's "Novel in Progress," I'd like to consider instead how the very incompleteness of the novel offers a unique opportunity to see Brown's aesthetic and ethical project laid bare, to consider a different set of questions that foreground the *work* of fiction in the world: what does Brown's work *do*? and *how* does it do so? Such a shift in critical perspective shows us Brown engaged in a painstaking process of turning everyday experience into what Dewey describes above as an aesthetic experience, one in which the day-to-day rhythms of working life become the material of a democratic art. "The intelligent mechanic engaged in his job," Dewey explains, is simultaneously "interested in doing well and finding satisfaction in his handiwork, caring for his materials and tools with genuine affection"; he is, finally, "artistically engaged" (5). The description aptly captures Brown's own sense of his work as writer, as well as his belief that these are lives that matter, and that to deny character, author, or reader the pleasures of art is to promote the worst kind of moral and aesthetic elitism. The critical shift I am suggesting will likewise cast Brown as something of an "autoethnographer" of working-class Southern life. The term is oppositional and comes from Mary Louise Pratt's attempt to account for the way that colonized others—and, certainly, Brown's New South characters live on the margins of contemporary national discourse— construct texts "in response to or in dialogue with those metropolitan representations" (7). Not unlike Zora Neale Hurston's fiction, Brown's captures from the ground up the layers of moral complexity revealed through regional language, gesture, and practice. This interpretive move will also examine how the elaborate enterprise to produce *A Miracle of Catfish*—clearly conceived to be mainstream at the same time that it challenges mainstream assumptions about rural and working-class life—points to a curious thematization of the socially constructed and ethical nature of art, experience, and literary meaning throughout Brown's work.

II.
Looking for the "Good Stuff":
Shabby Melodrama or Post-Southern Irony?

Some people have the notion that you read the story and then
climb out of it into the meaning, but for the fiction writer himself

the *whole* story is the meaning, because it is an *experience*, not an abstraction. (73; emphasis added)

—Flannery O'Connor

The already-vexed hermeneutic and scholarly project of literary interpretation is made all the more troublesome by a work that is quite explicitly and forever unfinished. Because it is not "whole" in the conventional sense, it does not quite allow for the usual experience of reading a novel. This is not to say that *A Miracle of Catfish* does not allow for an experience in both O'Connor's and Dewey's sense, a bringing into coherence, an understanding of oneself, others, and the world. But the novel as readers experience it betrays conflicting impulses that generate a simultaneous forward and backward movement alternately focusing on the prospects of Brown's literary future and carefully maintaining his posthumous memory. With few exceptions, the assessment from reviewers has been overwhelmingly positive, almost reverent, and the novel itself finally put Brown on the *New York Times* Bestseller List. But reviewers have also been cautious in making any value claims about the work, instead invoking its editorial front matter, even paraphrasing Shannon Ravenel's "Editor's Note" to comment on what she calls Brown's propensity "to write more than he needed. Having honed his skills on the short-story form, he reveled in the wide spaces that novels offer. I rarely found reason to suggest expansion. But I did find places I thought would gain by careful snipping and shaving" (xiii). This "snipping and shaving" winnowed some 33,000 words from the manuscript, opening still further questions of how the work should be placed critically. A quick sampling of review titles suggests a number of potential generic and critical categories for the novel: "The One That Got Away" (*New York Times*); "'Catfish' Swims in Endless Waters" (*USA Today*); "'Catfish' Is Not So Miraculous" (*Wichita Eagle*); "The Final, Unfinished Novel of the Late, Great Larry Brown; Fire Engine Redneck" (*Independent Weekly* [Raleigh-Durham]); "Hard Luck, Hard Living in Brown's Corner of the South" (*Boston Globe*). Part fish story, part "grit lit," part scholarly interest piece, part literary memorial, the book is the joint project of Ravenel, Brown's longtime editor; Brown's widow and literary executor Mary Annie Brown; and two of his friends, now advisors to his wife in her role as literary executor, Tom Rankin and Jonny Miles. The trouble with entering interpretive waters with this, Brown's last work, however, comes of course from its very incompleteness and the impossibility of ever landing a definitive interpretation. Brown's untimely death before completing the manuscript inflects the reading of the novel with a profound sense of loss and constantly threatens to close down a narrative concerned with stalled lives and missed connections. After all, there's only so much pressure a hermeneutic circuit can take before it gives out or wears thin.

Nonetheless, to paraphrase the opening of Brown's "Roadside Resurrection" (1991), this story remains forever open. Through an examination of the mundane, quotidian—or, in the view of some critics, "meandering"—details of contemporary rural working-class life, the novel attends closely to the materiality of several characters whose lives and stories intersect or sometimes just barely miss each other during a single year on the small stretch of land Brown has sketched out in a hand-drawn map on the novel's opening page. But it also self-consciously and even playfully engages the pop-culture constructs of regional and masculine identity, particularly by way of nine-year-old Jimmy's obsession with country singer Kenny Chesney. Brown does not *quite* write us into impossible fantasies of rough-hewn sentiment, of, for instance, two hard-bitten men talking in a bar—over cold glasses of milk—about the women they love and have lost (the scenario of Chesney's own "The Good Stuff"). Nor does he allow for swaggering macho bluster. But the novel's frequent invocation of Chesney does create a tropic shorthand for a certain kind of unapologetic embrace of cliché and sentiment deployed in a successful embrace of New South culture.[1] In Brown's transformation of this shabby but knowing sentimentalism, what we have is a more elaborate negotiation of the self-parody and earnestness that mark the highly mediated nature of contemporary Southern and working-class life.

Cortez Sharp, a septuagenarian haunted by his personal and racialized Mississippi past, dogged by his moribund wife, disappointed by his grown daughter, begins the action by building a catfish pond. It's an enterprise that has been taking shape in his mind for some time, and in the course of the ensuing year his vision will expand to take in at least some tangential perspective of the lives of the other chief characters. Down the road in a trailer, Jimmy tries to navigate the vagaries of New South masculinity. The emotional heart of the novel, Jimmy is a boy who "loved his daddy so much that he couldn't *stand* for his daddy to be mad at him, although he often seemed to be mad at him" (57). He doesn't know, though, if he wants to follow in the steps of his father or of the older boys who speed up and down their cut-off in "jacked-up" pickup trucks, leaving Jimmy's daddy's '55 in a cloud of dust.

Early in the novel Jimmy experiences what at first seems a simple childhood version of nostalgia in the face of decay and ruin but what soon captures in miniature this twin desire for family and the commodities of conspicuous consumption. After engineering his own "night-time running light," an old flashlight secured to the front of his go-cart, Jimmy takes a moment to consider what he has and what he's lost: "he sat down in the seat and looked at his once-clean machine. It had become battered. Dusty. Greasy and gravel specked, the red paint rock pecked here and there. A sad machine now where once was shiny and bright" (54). In its brief shift to passive construction and layers of appositives, the narrative here shows Jimmy discursively resisting the impulse to attach blame for the go-cart's condition. How or why "[i]t had become battered" is located outside the care or responsibility of Jimmy and especially his father, though his father repeatedly refuses to help his son fix a simple loose chain.

Instead of worrying over who should be responsible (himself? his father? the unfairness of the world at large?), Jimmy moves toward a makeshift restoration through selective memory, imagination, and desire: "He turned the steering wheel in his hands. He wished it was still new. He remembered how good it ran when it was new. How quiet and fast. Back then he could go up in the woods with it, or up and down the dirt road in front of the trailer as swiftly as he wanted, and it wouldn't matter. The wind would fly in his hair and he'd know a feeling of freedom such as he'd never felt or known was possible" (54). This preoccupation with driving, as Jay Watson notes in "Economics of a Cracker Landscape," is part of the poor-white discourse of contemporary Southern life and "offers the pleasures and privileges of self-extension in at least two ways: through physical movement and through conspicuous consumption" (505). Brown might add to this assessment the imaginative dimensions of art and the ethical consequences of a self-extending "drift." For Jimmy's remembrance of his go-cart is a fantasy of restoration to an impossible utopian wholeness; we know from earlier chapters that it was never quite this good. Likewise, we know that Jimmy's daddy's own project of self-extension—the '55 Chevy—comes at the expense of his son's happiness, and in the novel's final pages, he even sells Jimmy's beloved go-cart to pay for the Chevy's new transmission. This betrayal comes despite or perhaps because of Jimmy's daddy's own realization late in the novel that he is "nothing but a fuckup, would never be anything but a fuckup, and never had been anything but that" (426).

Other characters help move what little action there is slightly forward: there's Tommy Bright, the fish man, who travels the South stocking ponds with an assortment of fish, especially catfish. He's also an inveterate gambler on his way to losing everything, although, as he reminds himself, only half-believing, "He wasn't dead yet. And if you weren't dead there was always hope, wasn't there?" (83). There is also Cleve, an old hand at violence who sometimes works for Cortez, and whose plan to avoid a third prison sentence is simply to "stay away from the white man unless he had something you needed" (346). Certainly the five illustrate a spectrum of Southern masculine—and especially working-class—ethos, especially that of the working class. Insofar as the truncated narrative allows, each man lives out some of the options that might be available to young Jimmy as he grows to young adulthood. But this is no plot-driven novel. Indeed, for most of the book nothing much happens—or, to be more precise, nothing much happens that is out of the steady and often deadening routine of working-class life.

The focus, rather, as in all of Brown's fiction, is on character, particularly on the desire these characters have to establish bonds of kinship and connection with anyone who can help them stave off a descent into economic and emotional collapse. They seek paths not just of self-extension but of contact with an other who is decidedly not the self. As David Shipler notes in *The Working Poor: Invisible in America*, such bonds of kinship "in [their] broadest meaning, extending further than blood and tribe into a larger affinity and commonality . . . can blunt the edge of economic adversity. . . . It's a safety net that improves the material dimensions of life; for those who have that network of connectedness and caring within a family and beyond, the brink of poverty is a less dangerous place. . . . Its absence facilitates collapse" (179, 180). Within the first few chapters of *A Miracle of Catfish*, we begin to realize that these characters, though living so close to one another and having such overlapping interests, needs, and desires, are desperately alone. In Brown's earlier works, such narrative openness helped generate an ethical appeal for empathetic connectedness. Here, it gives way through the literal open-endedness of the "Novel in Progress" to a more participatory narrative positioning in which Brown brings us as readers closely into the thoughts of his characters. He creates for us a regionalist aesthetic which,

as I've argued elsewhere, lets us move from an "'objective' stance of the out-
sider *looking in* to a 'subjective' or engaged view of the insider *looking closely
at* his or her locale" (45)—and through this shift in perspective it calls us to
take seriously these regional lives.

Brown's commitment to the representation of these working-class
Southern lives comes at a time when the sense of an authentic local identity is troubled by the postmodern unsettlings of global capitalism. As
Aaron Fox notes in his ethnography *Real Country: Music and Language in
Working-Class Culture*, the "emplacement, embodiment, the organization
of temporal experience and memory, and normative local understandings
of emotion, subjectivity, and proper sociality" all comprise the "culture" of
contemporary Southern life (21), especially in a present historical moment
"in which American blue-collar workers and small-town communities feel a
profound sense of political disempowerment and economic and cultural insecurity, and *in which the dignity of embodied labor is in question as never before*" (25; emphasis added). Brown's affinity for these characters, their work,
and this region—and, famously, its music—of course derives in part from
his own familiarity with the terrain. His fictional mapping of his characters'
lives at times amounts to a transparent overlay of his own long emplacement amid the rural outskirts of Oxford, Mississippi. He and his characters
don't just walk the same lines; they drive the same backroads. A number of
his interviews even include his pointing to a house, a stand of trees, a road-
house, or some other physical landmark as he drives interviewers around,
telling which of his characters meets a particular fate there.

In the stories and "riffs" comprising *Billy Ray's Farm: Essays from a Place
Called Tula* (2001), for instance, we see much of the same description of
the landscape we find in *A Miracle of Catfish*. Several of the essays create
thinly veiled pseudonyms for Brown's family and friends (e.g. 'Bobby Ray'
for son Billy Ray; 'Marlana Antonia' for wife Mary Annie) to offer a sort
of heightened rendering of everyday experience. And we even get a paean
to Southern-fried fish: "give me fish, bream or crappie or catfish, even bass,
fried, with taters on the side, a small brown mound of hushpuppies, but
mainly . . . give me crisp meal-coated flakes of fish, white and steaming under the tines of the fork as it twists the once-swimming flesh from the thin
bones" (116). Though the details are perhaps at times excessive for a reader
not fully invested in Brown's everyday life, the attempt reveals a man taking seriously Thoreau's injunction to make his life, especially in the details,
"worthy of the contemplation of his most elevated and critical hour." The

collection's final essay, "Shack," itself captures a Thoreauvian enterprise to carve out a place in the country where one can join art and nature to live deliberately and fully. In the essay, the writing cabin itself remains unfinished, but Brown imagines what it might become, and in imagining sees it as a full experience. "[T]he little house sits windowless but roofed," he writes. "I've still got to get those windows in, build the cornices, hang the door, build the decks and finish all the outside, then the inside. It'll be years at this rate. But it's okay. It's something to keep looking forward to. One day, maybe I will eventually sit in it and either write something on a piece of paper or play a few chords on a guitar" (205). Brown never did get much of a chance to write there, according to his widow: "He moved the furniture into the cabin one week, and died the next" (Watkins). Despite this tragic irony, as Brown indicates in the close of the essay (and the collection), this particular end is somewhat beside the point; the *experience* of the cabin lies not in its use as a writing room but in its relationship to the natural world around it. "I go over there all the time," Brown writes. "I look across the pond at it when I drive up. In the summer you can barely see it. I like that. I go and sit in it if I know a rain storm is coming. It does not leak" (205). Despite the gaps and excisions in the narrative—all marked by Ravenel's bracketed ellipses—*A Miracle of Catfish* similarly sustains readers, bringing us a solid inside look on the lives of his regional characters.

III.
"No Shoes, No Shirt, No Problems": Narrative Absences and Presences

Something was pulling really really *really* hard and Jimmy didn't know what to do. . . . So he just stood there tugging on the rod, trying to raise it, but whatever had taken his little catfish was going deeper and deeper and deeper. . . . Jimmy was forced to hold it straight out and he knew that he couldn't hold it because it was pulling too hard and he almost cried out for some help and then the line went *zing!* and broke. . . . Jimmy stood there, stunned, his line lying limp in the water. He reeled it in and looked at it. . . . *Something mighty funny going on here*, Jimmy thought. *Mm hmm.* (369–70)

The subjective rendering of the characters in *A Miracle of Catfish* emerges largely through a series of interior monologues,[2] as we've seen above, and through their movement through Brown's richly detailed material world. Though the cultural idiom is largely internal here, such language-in-use reveals the discursive and cultural emplacement of the native population. As we've seen above with Jimmy and Jimmy's daddy, when Brown's characters talk, whether to themselves or to each other, they move through and engage the material of their lives, bumping up against what sociolinguist James Gee identifies as the "other stuff" that accompanies language-in-use to create what he calls "Big D" Discourses. "The key to Discourses," Gee notes, "is 'recognition' . . . as a particular type of who (identity) engaged in a particular type of what (activity), here-and-now" (27). The "Discourse" these characters participate in is of course one of Southern male identity, which also includes, as we see in Jimmy's chief desires (e.g. to maintain the love of and for his father, to see Kenny Chesney in concert, and to one day drive a "jacked-up" truck), the carefully packaged and commodified culture of "Country" and "Southern" masculinity—the sentimentalized machismo of pop-country music, Promise Keepers, and NASCAR Dads. These are not the history-obsessed denizens of Southern modernism; theirs is a culture of forgetting the past, themselves, and most significantly their obligations to one another. We see Jimmy's daddy, for instance, at the very moment he turns his '55 around in the parking lot of Old Union Baptist Church as the congregation is leaving, deliberately silence the "little voice that whispered inside his head . . . because it was usually telling him that he was messing up in some way or another." The voice attempts to remind him of his obligations: "[L]ook at you, riding around drinking beer while other people are in church. And not only that, but you're also thinking about screwing somebody. And you don't treat your kid right. Give him shit about drinking the last Coke. Why don't you just buy some more Cokes, asshole?" Just after this willful attempt at forgetting, Jimmy's daddy is "nearly run over by a jacked-up pickup that came hurtling over the hill" (180). Instead of calling him to change his current path, this near-miss seems to propel Jimmy's daddy further down the road to ruin, landing him at the door of a co-worker for an assignation. This flight from attending to the obligations of the here and now makes the "enactive work" of recognition-in-Discourse all the more difficult, for the characters seem to eschew any opportunity to direct their own lives, to choose, in Gee's terms, just "who" and "what" they will be.

A Miracle of Catfish *and the Recursions of Art*

In this respect, these characters also take part in another longstanding Southern discursive and religious tradition; they seem to be living out—again both in earnest and in the face of stereotype, irony, and parody—the very dilemma of St. Paul's divided human consciousness: "I do not do what I want, but I do the very thing I hate," Paul laments in his epistle to the Romans; "I can will what is right, but I cannot do it" (Rom 7.15, 18). Jimmy's daddy's own Damascus-like encounter as he exits the lot of the Baptist church captures the dilemma nicely, even down to the portentous warning of the pickup's Yosemite Sam mud flaps, which read "BACK OFF!" (180). Given the religious connotations of the novel's title, in fact, this convergence of Discourses suggests the difficulty of salvation and redemption for these apparent social and cultural "bottom-feeders," who are, as one reviewer remarks of Ursula, the enormous brood-catfish of the title, "beauteous eaters of their own species" (Lowry). Paul's own warning in the epistle to the Galatians invokes a similar image: "If you go snapping at one another and tearing one another to pieces, take care: you will be eaten up by one another" (Gal 5.15).

In addition to this deep concern for rendering faithfully the nuances both sacred and secular of working-class life on the rural fringes of the New South, Brown's aim on behalf of such characters has always been ethical. He frequently talks about his characters in a way that suggests a deep connection to their struggles, even a sense of obligation to help them out of their difficulties—echoing, though often more literally and less religiously, Paul's own injunction for the faithful to "Carry each other's burdens" (Gal 6.2). If Brown is something of an ethnographer of those struggling to negotiate life at the edge, as I've suggested above, then he is also most certainly a participant-observer, one who is invested in the outcome of his characters. He tells Tom Rankin in a 1995 interview, for instance, that the pain of ending a novel for him is always in "knowing that for some [characters] there's not going to be an easier way out—that some of them are going to have to pay the price, the human price," a realization that carries for Brown both aesthetic and ethical questions: "You always wonder if you've done the right thing" (117). These sometimes competing impulses of the sentimental moralist and the hard-eyed observer, I would argue, are at the heart of Brown's work, and any consideration of his final narrative—indeed, his work as a whole—needs to locate in the very rambling, melodramatic, and undisciplined appearance of his narrative a site of inquiry into what such tropes of movement, sentiment, and moral and artistic slippage might mean, as well as how they operate on us.

Jimmy's struggle with Ursula on his first attempt at fishing offers a fitting metaphor for the reader's experience with this novel, trying to dredge up meaning—about the characters, the novel, even Brown himself, perhaps—with only insufficient information and textual material to put it into relation with other works. But meaning-making for Brown is always an elusive and negotiated process, one that calls readers to move toward some larger action, feeling, or understanding. *A Miracle of Catfish* is, after all, a "Novel in Progress." Progress borne of narrative empathy can come only if readers recognize in the text something of their own realities and thereby commit to a process of readerly refiguration that allows the world of the text to alter or cast into heightened relief their own. Brown's fellow Mississippi writer Eudora Welty argues that this transaction occurs only when the reader has a lived sense of the reality of the fictional work. "Making reality real is art's assignment," she asserts, an assignment the writer fulfills primarily through use of place, for "[l]ocation is the ground conductor of all the currents of emotion and belief and moral conviction that charge out from the story in its course" (128). For Welty, place goes beyond the mere intersection of time and space and finds in region a wellspring for moral action.

Welty's definition locates a number of provocative claims about the interrelations among form, ethics, and region that recur throughout the practice of regionalist literature. The definition asks what it might mean, for instance, for art "to make reality real" at all, the repetition of "real" revealing the particular problem faced by any regionalist artist who would attempt to bring an imaginative (and perhaps alien) reality to life for readers from other parts of the country or from other political, social, or religious dispositions than those of the characters. Embedded in Welty's prescription is the claim that regionalist subject matter must have something like the religious notion of "presence," an animating force that makes itself known, that demands to be recognized. As George Steiner notes, "presence" reaches into the theological realm of understanding: it makes a "wager on the meaning of meaning, on the potential of insight and response when one human voice addresses another . . . when we encounter the *other* in its condition of freedom. . . . It supposes a passage, beyond the fictive or the purely pragmatic, from meaning to meaningfulness" (4). Whether that passage in Brown's work is in fact theological is largely irrelevant, however, for it is decidedly a human move.

A Miracle of Catfish *and the Recursions of Art*

The reader's experience, Brown observed in a 2003 interview with Charles Blanchard, should mirror the same discoveries and encounters with his characters the writer makes while writing: "I want to find out what the story is day by day. If you think about it, what happens to the reader is the same thing that happens to the writer, except in a much more condensed form. It's not six hours here, and fourteen hours there. It's a couple of days of reading the book" (175). What's more, the reader should also experience the same sort of ethical awakening and commitment to characters' lives that Brown sought through his oft-described strategy of "sandbagging" his characters to find out how they respond to trouble. Connecting our aesthetic impulse to this ethical question, Brown moves readers toward a refiguration of their subjective encounters with both their worlds and that of the text. Unlike Jimmy's memory of his go-cart, however, this is not an act of creative nostalgia, an imaginative production of a utopian space to fill the characters' lack. Rather we are engaged in an enterprise of refiguration which imagines out of present material circumstances possible, but realistic, alternative versions for what is and what has already been. No amount of desiring a different narrative path is likely to bring Jimmy and his father together, for instance, but seeing the split perspectives of their near-misses at father-son connections helps us to recognize just how and why they go awry. Through such narrative empathy in those moments we likewise glean real-world analogues and are being called, finally, to attend to others in their need.

IV.
Versions and Recursions: Experience as Art

The pony kept walking in a circle and between his knees Jimmy could feel the little animal shivering. He could feel himself shivering in his wet clothes. And if you were a pony you couldn't take a towel and dry off. He wondered if the man would take a towel and dry the ponies off before he loaded them back into the rusty horse trailer sitting there hooked to the man's pickup. The man and Jimmy's daddy were still talking and the pony kept walking. [...] On and on. Shivering. It went on for so long that it was all Jimmy could do to keep from asking somebody to please make it stop. (446)

In a July 2004 interview with Orman Day for a forum on working-class literature, Brown offered a quick catalogue of the many blue-collar jobs he'd held, among them grocery *sacker*, house *painter*, hay *hauler*, truck *driver*, and fire*fighter*, the titles capturing both the *do-ing* of work and a curious sense of working *against* or in opposition to the material world. As Brown reflected on what he has learned from those jobs, his focus moved from self, to family, to community at large, and finally to the genesis of his desire to become a writer: "I guess the main thing I learned was that I didn't want to work with my back for the rest of my life and wanted to use my mind instead," he explained. "I didn't want to remain poor. I wanted my children to have better opportunities than what I had. I wanted to work for myself. I saw people work their whole lives in factories, standing on concrete forty hours a week, and I didn't want that life. I wanted more than that from life. I thought I could find it in writing" (192). It is a story that recurs in many of Brown's interviews, but what stands out in this late version is how explicitly this trajectory from his own interests to the interests of others ultimately redounded upon the aesthetic and ethical goals of his fiction. This circuit from experience to writing clearly derives from a desire to break the cycle of poverty, and as we see with Jimmy's grim realization on his seemingly endless pony ride, we begin to move into a new path only when we recognize and attempt to empathize with the suffering of others.

Brown made this connection still more explicit with what at first seems a bromide about "the American worker," but what soon moves toward a critique of the forces responsible for the economic conditions of blue-collar workers: "I have great sympathy for the good people of the working class," he said. "They have a hard time making ends meet, even when they work very hard and the fat cats in this country just keep getting fatter and not paying their fair share of income tax because the government allows it to be that way and gets rid of American jobs and gives them to foreigners. There's much injustice" (192–93). This is the same "real country" discourse of "political disempowerment and economic and cultural insecurity" that Fox notes (25), and it clearly hints at Brown's own anger and frustration over the situations his characters inhabit. As he concluded his reflection, we see him tempering his critique, giving brief utterance to a longstanding (though contested) discourse about education's role as an avenue out of the cycle of poverty, and finally returning to the characters and settings that would become *A Miracle of Catfish*: "The little man is kept down by the big man, and it's always been that way, and it always will probably. The factory worker can't find anything better, or figures he has no right to hope for anything better since that's what his daddy did and what all the people around him do. I was exactly of that mindset, but I changed over the years. Education is the only answer. For those that want it, I mean. I consider myself a working-class person who lucked out. I'm exploring some of this in the novel I'm working on now. I have a main character who works in that same stove factory [where both Brown and his father worked]" (193). Brown's comments are instructive for both their insight and for their participation in the on-going discourse about work, poverty, and education. He begins with a resignation to "the way it's always been" and ends with a transformation of his own experience into an artistic demonstration of someone who believes in his own fated consignment to a life of dispiriting work—the character who will eventually become Jimmy's daddy. What separates Brown's experience from his character's, however, is less important than seeking to bridge that distance between someone like Jimmy's daddy and Brown's readers. Like Jimmy's understanding not just of the pony's suffering but of his own position in a cycle of suffering and abuse through willed neglect, Brown's narrative is designed to force readers to recognize their shared fate with his characters, but not so we can redeem them—the story, even if unfinished, has already been written; the discourse only awaits our participation in the utterance to enact our recognition—but so we can possibly save ourselves from going along with or giving in to these forces of division.

V.
Conclusion: Seeing Another / Being Seen

> The old man looked around. There were two sloping walls of
> trees, a natural place to build a pond. Cortez Sharp could see it
> plain as day. He'd been seeing it for a while. (1)

Long after Cortez Sharp has realized his vision of the catfish pond, Jimmy is trying to bring the pond into a certain focus of his own. After seeing Tommy Bright's Big Red Fish Truck make a delivery to Mr. Sharp, Jimmy begins to spy on Cortez, secretly using his father's binoculars to try to figure out what is happening at the pond. The process not only involves an exercise in the discipline of the long stare while lying still but allows us to watch as one character tries to understand another, even if only from a safe and comfortable distance. Throughout the scene, Brown tells us, Jimmy just "sat there in the woods and watched the old man," until at last "Jimmy felt some sort of strange feeling from watching him and knowing the old man didn't know it" (308). This recognition of his voyeuristic power over another causes Jimmy first to wonder what Cortez is doing and then why, what his emotional motivations might be: "What was that stuff in the garbage can and what was he doing with it? And why was he just sitting there? *Was he sick?* Jimmy's mama had told him that the old man's wife had died a while back. . . . Jimmy knew he was looking at Mr. Sharp. And that Mr. Sharp was probably pretty sad, missing his dead wife. *He didn't look that mean from here*" (309; emphasis added). This distant inspection, rendered close through binoculars, moves Jimmy to begin seeing Sharp not just on Jimmy's terms (as the mean old man who had yelled at him), but also in something approximating Cortez's own terms. Out of this opening view, Jimmy is able to emerge as Cortez's rescuer a few chapters later, when Sharp's tractor turns over into the pond and pins him in. Spying once again, Jimmy doesn't sit idly observing this time but rushes to action, calling emergency workers and then going to Mr. Sharp himself, wading into the pond and staying with him until help arrives, even though he doesn't know how to swim.

It seems likely that this connection between Cortez and Jimmy would have generated the novel's eventual resolution and, if not a happy ending, at least not the bleak ends that meet so many of Brown's other characters. Brown's notes for the final chapters indicate a scene in which Cortez and Jimmy fish a local river early in the day that Jimmy's daddy is stopped for drinking and driving. How their continued interaction would sustain them we can't know, of course, but since they are the only characters who seem to sense the ghost of Queen (the lover Cortez poisoned rather than relinquish his white privilege in segregation-era Mississippi), Cortez's own murderous past and Jimmy's continued neglect and abuse at the hands of his parents would likely have figured into any mutual attempt to see each other on his own terms.

The possibilities for the novel's resolution are not endless, but they do remain open and call for us to maintain contact between and among narrative strands. Not the result of having to make sense of an unfinished manuscript alone, this readerly refiguration is again Brown's strategy to call us to attend to the lives of others. What Brown calls his readers to witness is often unpleasant—amid the sweet sentiment of Jimmy's rich interiority is the physical abuse and callous neglect of his parents, for instance—but it is always made more easily *visualizable* by the participatory voice of his regional narrators. Although his stories and novels have long been praised for a gritty realism that refuses to look past the grim details of local life, Brown refuses to allow those details to portray the regional subject as an object of ridicule for his readers. Instead, he focuses on those structures of community that establish (and threaten) regional identity, particularly the familial and social bonds that alternately stifle and enable individual self-realization. In *A Miracle of Catfish*—and, indeed, in many of the essays comprising both *On Fire: A Personal Account of Life and Death and Choices* (1994) and, especially, *Billy Ray's Farm*—Brown configures for his readers a sense of community grounded in a visualizable space, marking the limits of that space as it attempts to circumscribe the subjectivity of working-class men and women and other overlooked persons in the name of community. Region in his fiction is a place imbued with the presence of local life. His characters effect empathy not because of their exploits, detailed through plot-driven stories, but because of who they are and what they do for each other, revealed through minutely-rendered characterizations by a narrator who has known them as neighbor, father, son, and friend.

With *A Miracle of Catfish* Brown again and with finality confronts the thematic perception that has always—and continues to—beset regionalism. The novel refuses to let these characters be subsumed into the sprawl of national and homogenizing discourses, and its representations of working-class men and women of the rural South demand a broadening of the reader's own world to include the perspectives of both a factual and a fictional "Tula." Like the cabin Brown sought to build with his own hands on family land, it is a place whose details warrant contemplation, a site where the living are both haunted by and can remember the dead. But more important, when we become engaged and empathetic readers of the narratives around us, it is a place to sustain us in our work together, even at the bottom. And that, in the end, is the miracle of catfish.

Notes

1. The enormous popularity of Kenny Chesney's quadruple-platinum *No Shoes, No Shirt, No Problems* (2002), including such hits as the title track, "Young," and "The Good Stuff," during Brown's work on the novel no doubt figured into Jimmy's musical preferences.

2. Watson notes in his introduction to *Conversations with Larry Brown* that "[c]ritics, reviewers, and Brown's own writing peers often point to his pitch-perfect ear for southern working-
class dialect and idiom as an important source of the authenticity so many readers found in his
work" (ix).

Works Cited

Blanchard, Charles. "Pulling Rabbits out of a Hat: An Interview with Larry Brown." Watson, *Conversations* 173–79.

Brown, Larry. *Billy Ray's Farm: Essays from a Place Called Tula*. Chapel Hill: Algonquin, 2001.

———. *A Miracle of Catfish*. Chapel Hill: Algonquin, 2007.

Day, Orman. "That Secret Code." Watson, *Conversations* 190–96.

Dees, Jim. "The Rough Road of Larry Brown: Smith and Wesson Meets Smith and Corona." Watson, *Conversations* 163–67.

Dewey, John. *Art as Experience*. 1934. New York: Perigree, 1980.

Dold, Gaylord. "'Catfish' Is Not So Miraculous." Rev. of *A Miracle of Catfish*, by Larry Brown. *Wichita Eagle* 20 May 2007. http://www.kansas.com/entertainment/books/v-print/story/74540.html.

Dufresne, John. "Hard Luck, Hard Living in Brown's Corner of the South." Rev. of *A Miracle
of Catfish*, by Larry Brown. *Boston Globe* 22 Apr. 2007. http://www.boston.com/ae/books/
articles/2007/04/22/hard_luck_hard_living_in_ browns_corner_of_the_south.html.

Fox, Aaron A. *Real Country: Music and Language in Working-Class Culture*. Durham: Duke UP,
2004.

Gee, James. *An Introduction to Discourse Analysis: Theory and Method*. 2nd ed. New York: Routledge, 2005.

Lowry, Beverly. "The One That Got Away." Rev. of *A Miracle of Catfish*, by Larry Brown. *New York
Times* 29 Apr. 2007. http://www.nytimes.com/2007/04/29/books/review/Lowry.html.

Minzesheimer, Bob. "'Catfish' swims in endless waters." Rev. of *A Miracle of Catfish*, by
Larry Brown. *USA Today* 21 Mar. 2007. http://www.usatoday.com/life/books/reviews/
2007-03-21-larry-brown-catfish_N.htm.

O'Connor, Flannery. "The Nature and Aim of Fiction." *Mystery and Manners*. Ed. Sally and Robert
Fitzgerald. New York: Farrar, Straus & Giroux, 1961. 63–86.

Pratt, Mary Louise. *Imperial Eyes: Travel Writing and Transculturation*. London: Routledge, 1992.

Rankin, Tom. "On the Home Front: Larry Brown's Narrative Landscapes." Watson, *Conversations*
99–118.

Shipler, David. *The Working Poor: Invisible in America*. 2004. New York: Vintage, 2005.

Sobsey, Adam. "The final, unfinished novel of the late, great Larry Brown; Fire Engine Redneck."
Rev. of *A Miracle of Catfish*, by Larry Brown. *Independent Weekly* 11 Apr. 2007. http://www
.indyweek.com.

Staunton, John. "Shadowing Grace in the Post-Southern South: 'A Roadside Resurrection' and
Larry Brown's Narratives of Witness." *Religion and Literature* 33.1 (Spring 2001): 43–74.

Steiner, George. *Real Presences*. Chicago: U of Chicago P, 1989.

Thoreau, Henry David. *Walden*. 1854. *Walden & Other Writings of Henry David Thoreau*. New
York: Modern Library, 1937.

A Miracle of Catfish *and the Recursions of Art*

Watkins, Billy. "Words (Even His) Can't Express Loss." *Clarion-Ledger* 18 Mar. 2007: 1F.

Watson, Jay. "Economics of a Cracker Landscape: Poverty as an Environmental Issue in Two Southern Writers." *Mississippi Quarterly* 55.4 (Fall 2002): 497–513.

———, ed. *Conversations with Larry Brown*. Jackson: UP of Mississippi, 2007.

Welty, Eudora. *The Eye of the Story*. New York: Random House, 1977.

Fireman-Writer, Bad Boy Novelist, King of Grit Lit

"Building" Larry Brown(s) at Algonquin Books of Chapel Hill

KEITH PERRY

The photo shows a man of about forty sitting at a table in a firehouse. He has a dark mustache and is wearing a uniform complete with patches, a badge, and a nametag, and atop his head is a baseball cap bearing the outsized letters "OFD." He looks tired, perhaps even weary, but he stares directly into the camera and leans forward rather than slouching back. His eyebrows slightly raised, his head slightly tilted, he not only seems to challenge the photographer but looks as if he is about one photo shy of asking him to step outside. In the article underneath, dated November 12, 1989, Sid Scott of the *Northeast Mississippi Daily Journal* tells a story that had begun almost a decade earlier, when the man in the photo, then a twenty-nine-year-old firefighter living just outside Oxford, Mississippi, had realized that "if I didn't find something to do with my life, I was never going to amount to anything." Curiously—for though he had always been a reader, Larry Brown had never been much of a writer—he one day decided that he would become a novelist. In October 1980, he therefore borrowed his wife's typewriter, set aside some downtime, and simply started banging out fiction. Two years and a legion of rejection slips later, he saw his first publication, a short story in the motorcycling magazine *Easyriders*. Another story, this one published in *Twilight Zone Magazine*, followed a year later—but then he "quit writing that kind of stuff and concentrated on trying to write literature." Three years passed, Brown writing and fighting fire all the while; then entered Shannon Ravenel, senior editor, at the time, at Algonquin Books of Chapel Hill (6F). After reading "Facing the Music," one of Brown's more recent, more ambitiously literary stories, published in the *Mississippi Review*, she contacted the author and, from the hundred or so he had then written, helped him select the ten that would constitute his first collection, *Facing the Music*, published shortly thereafter in 1988. Scott's article concludes with Brown's thoughts on his newfound struggle finding time to simultaneously fight fire, write and promote his fiction—his first novel and second book, *Dirty Work*, had just been published—and help his wife raise their three children. "It's hard, you know. It's hard," he said (7F)—a comment that may also explain why, in the photo of him on the article's first page, sitting still in front of the camera seems to irritate him so.

But, then, there is also another possibility. Four months later came another article, a much higher-profile piece published in the *New York Times*. In it Peter Applebome tells a story that begins, much as Scott's does, with a twenty-nine-year-old firefighter simply making up his mind to become a writer. As had Scott, Applebome explains that there was little in that firefighter's past "even to hint at" such an undertaking. Brown had grown up, after all, the son of a sharecropper little interested in his son's schooling, had enlisted in the Marines instead of enrolling in college, and thereafter, instead of writing, had fought fire full-time and managed a small store, cleaned carpets, built fences, cut wood, and hauled hay part-time. And yet, "with no real idea where his life was going, he came upon an odd notion...." Applebome tells readers that Brown had spent his first seven months at that borrowed typewriter on a novel, set in Yellowstone National Park, about a killer bear on a bloody rampage. It was "horrible," Brown admitted, "327 single-spaced pages of sex and man-eating." There had also been nonfiction, essays on hunting that he had sent to *Outdoor Life*, but nobody had wanted those either. But then, as that pile of rejection slips continued to grow beside his wife's typewriter, a second notion struck him: "Having begun with visions of being the next Stephen King, he decided he would rather be the next Flannery O'Connor." He therefore set aside his Louis L'Amour and Harold Robbins and took up Cormac McCarthy and William Faulkner, later even taking a creative writing course from Ellen Douglas at the University of Mississippi. Then—as in Scott's article—came Shannon Ravenel, *Facing the Music*, and *Dirty Work*. Applebome's version of Brown's story thus differs little from Scott's; writing in early 1990 instead of late 1989, though, Applebome could report that in January, Brown had left the firehouse to write full-time—and that articles like Scott's and photos like the one accompanying it may well have influenced his decision. "I did a lot of interviews at the fire station and had a lot of pictures taken there," Brown said, "and I got tired of that whole angle." He had resigned not just to devote more time to his new career, but, as Applebome emphasizes, to make "a statement about who he is and what he wants to do with his life." Significantly, the photo accompanying the article shows Brown in street clothes, standing in front of the Lafayette County, Mississippi, courthouse: readers see not the firefighter Scott had shown them but a man distinguished primarily by receding brown hair and a full beard. "I don't want to be known as Larry Brown, the fireman writer," Brown concluded. "I [resigned because I] wanted to be known as Larry Brown, writer. That's what I want to do with my life" (B1).

Surveying the promotional campaigns, author profiles, and book reviews that his decade and a half with Algonquin Books generated, however, one often finds Brown himself one of the few to "g[e]t tired of that whole angle." Even the most cursory glance at materials surrounding his published works reveals that those writing about them could not always see past his biography to focus on the novel or short story collection more immediately at issue. The story of such materials is thus one of representation as much as reception, or, rather, of representation as reception: not just of how Brown's work, but how Brown himself was presented first to reviewers, then to readers. In the end, one of the best gauges of his reputation as a writer is thus the lack of representation that references his early years and all but one of the ways he made his living as an adult, is thus his publicists' and reviewers' abilities to bypass "Larry Brown, the fireman writer"—if not the Oxford native, the sharecropper's son, the former marine, or any of his other extraliterary incarnations—to tell their readers about "Larry Brown, writer."[1]

Two years before either Scott's or Applebome's article would appear, "that whole angle" had been born, and innocuously enough, in the Chapel Hill, North Carolina, offices of Brown's publishers. Ravenel wrote in 1993 that, in "a tiny company like Algonquin Books, the editor's job is not confined to acquiring books to publish. That's a big part of the job," but the "really *hard* work" begins only after author and publisher sign the contract (Brown et al 45). Shortly after finalizing that for *Facing the Music* in October 1987, Algonquin introduced Brown to booksellers and reviewers by way of an eight-page booklet, "Facing the Music" the entirety of its contents, that marked the first published pairing of Brown's name and the Algonquin Books colophon. On its inside rear cover was one of the publisher's first attempts at rendering its new author's life in words: "Larry Brown was born in Oxford, Mississippi, in 1951. He served in the Marine Corps from 1970 to 1972, and joined the Oxford Fire Department in 1973. He and his wife, Mary Annie, have a small country store at Tula. His short stories have been published in *Mississippi Review*, *St. Andrews Review*, and *The Greensboro Review*, which awarded its 1988 Literary Prize to 'Kubuku Rides (This Is It),' another of his stories collected in *Facing the Music*." The back of the booklet featured three blurbs: after one from Willie Morris and one from Ellen Douglas, Barry Hannah wrote that "Larry Brown, a captain of the firehouse in Oxford, Mississippi, rediscovers real stuff, like great writers do." Upon his introduction to booksellers and reviewers, then, Brown was a thirty-seven-year-old native of Oxford, a former marine, a firefighter, and a country store owner who had published three stories in literary magazines, impressing three of Mississippi's most celebrated living authors along the way. Other than that, the booklet told readers nothing more about him—and neither did the first-edition hardback of the complete collection, published September 30, 1988. The front jacket flap, slightly revising a letter that Ravenel had sent out with the booklet, emphasized the interdependence of Brown's dual vocations: "Since 1973, Larry Brown has spent his working life as a fireman in Oxford, Mississippi. Clearly, his job has been a rich source of material for his art. Brown is called forth to fight more than house fires and he has seen more than destruction and chaos. His stories are evidence that he sees behind the face of crisis and that he hears the music to which his victims march." The rear jacket flap bore a similarly revised version of the author's biography from the booklet: again, he was a native of Oxford, a former marine, a firefighter, and a country store owner with a handful of publications. Under a photo of Brown as writer, not firefighter—he wore a dress shirt and jacket and leaned against the balcony railing outside Oxford's Square Books, the Lafayette County courthouse in the background—the rear of the jacket bore the same blurbs as the booklet. He now had a face, but the writer Algonquin introduced to readers of *Facing the Music* was essentially the same one they had introduced to booksellers and reviewers.

Looking back some five years later at their efforts to promote *Facing the Music*, Ravenel would confess that "We shamelessly used the fireman-turned-writer hook." And, she would continue, "it worked." Dozens of high-circulation media outlets reviewed the volume, an impressive outcome given the fact that Brown had debuted with a collection of short stories rather than a novel (Brown et al 46). The question, though, is whether Algonquin's "hook" worked too well, whether Brown's biography made more of an impression than his writing itself did. Most reviewers could not avoid mention of it in some small dose—*Publishers Weekly* introduced him as a "fireman-turned-writer" (40), the *Albuquerque Journal* as a "fireman who writes (or writer who fights fires)" (Gage G8)—while it seems to have left the occasional reviewer positively distracted. Under the headline "Firefighter Larry Brown is first rate at his second calling," Sam Hodges began his *Orlando Sentinel* review with praise for firefighters in general, only later taking up the single firefighter relevant. "Fireman Brown has made himself into a very good short story writer," he wrote. "In fact, if his first book . . . were itself a fire, it would require five alarms. The stories are that strong" (F7). No matter how generous his praise, though, Hodges's implication, touted first by that headline—in which Brown was a fireman who wrote, not a writer who fought fires—was that what made the author remarkable was less his fiction than his writing it only when not fighting fire. Joyce Slater, also obviously taken with Brown's biography, began her review, published in the Cleveland *Plain Dealer*, with an anecdote about encountering a fireman in a grocery store. After the cashier had praised his bravery, he had replied, "'Oh, I don't know. I think you've got to wonder about a guy who runs *into* burning buildings.'" We therefore have to wonder about Larry Brown as well, Slater wrote, for he "hurls himself into his writing with all the eager recklessness of a rookie battling his first apartment house blaze. Readers may come away from *Facing the Music* feeling a little scorched themselves" (11F). As had Hodges, Slater ultimately devoted most of her attention to the collection, as did a score of other reviewers. Still, what attracted the most animated attention, what most fascinated so many of their fellows, was the story Brown had lived—its heat- and smoke-filled sections in particular—rather than the stories he had written.

Algonquin, as Ravenel would put it, had used only one "hook" in marketing *Facing the Music*. Their frequent references to Brown's birth in Oxford—rather than to his residence just outside it—though, often garnered as much attention as those to his full-time job. Some reviewers mentioned the city only in passing, only to place on the map those fires he was fighting, but others, as anyone who knows anything about Oxford might expect, could not stop just there. Oxford, after all—as *The State* (Columbia, South Carolina) so coyly put it—had also been home to "another pretty well-known author" (Starr 1I). This geographical coincidence set several reviewers, among them Dan Ahlport of the Greensboro, North Carolina, *News & Record*, on a search for correspondences they otherwise may not have considered: "While overall comparisons to Oxford's most famous writer are entirely inappropriate," Ahlport wrote, "there is at least a freshness of vision and technique here that is reminiscent of Faulkner's experiments in narrative structure and point of view" (E5). Reviewing the collection for the *Winston-Salem Journal*, Betty Leighton set out to silence all such comparisons, even began by satirizing them. "William Faulkner, move over," her first sentence read. "Make room for a new son of Mississippi soil, one from your own town of Oxford, no less." Leighton's most immediate source of irritation was an Ole Miss newsletter that, in announcing Brown's debut, had declared, "Nearly four decades after William Faulkner won the Nobel Prize for Literature, many readers and scholars still wrestle with questions about how such an amazingly talented literary artist could have come from a rural county in northern Mississippi. Now these questions are being asked about another writer from Lafayette County—Larry Brown." Although it's "fitting" that "a new talent be heralded," Leighton countered, "why not allow Larry Brown to be Larry Brown, not a contender thrust into the ring with one of the heavyweights in American literature?" Subsequent commentators should "do him the courtesy of allowing him to stand on his own two feet without any props" (H4). The difficulty, though—or godsend, if you work for Algonquin—is that when a writer claims Oxford, Mississippi, as his birthplace, he's impossible to introduce without at least one "prop," even if you don't want to grant it status as a "hook." David Nicholson of the *Washington Post* would write five years later that "the publicist assigned [*Facing the Music*] must have thought she'd died and gone straight to heaven. It wasn't simply that Brown could write. There was also the kind of features-page angle that couldn't have been invented" (C2). Indeed, upon his introduction to the reading public, Larry Brown was almost as much a fireman and native of William Faulkner's Oxford as the author of a new short story collection.

Dirty Work, Brown's first novel and second book, followed some eleven months later, and Algonquin's campaign in support of it began with a letter to book review editors dated June 12, 1989. In it Ravenel announced first the novel's publication, then the fact that *Facing the Music*—one selection from which would soon appear in *Best American Short Stories*—had won the Mississippi Institute of Arts and Letters Award for Literature. Only toward its end did she include a two-sentence biography: "The son of a Mississippi sharecropper, Brown graduated from high school in 1971 and spent two years in the Marines. In 1973 he became a professional firefighter and now serves as a captain in the Oxford, Mississippi, Fire Department." Press releases also introduced both earlier and more recent Larry Browns. In entitling one "First novel by Mississippi firefighter leads Algonquin's fall list," publicists effectively joined those reviewers of *Facing the Music* who implied that Brown's fiction was less distinctive than the circumstances surrounding its creation. Many who were mailed these materials also received what Algonquin calls an F&G of the novel, a softbound set of the folded and gathered sheets soon to become the pages of the first-edition hardback. Its front cover said little about Brown, only that he had also written *Facing the Music*, but a review excerpt on the back cover told readers that he was "a fireman in Faulkner's town of Oxford, Mississippi." Shortly thereafter, on August 25, came the first-edition hardback itself, its jacket flaps—unlike those of *Facing the Music*—telling readers little about its author. Only those with previous knowledge of Brown's resume would recognize the excerpt from Hodges's *Orlando Sentinel* review—"if his first book . . . were itself a fire, it would require five alarms"—as a more than ordinarily pregnant metaphor. On the rear cover, under a photo of Brown in a white button-up shirt and jeans, sitting at a picnic table—he was a writer, again, not a firefighter, and one this time without the Lafayette County courthouse inevitably suggesting ties to Faulkner in the background—appeared a biographical sketch that again promoted the Oxford native, the former marine, the fire department captain, and the award-winning author. Most curious among promotional materials for *Dirty Work* is the fact that, given the novel's military subject matter, the former marine stood as quietly beside the much more conspicuous firefighter as he had during the promotion of *Facing the Music*, was even displaced this time by something of an upstart, the sharecropper's son, who in one press release was asked to confer upon the novel an authenticity the former marine apparently could not. "Like Brown himself," it read, the novel's main characters "share a background in the cotton fields of Mississippi." That all three had also served in the military—a far more salient point, it would seem—was left for readers to make on their own. Again, nonetheless, the writer was only one of many Larry Browns asked to shoulder his promotions.

Brown's biography, consequently, continued to inspire author profiles—the publication of *Dirty Work*, as had that of *Facing the Music*, occasioned an array of features articles—but it failed to bleed over into reviews of the novel as often as it had those of the collection. Still, the odd review at least began like something more about the author than his works. Dan Cryer's review in Long Island's *Newsday* began, "That Larry Brown is an author at all is something of a miracle. Born of poor white folk in Mississippi and Memphis, Brown barely managed to graduate from high school and taught himself to write only after many years of reading fiction and groping to create his own." Cryer then went so far as to invent his own Larry Brown. Algonquin may not have asked the former marine to confer authenticity on *Dirty Work*, but *Dirty Work*, ironically, conferred authenticity on the former marine—who had served *during* the Vietnam War, but never *in* Vietnam. "Clearly," Cryer wrote, "the author writes out of experience." As "a Vietnam veteran, he is . . . sickened by the cruelty and waste of war" (16). After introducing Brown as "a novelty, the redneck who made good in an intellectual world without any of the usual credentials," Susan Wood, reviewing *Dirty Work* for the *Houston Post*, went on to make the same assumption. One of Brown's "great strengths," she wrote, was "his honesty and directness, his refusal to look the other way no matter what brutality he sees, things a sharecropper's son, fireman and Vietnam vet is bound to know something about" (C6). For the most part, though, reviewers this time seemed more interested in the book than its author. Though a few continued to identify Brown as a fireman or ex-marine, as many if not more said nothing of any Larry Brown except the writer: the *Atlanta Journal-Constitution* (Johnson L10), *The New York Times Book Review* (Bass 15), and *USA Today* (Allen 4D), for instance, ignored even the fact that Brown spent so much of his time fighting fire. Reviewers, it seems, were at least beginning to find the writer telling a more compelling story than he lived.

His biography had hardly lost its hold on the press as a whole, however. Less than a month after the publication of *Dirty Work* came the first of several high-profile features pieces that, taken together, constitute a coup for Brown and Algonquin. "Country Boy Hits Big Time" occupied the entire front page of the *Los Angeles Times* features section on Sunday, September 17, 1989. Beside a photo of Brown perched—if not posed—on the running board of a fire truck, pen and clipboard in hand, gazing off into the right-hand margin as if in search of inspiration, Berkley Hudson began with more of that condescension that at least one reviewer had already decried (see Wood). Hudson's Larry Brown was "a local literary hero," an "unlettered country boy who has become a self-taught man of letters," but one who at the same time sounded as if he could hardly have found success, especially in the literary world, in the first place. The piece focused more on his biography than his fiction—it was a profile, after all, not a review—but even if it did devote a quarter of its column inches to *Facing the Music* and *Dirty*

Work, it still seems preoccupied with the fact that Brown was born the son of an alcoholic sharecropper; that he lived on land "surrounded by soybeans, cows, cotton, catfish ponds, and pecan trees"; that his hands had "short, stubby fingers . . . more like those of a working man than a writer"; and that "His way of talking, his manners bespeak rural Mississippi." In one of the few instances in which Hudson—whose prose often mimicked the way he seemed to hear Brown—let the author speak for himself, he quoted him as saying, "Flaubert. Is that how you say it?" as if a "Southern-accented version of the French author's name" were more ludicrous than merely amusing (1). Some six months later came Applebome's *New York Times* profile, introduced above, another to be accorded the front page of a Sunday features section. Applebome took up much the same material Hudson had but treated it with more consideration, refusing to turn Brown into a caricature. He wrote relatively little about *Facing the Music* and *Dirty Work*, focusing instead on the "astonishing literary odyssey" by which Brown "essentially willed himself to become a serious writer." He quoted Barry Hannah, who called his fellow Mississippian "one of America's great stories. . . . Something happened in about five years that's quite a miracle. He's become his own genius" (B1). Either a once-unlettered redneck lately taken root among the literati or a blue-collar prodigy writing his way into the American literary pantheon, Brown was the subject of subtle—and often not-so-subtle— derision in the former profile, occasional aggrandizement, perhaps, in the latter.

Readers met yet another Larry Brown in Mary T. Schmich's "Getting a late start,"[2] a two-page profile published in the June 19, 1990, *Chicago Tribune*. A photo on the first page showed Brown, again in street clothes, again leaning on the balcony railing outside Oxford's Square Books. As the photographer had shot him from his left side rather than straight on, however, the Lafayette County courthouse did not appear in the background. Absent, in other words, were both firehouse and courthouse, as if Brown were consciously distancing himself from all readily visible associations with firefighting and William Faulkner. Again not a fireman but a writer, he was this time, and for one of the first times, his own writer. The article's subheading, "A former firefighter finds success in writing by stoking the flame within," said almost as much about his former occupation as the article itself did. Schmich's Larry Brown began as "just another one of the guys over at Oxford Fire Station No. 2 . . . just an ordinary, small-town fellow" who, at age twenty-nine, "peered down the old highway of life and saw a scary sight:

middle age hurtling toward him like an 18-wheeler with the brakes gone bad." Nine years later, "Brown has achieved the kind of literary success that thousands of better-lettered writers would trade their Ph.D.s for" (11). The media, Schmich wrote—as if in direct response to Hudson, Applebome, and so many of Brown's reviewers—had "reduced" him to "a tidy wad of marketable contradiction . . . Larry Brown: firefighter, ex-Marine, the share-cropper's son who flunked high school English, the next William Faulkner." And yet, Schmich herself could not quite reconcile the disparities between *Facing the Music, Dirty Work*, and the man sitting quietly in his living room, Marlboro in one hand, Budweiser in the other, politely answering her questions. His subject matter, she wrote, was "apt to convince readers that he is a tormented man who has staggered to hell and back in a blur of beer and bourbon." Up close, however, his life looked "as placid and ordinary as a 1950s sitcom." His house, "comfortable but plain," rested amid acres of green farmland, and at one point during the interview he called to his wife Mary Annie, beginning, "Hon . . ." to get her attention (15). Schmich let Brown speak for himself more than Hudson had, more even than Applebome had, and in the process created neither ridicule nor wonder. He may have seemed an "ordinary, small-town fellow," but in the end he resisted even that characterization as he was also an accomplished and justly celebrated novelist who had taken an unconventional, many might say improbable path to literary acclaim.

Schmich's editors at the *Chicago Tribune* most likely spent June 18, 1990, finalizing articles—her profile of Brown among them—for the next day's various editions. Roughly eight hundred miles to their southeast, one particular editor at Algonquin spent that same day finalizing yet another letter to reviewers. After announcing the publication of Brown's third book, summarizing its subject matter and predominant themes, Ravenel concluded, "We at Algonquin believe that Larry Brown is an important writer and that the stories in *Big Bad Love* are important to understanding his art." For the first time in such a missive, Brown was not a firefighter—current or former—not an Oxford native or a former marine, not even a Mississippian: he was a writer and a writer only. One of the press releases that followed also reflected this shift away from all Larry Browns but one. Far from "First Novel by Mississippi firefighter leads Algonquin's Fall list," "Larry Brown Collects Ten New Unsparing Stories" said only this about the author: that he was a thirty-eight-year-old, self-taught, and now full-time writer and a former captain in the Oxford, Mississippi, Fire Department. The bound

galleys of the first edition contained no biographical information whatso-
ever, and the first-edition hardback, published September 30, contained
only the following: "Larry Brown lives at Yocona, Mississippi, with his wife
and three children. He was a professional firefighter in Oxford for sixteen
years, but left the fire service in January of 1990 to write full time." The word
"Oxford" continued its inevitable associations with Faulkner, but, significantly, this was the first such description to place Brown anywhere but in the
town the two writers shared. As the back of the jacket cropped the photo
published eight months earlier with Applebome's *New York Times* article,
though, viewers saw Brown—as if Algonquin were not quite ready to completely sever his implied ties to Faulkner—standing in front of the Lafayette
County courthouse. Superimposed on top of the photo were excerpts from
ten reviews of *Dirty Work* and five of *Facing the Music*, but unlike the blurbs
from those two books, none mentioned or even alluded to Brown's biography. Only eight months after arguing in the *New York Times* against the
fireman-writer designation, Larry Brown—at least as far as his promotions
were concerned—was beginning to become "Larry Brown, writer."

Many who reviewed the collection were content to say nothing about its
author beyond the fact that he had written it, *Facing the Music*, and *Dirty
Work*; many of their colleagues, however, could not stop just there. Reviewers for the *Dallas Morning News* (Bass 8J), the *Boston Sunday Herald*
(Cohen 52), and the *Los Angeles Times* (Crews 3), among others, avoided
even the word "fire" and all derivations thereof. Some, however, seemed
content only upon summarizing much of his biography. Michael Skube of
the Raleigh, North Carolina, *News & Observer* complained that the story of
Brown's life was so "striking" that it was "get[ting] in the way of a disinter-
ested consideration of his work"—and then, ironically, told that same story
himself, reviewing *Big Bad Love* only afterwards (4J). Jack Reese's review
in the Knoxville, Tennessee, *News-Sentinel* began more like one of Brown's
first book than his third, touching on everything from his former tastes in
drugstore paperbacks to his never-published man-eating bear novel (19).
Algonquin, as we have seen, incorporated less biographical detail into each
successive campaign for Brown's first three books. Reviewers of *Big Bad
Love*, however, often amplified what Algonquin had attenuated—and quite
possibly because of autobiographical content that, whether truly present or
not, so many of them read into the collection. The *Arkansas Gazette*, in calling certain stories "so authentic" that readers "may suspect" them of being
"autobiographical" (Knutson 7G), was representative. Even if only touched

upon in promotional materials, even if only hinted at in the work itself—by
way of its time and place, its characters and their concerns—then, the story
of Brown's life was so compelling, had been so often and so well told that,
de-emphasize it though Algonquin did, it often assumed an all but central
role in many reviews. And yet, that fact did not necessarily imply that reviewers would get its details correct: *The State* joined earlier newspapers in
turning Brown into a Vietnam vet (1F), while others romanticized his story
still further by characterizing him as "a high-school dropout" for whom
publishing in "biker magazines"—not just one, and not just once—was apparently some sort of early métier (Sigal 11; Neal 6L). Lacking one fully
limned by his publisher, reviewers, it seems, could not help but create their
own Larry Browns.

As reviews of *Big Bad Love* began to dwindle toward the end of 1990,
the *Washington Post* devoted two pages of its Sunday, December 9, editions
to "The Back-Roads Blue-Collar Artiste: Mississippi's Larry Brown, Bent
on Becoming a True Voice of American Fiction," the fourth such feature
Brown's story had inspired since mid-September 1989. In its photo of the
author readers saw neither firehouse nor fire truck, neither courthouse nor
Square Books balcony: Brown simply sat facing the camera, his arms across
the back of a chair, a pack of cigarettes in his pocket. Its Washington, D.C.,
setting the most likely reason for the spareness of the frame—Brown was
on tour to promote *Big Bad Love*, and the photographer had caught him in
some bland, relatively public space—the photo implied more clearly than
any since the jacket of *Dirty Work* his growing distance from the stock props
of his biography. The article itself, by Judith Weinraub, trotted out many of
those same props but did so in a way that celebrated Brown's accomplish-
ments without condescending to or overly lionizing him. Weinraub began
by calling him "an American original" and writing of his childhood, his volunteering for the Marines, his sixteen years as a firefighter, and his early attempts at fiction (F1). On the subject of the latter, Brown commented that
"all the stuff I wrote for years and years was bullshit. . . . It was artificial, and
it wasn't honest. It took me a long time to learn that the main thing to write
about is people's emotions." Weinraub concluded the article with Brown's
thoughts on what she called his "astounding path from the backroads of
Mississippi to literary salons across America." As he saw it, she wrote, it was
more a function of determination than talent: "'If you want to be a writer,
there is nobody who can help you but yourself,' he says. 'When people say
I'm a born writer, I say no, that's not right. I just wanted to do it and I taught

myself how. I think it can be learned; I don't think anything is going to make it for you except you sitting in a room by yourself and writing'" (F4). Though Brown had been the subject of three other such profiles in the previous fifteen months, only Weinraub gave him the chance to speak at such length about issues so far removed from her predecessors' seemingly circumscribed subject matter, highlighting in the process aspects of his character, and especially his career, that journalists less interested in presenting an individual than a caricature had rarely let readers see.

And yet, no more than a few months later, Algonquin enlisted Weinraub's assistance in a campaign that could hardly help but turn reviewers' heads back toward his less literary alter egos. Believing that *Joe*, Brown's second novel and fourth book, "could very well be Larry's break-out book"—as Ina Stern, then marketing director at Algonquin, had put it—they launched an especially ambitious promotional campaign, scheduling more than the usual number of author appearances, buying more than the usual amount of advertising space, even creating point-of-sale giveaways (Brown et al 50). A *New York Times Book Review* ad, roughly half of which was devoted to the novel's jacket photo—in which Brown, wearing a white shirt and leather jacket, leaned against a nondescript wall—featured excerpts from reviews that called him "a major writer," "a writer of stature," and "a novelist of universal power," but not an Oxford native, a sharecropper's son, a former fireman, or anything of the sort. The same was true of a *Publishers Weekly* ad, which featured excerpts from thirty-six similar reviews. As the lead novel on Algonquin's fall list, *Joe* also benefited from promotional efforts at one of the publishing industry's premiere events, the annual convention of the American Booksellers Association. At the Algonquin booth, the backdrop to which was a ten-times-life-size headshot of Brown, booksellers and reviewers could pick up *An Affair of Honor: Larry Brown's Joe*—a four-page pamphlet that Cleanth Brooks had written in praise of the novel—as well as specially designed F&Gs (Brown et al 50), the rear covers of which informed them that Brown, according to Baltimore's *Evening Sun*, was "one of the most authentic literary voices of our generation." The F&G said nothing else about its author, and, indeed, did not need to—for also available were specially produced booklets containing, among more than fifty excerpts from reviews of Brown's first three books, four profiles, each reproduced in its entirety, complete with photos: Hudson's "Country Boy Hits Big Time," Applebome's "Larry Brown's Long, Hard Journey," Schmich's "Getting a late start," and Weinraub's "The Back-Roads Blue-Collar Artiste." As had those for *Big Bad Love*, other materials—the advance uncorrected proofs, an undated press release, the first-edition hardback among them—stressed the books more than the author. Hudson, Applebome, Schmich, and Weinraub, however, had stressed the author far more than his books; and as Brown's reviewers had not always proven adept at focusing on the matter most immediately at issue, that "tidy wad of marketable contradiction"— "Larry Brown: firefighter, ex-Marine, the sharecropper's son who flunked high school English, the next William Faulkner"—had as much as been reborn, and months before even the first review of his new novel.

For all those who had missed Brown's admonition upon its original appearance in Applebome's profile or, upon its reprinting, in one of the booklets designed to promote *Joe*, one of the first features stories the new novel generated, a profile published in the Memphis *Commercial-Appeal*, began, ironically, "Don't call Larry Brown the writing fireman." That, Brown repeated, "was an angle everybody liked to use for a while.... It probably helped me early on, but I wanted to be known just as a writer" (Koeppel G4). Clear enough—again: and yet, most reviewers of the novel either seemed not to have heard him or simply chose not to comply. A few reviewers—those for *Washington Post Book World* (Woodrell 9) and the *New York Times Book Review* (Rooke 25), for instance—confined their comments to the novel, but those who also addressed its author's biography ultimately outnumbered them by far. *Time* called Brown "a onetime Mississippi fireman" (Skow 96), the *Detroit Free Press* a "high-school-educated firefighter in tiny Oxford, Miss." (Tucker 7G). For Richard Eder, writing in the *Los Angeles Times*, Brown had never even become a full-time writer, was still "a Mississippi fireman" (E8). Rather than read any malice into such an apparent desire for reversal, if not reverses, though, it seems more fitting to point out that the review of a book by "a onetime Mississippi fireman who reinvented himself a few years ago as a talented fiction writer in the whiskeyish, rascally Southern tradition" simply makes for better reading than the review of one by someone introduced merely as "[t]he author of *Dirty Work*" (Skow 96; Hart 141). Upon the publication of *Joe*, nevertheless, the writer was again beginning to seem less compelling than his less literary alter egos—or, at the very least, was again beginning to seem more compelling in their company than when on his own.

Reviews of the novel also remind us that a son of Oxford can generate more compelling copy than a writer born anywhere without such a legacy. The effects of praise from so eminent a scholar as Cleanth Brooks, whose

name alone is enough to make a certain kind of reader think of Faulkner—
and whose identification in *An Affair of Honor* and on *Joe*'s dust jacket as
one of the foremost authorities on the author would clue in all others—
cannot accurately be gauged, but reviewers who placed Brown's hometown
in Oxford greatly outnumbered those who, in spite of the novel's rear jacket
flap, placed it in Yocona. W. Kenneth Holditch, writing in the *Chicago Tribune*, was more accurate on the subject than most, but his overall perspective was nonetheless representative: "Drawing a parallel between [Brown
and Faulkner] seems inevitable," he wrote, "for Brown lives near Oxford,
Miss., and some have proposed him as heir to the Sage of Yoknapatawpha"
(4). Writing in *Entertainment Weekly*, Gene Lyons catalogued still more
correspondences, and even if he did so only to undercut them—"That much
said," he concluded, "Brown is distinctive enough to be considered on his
own terms" (57)—every comparison of the sort, to paraphrase Betty Leighton's review of *Facing the Music*, ultimately refuses to let Brown be Brown.
Instead of a discrete quantity, a writer allowed to define himself on his own
terms, he becomes a quantity defined by his relationship to a venerated, if
not idolized predecessor: he is not as much Larry Brown, in other words, as
not-William Faulkner. More pernicious, of course, were reviews that turned
"Larry Brown, writer" into, again, the "son of a dirt-poor, alcoholic Mississippi sharecropper who died when Brown was a teenager; a small-town
fireman who never went to college and who got the ridiculous notion that
he could teach himself to be a writer" (Kimble 17), but, praise *Joe* as they
would—and almost all of them did—many reviews of it, in resurrecting
extraliterary Larry Browns that both Algonquin and certain reviewers had
earlier begun to leave behind, turned Brown into something other, almost
always something less, than what he had since become.

The publication of *On Fire* brought more of the same—the biographical,
after all, being imperative to reviews of the autobiographical—but, soon
thereafter, Algonquin began returning the writer to the center of their promotional efforts. The advance uncorrected proof of *Father and Son*, Brown's
third novel and sixth book, featured three pages of excerpts from reviews of
his first five works. One, from *Men's Journal*, informed readers that he "left
the Oxford, Mississippi, fire department after his first novel was published,"
and that the move "paid off," but only four others among the fifty total explicitly referenced Brown's extraliterary past. The sharecropper's son and
the ex-marine, it seems, had done what they could for the writer; the former firefighter and the son of Faulkner's Oxford, however, apparently still

had work they could do. A biographical sketch on the proof's first page contradicted *Joe*'s rear jacket flap—as well as the simple truth of the matter—by informing readers that Brown "lives in Oxford with his family," and an undated three-page press release entitled "'Bad Boy Novelist Larry Brown' Knows the Mind of a Killer"[3] said much the same. Materials aimed not at reviewers but readers focused on the same three Larry Browns. As the *New York Times Book Review* ad for the novel made clear, after a description of Brown as "the author of *Joe, On Fire, Dirty Work*, and *Facing the Music*," nothing else needed to be said about his biography. Much the same thinking seems to have been behind the design of the first-edition hardback, published September 30, 1996. The rear jacket flap reprinted the photo of Brown first published with Schmich's *Chicago Tribune* profile—in which, again, he was free from both firehouse and courthouse—then concluded with a short biographical paragraph in which he was an Oxford native, a former firefighter, an award-winning author, and a resident of Yocona. Only because it described a book he had written about the subject did it even intimate that he had once been a firefighter. The eleven blurbs on the rear of the dust jacket, moreover, never implied that he had ever done anything but write. More so than any since that for *Big Bad Love*, then, the promotional campaign for *Father and Son* presented a Larry Brown who, above all else, was a writer.

The press, however, did not always present that same Larry Brown to its readers. Profiles in general say as much about the past as about the present, but those surrounding the publication of *Father and Son* continued to skew markedly toward Brown's life before *Facing the Music*. *Newsday* devoted seventeen paragraphs to the sharecropper's son, the fireman-writer, and the "good ole boy" (Cryer C33), only seven to the now three-time novelist. Chicago's *NewCity* magazine gave *Father and Son* less than half the space it gave "Rattlers Roost," Brown's first published story (retitled "Plant Growing Problems" upon its appearance fifteen years earlier in *Easyriders*). The "bloody" tale, in Brown's words, of "some guy who was raising a patch of dope over in Georgia" and the "crooked sheriff [who] caught him and was gonna take his dope" (de Grazia 17), it added yet another subject to the list of those that apparently trump a growing number of acclaimed books as fodder for features articles. Reviewers, on the other hand, at least occasionally implied influence by Algonquin's attenuation of such material: the *Chicago Tribune* (Kunerth 5), the New Orleans *Times-Picayune* (Larson E7), and the *New York Times Book Review* (Quinn 11) said nothing about extraliterary Larry Browns. Not necessarily more numerous, but certainly more conspicuous, however, were reviews that exercised more overworked designations. The *Washington Post* referred to him as a "fireman turned writer" (Hynes C2), while *USA Today* introduced him—inaccurately, in part—as "a Vietnam veteran and Oxford, Miss., ex-firefighter now making a living as a writer" (Huffman 7D). Algonquin may have been promoting the current rather than any earlier incarnation of Larry Brown more intently than they had in the six years since *Big Bad Love*, but those previous incarnations were often what continued to inspire those writing about him. Even Alqonquin's adoption of the "Bad Boy Novelist" tag failed to make an impression on many journalists. In 1996, Sean Penn could be a bad boy actor, Dennis Rodman could be a bad boy athlete, but Larry Brown—at least as far as those writing his profiles and reviews were concerned—could only rarely break out of that "tidy wad of marketable contradiction" that had confined him for almost a decade.

Although again at the center of a marketing campaign, "Larry Brown, writer" was only one of the many Larry Browns Algonquin referenced in support of *Fay*, his fourth novel and seventh book. An undated promotional letter informed readers that he had been fighting fires when Ravenel first read "Facing the Music," but it makes nothing more of the fact, emphasizing instead his growing status as "a writer that aspiring writers and successful writers and the best of all writers admire." The novel's advance uncorrected proof reprinted selections from eleven reviews of his previous books, but only one, that from *Men's Journal*, excerpted above, referenced firefighting. In the ten others, Brown was a writer and only a writer, "one of the best writers we have," one who had "slapped his own fresh tattoo on the big right arm of Southern Lit." The back cover of the proof, next to a photo of the author in a short-sleeved white dress shirt and chinos, similarly reminded readers of his past but told them primarily of his present—of his status as "America's 'Bad Boy Novelist,'" the award-winning author of six previous books, and the subject of a recent documentary film. Only twice a former fireman in the proof, he was never anything but a writer in a three-page press release: one of the ten reviews it quoted called him "one of this nation's greatest living writers," "the immutable bad boy from the South"—implying that *Vanity Fair*'s sobriquet had gained at least some currency—and "a Faulkner for the twenty-first century," but neither Algonquin nor any of the other nine reviewers addressed a Larry Brown beyond "Larry Brown, writer." The first-edition hardback of the novel, published March 31, 2000, also promoted then-present rather than past Larry Browns. On the front jacket flap, he was "the reigning king of Grit Lit." In the biographical paragraph on the rear flap, under a headshot of him cropped from the photo on the back of the proof, conspicuously missing—and for the first time in his twelve years with Algonquin—was any reference to firefighting, even the implication that often came via citations of *On Fire*. As if Algonquin were unwilling or even unable to publish a book by Brown without at least some reference to his birthplace and first line of work, though, the *Men's Journal* excerpt made yet another appearance, this time on the back of the dust jacket. Evidence in Algonquin's campaign for *Fay* that its author had not always been a writer was not difficult to find, but alongside it was an equal if not greater amount of evidence that Brown was also a writer's writer, a "Bad Boy Novelist," and, of course, "the reigning king of Grit Lit."

Even with a spate of new designations to choose from, though, not every reviewer seemed content. Many clung to some of the first they had used— the *New York Times Book Review* identified Brown as "a former firefighter in Oxford" (Mobilio 18)—but some referenced Algonquin's more recent characterizations: *People* called him a "writer's writer" (Plummer 59), *Bookpage* called him "America's 'bad boy novelist'" (Dickerson 9), and *Library Journal* called him "the official 'king of grit lit'" (Hellman 260). One particular reviewer, as if finding all other labels lacking, invented his own. John Mort, from the beginning to the end of his advance review of *Fay* for *Booklist*, had nothing but praise for Brown's work. His last sentence, however, read, "This is awful, beautiful work from the King of White Trash" (833). The label is jarring, pejorative, ill-chosen at best—but, given the wholly laudatory nature of every sentence that precedes it, can only be seen as a well-intended but inadept attempt to heap further praise upon the author. Divorced from its original context, though, it can easily seem injurious. Not for nothing did Algonquin excise its latter half when reproducing the passage in the "Bad-Boy Novelist" press release and one of the print ads for *Fay*: both have Mort concluding, simply, "This is awful, beautiful work." Authors of at least two profiles, though, apparently preferred the original. Within a week of *Fay*'s release came a *USA Today* profile in which Brown— and in the article's headline, no less—is again "the King of White Trash." In the article itself, otherwise as laudatory as Mort's, however, Brown defused whatever vexation that readers familiar with his opinions on the "fireman writer" label or photos shot in firehouses might expect. When reminded, toward its end, that "*Booklist* calls *Fay* an 'awful, beautiful work from the

King of White Trash,'" Brown first laughed, then joked that he had told his daughter that his newly acquired title effectively crowned her the Princess of White Trash (Minzesheimer 7D). In a *Philadelphia Inquirer* profile published two weeks later, readers saw much the same. Identified under a photo as "Larry Brown, fireman turned novelist, 'King of White Trash,' writer's writer," he "doesn't shirk" the designation when asked about the second of the three. "I kind of like it," he laughed. "I told [daughter] LeAnne, 'If I'm the king, that makes you the princess'" (DeLuca F5). For a man who earlier and on more than one occasion had asked not be called a fireman-writer, the response is puzzling—and yet, pejorative though "King of White Trash" unquestionably is, Brown had at that point been talking to journalists for years and had several successful books to his credit. As Ravenel explains, he was simply "more secure about his reputation" in 2000 than he had been ten years earlier, and he "could laugh it off" (Ravenel). Even if he was still not "Larry Brown, writer" to the press, ten years and eight acclaimed books had evidently taught him that he could at least be "Larry Brown, writer"—and secure in that fact—to himself.

After their efforts on behalf of *Billy Ray's Farm*, which followed *Father and Son* in 2001, Algonquin did not again promote a new book by Larry Brown until late 2006. The Free Press published *The Rabbit Factory*, his fifth novel and ninth book, in September 2003; fourteen months later, on November 24, 2004, Brown suffered a heart attack and suddenly, unexpectedly, died. Algonquin's campaign for *A Miracle of Catfish*, his unfinished sixth novel and tenth book, therefore memorialized its author as much as promoted the work itself. Among materials in the promotional folder designed for reviewers and booksellers were photocopies of Brown's *New York Times*, *Washington Post*, and *USA Today* obituaries, and the first words in the novel's advance reading copy came not from an Algonquin staffer but from Brown's friend and mentor, Square Books owner, and now Oxford mayor Richard Howorth, who wrote that "Larry has a loving family and many friends in this community, and his loss has been great for us." Readers, Howorth emphasized, "felt a kind of suffering as well." Instead of a sharecropper's son, a marine, or a firefighter, Brown was a beloved family man, friend, and community member missed almost as much by those who read him as by those who knew him for years, and the novel was his valedictory "gift" to us all. After Howorth's letter came more standard promotional fare, four pages of excerpts from reviews of Brown's previous books, excerpts in which he was again a native of "Faulkner country," a "self-taught country boy," and a former firefighter. The back cover of the advance copy, beside a small headshot of the author, featured Algonquin's most recent—and, at this point, last—such attempt at his biography. The paragraph sounded many of the old notes, but in that it mentioned his "untimely" death and referred to his survivors, its tone was less promotional than elegiac. Except for the most superficial of changes, the same paragraph reappeared in the first-edition hardback of the novel, published March 20, 2007. Its front flap described Brown as "a force in American literature," then echoed the tone and import of Howorth's letter: "That Larry Brown died so young, and before he could see A Miracle of Catfish published, is a tragedy. That he had time to enrich the legacy of his work with this remarkable book is a blessing." The back cover carried encomia from fellow writers, all commemorating a friend as much as praising his last novel: Tom Franklin, for instance, wrote that "this generous work from one of America's finest writers is a gift to readers everywhere." In the wake of Brown's unexpected death, the promotional campaign for *A Miracle of Catfish* thus gave birth to yet another Larry Brown: the late, lamented Larry Brown, a much-beloved American master who left friends, family, and a legion of readers much earlier than any of them would have wished.

The writer reviewers took up upon publication of the posthumous novel was, similarly, equal parts esteemed author and subject of great loss. Perhaps as a result of genuine appreciation, perhaps as a result of what the Kirkus review service called "pre-emptive strikes against anticipated criticism" (3)— Barry Hannah's introduction and Shannon Ravenel's editor's note, which functioned in the first edition much as Howorth's letter did in the advance reading copy—few reviewers faulted the novel for being unfinished. No one referred to its author by any such derogatory designation as the King of White Trash, either: instead, the Charleston, South Carolina, *Post and Courier* called him "the quintessential Southern writer" (Barfield 6), the Associated Press called him "one of the South's most promising and interesting writers" (Talbot 2), and the *Roanoke* (Virginia) *Times* called him "perhaps the most authentic Southern voice of his generation" (Hicks H4). Even the rare negative review of the novel praised its author as "one of the greats" (Dold 6E). Most reviews did not adopt a tone as openly elegiac as that of the promotional materials, but almost all mentioned Brown's early death: John Dufresne, writing in the *Boston Globe*, closed, "We'll miss him terribly" (E5). And still, as it had been since the beginning, reviewers couldn't resist telling what one called Brown's "truly extraordinary personal story"

(Chitwood G4). Mary Jane Park, writing in the *St. Petersburg* (Florida) *Times*, began, "Mississippi writer Larry Brown was fifty-three when he died of a heart attack in November 2004. A native of Oxford,, Miss., he failed senior English in high school but taught himself how to write in adulthood. First, he became an insatiable reader. Then, he wrote dozens upon dozens of stories, every one of which publishers rejected." Three similarly biographical paragraphs later, Park seemed to recall her objective: "But this is not his obituary," she wrote. "This is about *A Miracle of Catfish*, Brown's latest tale" (1E). In the end, it was often difficult to tell the difference, and in far more reviews than just Park's—for though "Larry Brown, writer" and the late, lamented Larry Brown played the largest roles in such reviews, their earlier, extraliterary complements continued to make their by now nearly standard appearances.

In a memorandum written to energize Algonquin sales representatives soon to pitch *Father and Son* to booksellers, Ina Stern wrote in April 1996 that "Larry is a writer we've all been building—you, the Algonquin staff, the booksellers, and the reviewers." Implicit in this single statement is the degree to which Brown's success at Algonquin depended—and, one would imagine, any author's success at any publisher depends—upon an array of promotional efforts. Just as sales representatives had to build a Larry Brown who would generate orders among booksellers, booksellers had to build a Larry Brown who would generate sales among the public. Just as the Algonquin promotions staff had to build a Larry Brown who would generate interest among reviewers, reviewers had to build a Larry Brown who would generate interest among their readers. As divergent as these aims often were, though, all of them depended on each contingent's building the most remarkable Larry Brown possible. Luckily for them—one reviewer, as we have seen, wrote that his publicist "must have thought she'd died and gone straight to heaven"—Larry Brown was remarkable for a number of reasons. Algonquin's early campaigns therefore built a Larry Brown who was sometimes a native of William Faulkner's Oxford, sometimes a sharecropper's son, sometimes a former marine, but was always both a talented writer and, at the same time, a full-time firefighter. Later campaigns spent more time building the writer's writer, the "Bad Boy Novelist," and the "king of Grit Lit," but they never quite let reviewers forget that first, and for far more years, many had called him "Captain." Evidence that the Larry Brown built primarily for readers had also spent sixteen years fighting fire is apparent in all nine of his Algonquin titles, and even though those responsible for them increasingly attenuated the extraliterary material in them as well, it was not until the Free Press's 2003 publication of *The Rabbit Factory* that a Brown title appeared whose one and only reference to his past as a firefighter came implicitly, by way of *On Fire*'s obligatory inclusion in the list of his other published works. Less so at the end of his career than at the beginning, then, he was always to some degree Algonquin's (former) fireman-writer.

Without "Larry Brown, writer," though, no one would have built that fireman-writer in the first place. "Larry Brown, writer," though not always the most visible Larry Brown, was nonetheless the progenitor of and raison d'etre for every Larry Brown that followed, no matter the builder, occasion, or audience. And yet, as nearly two decades of book reviews clearly prove, there was so much interest in extraliterary Larry Browns that Larry Brown himself ultimately may have been the only one interested in a purely literary Larry Brown, may even have been the only one for whom a "Larry Brown, writer"—one born at the moment he borrowed his wife's typewriter and alive thereafter only when pounding away in front of it—ever existed. For so many others, the Oxford native and the sharecropper's son, the former marine and the firefighter, the "Bad Boy Novelist" and the "king of Grit Lit" and, now, the late, lamented American master all joined together to make the figure at the heart of these hundreds of narratives just that much more appealing. The story of a Larry Brown who was a writer and a writer only effectively forfeits its most distinctive constituent: the blue-collar, if not no-collar context that makes its central character's success as an author so unlikely for, and therefore so appealing to, so many readers. Thus, ironically, did Algonquin and the press build a more compelling Larry Brown than Larry Brown himself would have had them build. He said—and on more than one occasion—that he wanted to be known as "Larry Brown, writer," but readers, as both Algonquin and his reviewers apparently knew, had read stories about writers before. What they had not read was the story of the sharecropper's son who became the fireman later crowned the king of Grit Lit—a story much more worth the telling and, of course, the retelling (and retelling) than that of someone who had never done much of anything except write. One Larry Brown, *the* Larry Brown, died in late 2004; all other Larry Browns, composed as they are of ink and paper, not skin and bone, show no sign of following him anytime soon. And "Larry

Brown, writer"—to what likely would have been *the* Larry Brown's continuing chagrin—is still only one of them.

Notes

For assistance with this article I have to first thank Shannon Ravenel, retired director of Shannon Ravenel Books, an imprint of Algonquin Books of Chapel Hill, for allowing me to peruse promotions and review files at the Algonquin Books offices, for granting me access to unprocessed portions of the Algonquin Books Papers housed at the University of North Carolina-Chapel Hill, and for so quickly and agreeably answering the myriad questions I asked her about them. I also thank Ina Stern, associate publisher at Algonquin Books, for forwarding me additional promotions materials and answering still further questions, and Barbara Jones, assistant librarian at Dalton State College's Derrell C. Roberts Library, for securing me more than a hundred author profiles and book reviews via interlibrary loan. Without their invaluable assistance, this article would not exist in its present form, if at all.

1. As those promoting and reviewing Brown's autobiographical works *On Fire: A Personal Account of Life and Death and Choices* (1994) and *Billy Ray's Farm: Essays from a Place Called Tula* (2001) could not help but address the facts of his life—those being the very subject of both books—materials surrounding their publication will not be examined here.

2. Schmich's headline alluded to the title of the address Brown delivered at the Conference on Southern Literature held April 8, 1989, in Chattanooga, Tennessee. Published as an eight-page pamphlet, *A Late Start* was widely distributed to book page editors and reviewers, many of whom borrow from it freely, without acknowledgement, in profiles and reviews. One might well assume that nearly every reference to Brown's unpublished novel about the man-eating bear, for instance, mentioned nowhere else in Algonquin's promotional materials, derived from *A Late Start*.

3. The "Bad Boy Novelist" designation was *Vanity Fair*'s, from its one-sentence, September 1996 review of *Father and Son* (Schappell 254).

Works Cited

Ahlport, Dan. "'Music' is vital, entertaining." Rev. of *Facing the Music*, by Larry Brown. *Greensboro News & Record* 8 Jan. 1989: E5.

Algonquin Books of Chapel Hill. Papers. Southern Historical Collection, the Library of the University of North Carolina at Chapel Hill.

Allen, Bruce. "Vietnam aftershocks: 2 novel views." Rev. of *Dirty Work*, by Larry Brown. *USA Today* 8 Sept. 1989: 4D.

Applebome, Peter. "Larry Brown's Long, Hard Journey on the Road to Acclaim as a Writer." *New York Times* 5 Mar. 1990: B1.

Barfield, Rodney. "Quintessential Southern writer's final story." Rev. of *A Miracle of Catfish*, by Larry Brown. *Roanoke Times* 20 May 2007: Books 6.

Bass, Rick. "In the Hospital, Waiting for a Savior." Rev. of *Dirty Work*, by Larry Brown. *New York Times Book Review* 1 Oct. 1989: 15.

——. "Redneck woe in the swamps of north Mississippi." Rev. of *Big Bad Love*, by Larry Brown. *Dallas Morning News* 16 Sept. 1990: 8J+.

Brooks, Cleanth. *An Affair of Honor: Larry Brown's Joe*. Chapel Hill: Algonquin, 1991.

Brown, Larry. *Big Bad Love*. Chapel Hill: Algonquin, 1990.

——. *Big Bad Love*. Bound galleys. Chapel Hill: Algonquin, 1990.

——. *Dirty Work*. Chapel Hill: Algonquin, 1989.

——. *Dirty Work*. Folded and gathered sheets. Chapel Hill: Algonquin, 1989.

——. *Facing the Music*. Chapel Hill: Algonquin, 1988.

——. *Facing the Music: Stories by Larry Brown*. Chapel Hill: Algonquin, 1988.

——. *Father and Son*. Advance uncorrected proof. Chapel Hill: Algonquin, 1996.

——. *Father and Son*. Chapel Hill: Algonquin, 1996.

——. *Fay*. Advance uncorrected proof. Chapel Hill: Algonquin, 1996.

——. *Fay*. Chapel Hill: Algonquin, 1996.

——. *Joe*. Chapel Hill: Algonquin, 1991.

——. *Joe*. Advance uncorrected proofs. Chapel Hill: Algonquin, 1991.

——. *Joe*. Folded and gathered sheets. Chapel Hill: Algonquin, 1991.

——. *A Late Start*. Chapel Hill: Algonquin, 1989.

——. *A Miracle of Catfish*. Advance reading copy. Chapel Hill: Algonquin, 2007.

——. *A Miracle of Catfish*. Chapel Hill: Algonquin, 2007.

——. *The Rabbit Factory*. New York: Free Press, 2003.

Brown, Larry, Liz Darhansoff, Richard Howorth, Shannon Ravenel, and Ina Stern. "'Go, Little Book . . .': Getting a Book to Readers." *Publishing Research Quarterly* 9.4 (Winter 1993/1994): 41–52.

Chitwood, Michael. "Larry Brown's final novel." Rev. of *A Miracle of Catfish*, by Larry Brown. *News & Observer* 6 May 2007: G4.

Cohen, Judith Beth. "Tales of desperation: Men in 'Love' find salvation in storytelling." Rev. of *Big Bad Love*, by Larry Brown. *Boston Sunday Herald* 7 Oct. 1990: 52.

Crews, Harry. "Perfectly Shaped Stones." Rev. of *Big Bad Love*, by Larry Brown. *Los Angeles Times* 21 Oct. 1990: Book Review 3.

Cryer, Dan. "The Soldiers' Story." Rev. of *Dirty Work*, by Larry Brown. *Newsday* 20 Aug. 1989: 13+

——. "Tales of a Former Firefighter." Rev. of *Father and Son*, by Larry Brown. *Newsday* 20 Oct. 1996: C33.

de Grazia, Don Gennaro. "Fatherly Advice." *NewCity* 31 Oct. 1996: 17.

DeLuca, Dan. "Author Larry Brown goes and stares at human fires." *Philadelphia Inquirer* 18 Apr. 2000: F1+.

Dickerson, James L. "America's 'bad boy novelist' enters virgin territory with *Fay*." Rev. of *Fay*, by Larry Brown. *Bookpage* Apr. 2000: 9.

Dold, Gaylord. "'Catfish' is not so miraculous." Rev. of *A Miracle of Catfish*, by Larry Brown. *Wichita Eagle* 20 May 2007: 6E.

Dufresne, John. "Hard luck, hard living in Brown's corner of the South." Rev. of *A Miracle of Catfish*, by Larry Brown. *Boston Globe* 22 Apr. 2007: E5.

Eder, Richard. "The Moral Landscape of the Backwoods." Rev. of *Joe*, by Larry Brown. *Los Angeles Times* 24 Oct. 1991: E8.

Rev. of *Facing the Music*, by Larry Brown. *Publishers Weekly* 8 July 1988: 40.

Gage, Nancy. "Short Stories Filled With Skewed Despair of Southern Life." Rev. of *Facing the Music*, by Larry Brown. *Albuquerque Journal* 12 Feb. 1989: G8.

Hart, Lenore. Rev. of *Joe*, by Larry Brown. *Library Journal* Aug. 1991: 141.

Hellman, David. "Mud, Blood, and Beer: Grit Lit Classics." *Library Journal* 1 June 2001: 260.

Hicks, Brian. "Last trip to depressed South; An authentic voice silenced." Rev. of *A Miracle of Catfish*, by Larry Brown. *Post and Courier* 13 May 2007: H4.

Hodges, Sam. "Firefighter Larry Brown is first rate at his second calling." Rev. of *Facing the Music*, by Larry Brown. *Orlando Sentinel* 27 Nov. 1988: F7.

Holditch, W. Kenneth. "A Mississippi macho man from novelist Larry Brown." Rev. of *Joe*, by Larry Brown. *Chicago Tribune* 29 Sept. 1991: Books 4.

Hudson, Berkley. "Country Boy Hits Big Time." *Los Angeles Times* 17 Sept. 1989: VI, 1+.

Huffman, J. Ford. "Memorable 'Father and Son': Larry Brown explores love and hate in a hardscrabble world." Rev. of *Father and Son*, by Larry Brown. *USA Today* 21 Nov. 1996: 7D.

Hynes, James. "Southern Cross: In Rural Mississippi, a World of Anger and Loathing." Rev. of *Father and Son*, by Larry Brown. *Washington Post* 26 Sept. 1996: C2.

Johnson, Greg. "Stirring Story of Veterans' Painful Lives." Rev. of *Dirty Work*, by Larry Brown. *Atlanta Journal-Constitution* 3 Sept. 1989: L10.

Kimble, Cary. "Re-exploring Faulkner country." Rev. of *Joe*, by Larry Brown. *Milwaukee Journal* 27 Oct. 1991: I7.

Knutson, Karen. "Brown crafts tales of Mississippi men." Rev. of *Big Bad Love*, by Larry Brown. *Arkansas Gazette* 11 Nov. 1990: 7G.

Koeppel, Fredric. "Author, his 'tragedy,' spring from same North Miss. Turf." *Commercial Appeal* 22 Sept. 1991: G4.

Kunerth, Jeff. "Brown paints fine portraits in 'Father and Son." Rev. of *Father and Son*, by Larry Brown. *Chicago Tribune* 9 Oct. 1996: I5.

Larson, Susan. "Blood Simple." Rev. of *Father and Son*, by Larry Brown. *Times-Picayune* 6 Oct. 1996: E7.

Leighton, Betty. "No Faulkner: Strong Stories Show Dark, Partial View of Man." Rev. of *Facing the Music*, by Larry Brown. *Winston-Salem Journal* 8 Jan. 1989: H4.

Lyons, Gene. "Bad Behavior." Rev. of *Joe*, by Larry Brown. *Entertainment Weekly* 4 Oct. 1991: 56–57.

Rev. of *A Miracle of Catfish*, by Larry Brown. *Kirkus Reviews* 1 Jan. 2007: 3.

Minzesheimer, Bob. "'King of White Trash,' characters share thirst for life." *USA Today* 5 Apr. 2000: 7D.

Mobilio, Albert. "Biloxi Bound: A teenager hitchhiking in Mississippi finds life's highway full of bumps." Rev. of *Fay*, by Larry Brown. *New York Times Book Review* 16 Apr. 2000: 18.

Mort, John. Rev. of *Fay*, by Larry Brown. *Booklist* 1 & 15 Jan. 2000: 833.

Nicholson, David. "A Fireman's Memoirs: Hot Spots." Rev. of *On Fire: A Personal Account of Life and Death and Choices*, by Larry Brown. *Washington Post* 1 Mar. 1994: C2.

Park, Mary Jane. "More than a Fish Story." Rev. of *A Miracle of Catfish*, by Larry Brown. *St. Petersburg Times* 8 May 2007: 1E.

Plummer, William. Rev. of *Fay*, by Larry Brown. *People* 15 May 2000: 59.

Quinn, Anthony. "The Summer of Hate: Larry Brown's novel is a blue-collar tragedy set in the Deep South." Rev. of *Father and Son*, by Larry Brown. *New York Times Book Review* 22 Sept. 1996: 11.

Ravenel, Shannon. "Re: quick Larry Brown question." E-mail to the author. 1 May 2006.

Reese, Jack. "Author's 'late start' pays off with 'Big Bad Love' collection." Rev. of *Big Bad Love*, by Larry Brown. *Knoxville News-Sentinel* 11 Nov. 1990: Showtime 19.

Rooke, Leon. "Pistol Under the Seat, Beer in the Cooler." Rev. of *Joe*, by Larry Brown. *New York Times Book Review* 10 Nov. 1991: 25.

"Building" Larry Brown(s) at Algonquin Books of Chapel Hill

Schappell, Elissa. "Hot Type." Rev. of *Father and Son*, by Larry Brown. *Vanity Fair* Sept. 1996: 254.

Schmich, Mary T. "Getting a late start: A former firefighter finds success in writing by stoking the flame within." *Chicago Tribune* 19 June 1990: I1+.

Scott, Sid. "Special Delivery: Book begins new chapter in life of Larry Brown." *Northeast Mississippi Daily Journal* 12 Nov. 1989: 6F+.

Sigal, Clancy. "Looking for Love in All the Wrong Places." Rev. of *Big Bad Love*, by Larry Brown. *Washington Post Book World* 23 Dec. 1990: 11.

Skow, John. "Southern Pine." Rev. of *Joe*, by Larry Brown. *Time* 28 Oct. 1991: 96.

Skube, Michael. "Rednecks and rough honesty in Larry Brown." Rev. of *Big Bad Love*, by Larry Brown. *News & Observer* 9 Sept. 1990: 4J.

Slater, Joyce. "Off to a Roaring Start." Rev. of *Facing the Music*, by Larry Brown. *Plain Dealer* 1 Dec. 1988: 11F.

Starr, William W. "Larry Brown makes impressive debut." Rev. of *Facing the Music*, by Larry Brown. *The State* 11 Aug. 1988: 1I.

———. "Stories have Brown written all over them." Rev. of *Big Bad Love*, by Larry Brown. *The State* 16 Sept. 1990: 1F.

Talbot, Chris. Rev. of *A Miracle of Catfish*, by Larry Brown. *Prince Rupert Daily News* 26 Mar. 2007: Arts 2.

Tucker, Neely. "Mississippi Shadows: Sexism, racism, and poverty fuse as a way of life in a small rural town." Rev. of *Joe*, by Larry Brown. *Detroit Free Press* 13 Oct. 1991: 7G.

Weinraub, Judith. "The Back-Roads Blue-Collar Artiste: Mississippi's Larry Brown, Bent on Becoming a True Voice of American Fiction." *Washington Post* 9 Dec. 1990: F1+.

Wood, Susan. "Trying to answer the great unanswerable questions." Rev. of *Dirty Work*, by Larry Brown. *Houston Post* 27 Aug. 1989: C6.

Woodrell, Daniel. "Losers Take All." Rev. of *Joe*, by Larry Brown. *Washington Post Book World* 20 Oct. 1991: 9.

AFTERWORD

On *The Rough South of Larry Brown*

An Interview with Filmmaker Gary Hawkins

KATHERINE POWELL

Gary Hawkins, an independent filmmaker from North Carolina, began planning a documentary on the life and work of Larry Brown in the late 1990s. Hawkins saw the film as something of a sequel to a previous project, his Regional Emmy-winning documentary *The Rough South of Harry Crews*, produced in 1991 for North Carolina Public Television. After enlisting Brown's participation in the venture, Hawkins took three trips to Mississippi to visit the writer and his family. Brown's wife Mary Annie quickly became an integral part of the interviews that followed, and as the project progressed, Hawkins and Brown decided to film adaptations of three of his short stories, "Boy and Dog," "Wild Thing," and "Samaritans."

The result is a film of extraordinary power. Hawkins elicited sincere and revealing comments from both Larry and Mary Annie Brown, capturing them at their ease as they offered genuine insights into what it was like to be Larry Brown, a man who determined relatively late in his life that he wanted to write fiction. Near the end of the film, Brown admits that he still feels humbled by his literary heroes—Crews, William Faulkner, Flannery O'Connor, Raymond Carver, and Cormac McCarthy among them—but that, at the same time, he takes pride in the estimable success he himself has achieved. His wife Mary Annie, however, emphasizes how difficult it was for her and their three children to watch Brown struggle—with so much determination, for so many years—to see his work into print. Jeff Baker, reviewing *The Rough South of Larry Brown* for the *Oxford American*, asserted that the Browns' "forthrightness—along with a variety of visual resources including home movies, photographs, interview footage, and shots of rural

Mississippi that evoke Brown's life and work—is responsible for the intimate tone of the film" (43).

When asked how they came to feel so comfortable with cameras intruding into their daily lives, Larry Brown said that he had known Gary Hawkins for years, and that they "became friends." When Hawkins and his crew went to Oxford, "We let them stay here with us, along with most of the equipment and the cameras and the film. . . . I guess we just got used to having him around, and besides that, it was fun while it was going on." Mary Annie added, "I felt Gary was . . . a person who would not do anything that would be hurtful to us. I liked Gary the first time I met him. He was easy to talk to and seemed very caring of how the film would be true to us as a family and to Larry as a writer. He also put a crew together that felt the same as he did. They were very kind and considerate of us" (Brown and Brown). The Browns have positive feelings for the final product as well. Larry Brown said, "Hawkins put a lot of work into it and I think it's very well done. His use of different film stocks and different cameras works effectively. His adaptations of the stories are true to them. And he was able to capture a good impression of our life as it was then." Mary Annie Brown agreed that "Gary did an excellent job of capturing Larry as an individual and as a writer. He showed Larry as he really is. I loved the way Gary intertwined Larry's work with our lives" (Brown and Brown).

After completing *The Rough South of Larry Brown* in early 2000, Hawkins premiered it at the 2002 Full Frame Documentary Film Festival in Durham, North Carolina. He subsequently entered it in a number of regional film festivals, including the 2002 Ohio Independent Film Festival, where it won an Off-Hollywood Oscar for Best Feature Film; the 2002 Savannah (Georgia) Film and Video Festival, where it was judged Best Feature; and the 2003 Oxford (Mississippi) Film Festival, where it was voted Best Documentary. Hawkins also screened the film for an enthusiastic audience at the 2002 Southern Literary Festival in Nashville, Tennessee, a screening after which both Browns answered questions. Just after Larry Brown died in November 2004, Hawkins returned to Oxford to attend his viewing and burial at Tula, later adding footage from that trip, as well as a subsequent interview with Mary Annie Brown, to his original film. Her words express a great sense of loss, even help to focus the viewer's own grief. After her husband's unexpected and premature death, the value of Hawkins's film has only increased: it is the only full-length documentary on the life and career of Larry Brown yet produced, and it will remain the only such work produced during his lifetime.

Jean W. Cash

In September 2003, Hawkins screened *The Rough South of Larry Brown* at the Southern Writers Symposium at Methodist College in Fayetteville, North Carolina. Katherine Powell of Berry College assisted him and afterwards conducted the following interview.

POWELL: Is there a definition for "Rough South," or do you just know it when you see it? How did you come to this project? Why this writer? Do you envision more films in this series? Do you have other writers in mind?

HAWKINS: The closest I've come to a prototypical Rough Southern author is Larry. He was born and raised in a Southern state. His upbringing was rural. He's working-class and despite the acclaim, remains so. He's largely self-educated and writes about the local landscape. Those qualities define Rough South, I suppose. I didn't intend "Rough" as a description of Larry's writing, which can be delicate or florid or seductive or minimal or whatever he needs it to be in order to get its point across. "Rough" refers to the rural Mississippi landscape and the characters who populate Larry's stories.

POWELL: How did the film come about?

HAWKINS: Back in the late eighties I pitched a series of one-hour shows to UNC-TV. I called the series *The Rough South*. In the first half-hour we'd meet an author, and in the second half-hour we'd see a dramatization of the writer's work. UNC-TV lacked the budget (and the mandate) for full-blown drama, so they quickly dropped the fiction element. Also, the management wanted to see only North Carolina authors in the series, so the regional aspect was compromised, too. Come to think of it, they didn't much like the "Rough" part either.

Harry Crews—my first Rough Southern entry—is a Georgia-born writer working in Florida. Larry is Mississippi all the way. The only North Carolina authors who satisfied my Rough South requirements were Jim Grimsley and Kaye Gibbons. I'd consider overseeing a series of *Rough South* episodes, but the days of handcrafting each individual episode are over. There's just no money in it. I'd grow old and poor and have nothing to show for my effort but occasional pats on the back. These shows are time-consuming, and I'm no spring chicken anymore.

POWELL: What is your responsibility as a documentary filmmaker?

HAWKINS: The filmmaker's responsibility to both his subject and his audience is to state clearly the rules of the presentation, then stick to them. The rules of the presentation are not "The Truth," because the truth is always in question when you make a documentary. I think it's very telling that we refer to this truth as "non-fiction," as if fiction is the standard and non-fiction the anomaly. That's saying a lot with terms, and I for one agree with what's being said. Because you never know. Maybe the guy is telling the truth to the best of his ability, but he doesn't remember exactly what happened. You run into this stuff every time you go out and you try to be as honest as possible, knowing full well that you'll fail. True, the camera records actualities, but the arrangement and presentation of those actualities are purely subjective. You said in an earlier conversation that you were struck by my invisibility. Well, I'm there, all right. I'm the guy behind the curtain doling out the information, exactly the way I want it doled out.

POWELL: How does your background as a painter inform your filmmaking?

HAWKINS: I guess my quick answer is that painting trained me to see. When you draw or paint you tend to develop a sensibility, which I define as the ability to see the world in terms of art. Now what the hell does *that* mean? It means that you tend to compose images instead of just pointing your camera at something and capturing it. You create compositions, and your compositions exude qualities of balance, appropriateness, unity, and closure that life-at-a-glance rarely affords. Maybe you find it on a face. The door opens, and there *she* is. But a perfectly composed image is usually worked for. You handle your subject to get it to say what you want it to say.

The obvious difference between cinema and painting is that cinema moves. Cinema is always in a state of becoming. From camera start to camera stop you're capturing a changing situation. This record of *what happened* is factual, even if what you photographed is scripted and staged. The scripting and staging are factual. So cinema is factual. It's not completely illusory. Painting, for centuries, was completely illusory. In the twentieth century it gradually took on an added dimension—the record of a human hand moving across a canvas. In that way it's factual, but the effort to create recognizable images is *trompe l'oeil*, tricking the eye. Illusionism. Painters don't always make good filmmakers. Painters tend to get stuck on the beautiful image or an arresting image, and think, "that's good enough." It's not good enough. You've got to be willing to destroy your pretty pictures—to kill your darlings, as Faulkner says—to achieve the *right* image. The right image might not be a pretty image or even an arresting image. Cinematic images are verbs, not nouns. The filmmaker must always ask himself, "What is this image *doing*?" If it looks good but it's not doing anything, or if it's doing the wrong thing, or if it's just calling attention to itself, it's wrong. You gotta get rid of it.

Anyway, knowing how to draw does help you communicate with your camera operator. That much I do know. The third and final time I visited Oxford I took a few former students from the North Carolina School of the Arts with me. I seem to remember that everybody had his own camera. It was my way of dealing with the 24-7 pace at Larry's house. Well, Larry surprised me by requesting that we film him fishing. It was the only time in the whole process that he requested anything of us, so it threw me a little. I was tied up with Mary Annie, so I asked [cinematographer] Scott Gardner to go off with Larry and pick up a sixty-second overhead shot with the camera locked off. I wanted something resembling the pagan swimming to safety from Tarkovsky's *Andrei Rublev* [1969]. Scott didn't remember the shot, so I drew him a little sketch on a Hardee's wrapper. Scott went off with Larry and got the shot—and boy, did he get it. What a beautiful image it turned out to be. I can't help thinking the drawing on the wrapper helped.

POWELL: Both the camera and the filmmaker are invisible in this film. Was this something you were striving for?

HAWKINS: Yes, I was definitely striving for it. You hear me ask about the roses when Larry and Mary Annie are in the kitchen, but only because the scene wouldn't make sense otherwise. I admire a good first-person documentary—really liked Caveh Zahedi's *I Don't Hate Las Vegas Anymore* [1994], or anything by Ross McElwee—*Sherman's March* [1986], *Time Indefinite* [1993]. Orson Welles's *F is for Fake* [1974] is an amazing documentary. But I'm neither polished like Welles nor nerdy and put-upon like Zahedi and McElwee. So I've drifted more towards the Errol Morris style of filmmaking. The actors appear, explain themselves in complete thoughts, and depart.

POWELL: How, specifically, is the invisibility accomplished?

HAWKINS: How? Well, the director just has to stay out of the way. You want your subjects to speak in complete thoughts—that's how you lose the questioner—and it took me a while to figure out how to do that. The main thing is to put your subject at ease, relax him, and avoid questioning if possible. When I interview someone I tend to make statements, then sit back and listen. Listening is everything. I keep the agenda loose, especially in the early going, and just let the subject lead the dance. But I'm not above saying, "Please say that again in a complete sentence so the viewers know what the hell you're talking about." The more interviews you conduct, the more you tend to hear the "stand-alone" sound bites when they're spoken.

POWELL: How do you get people to lose their awareness of the camera?

HAWKINS: I don't know that it's possible to get a subject to lose his awareness of the camera. A film camera is about the size of a sewing machine, and it sits on a tripod, and it's occupying a space in your living room where the rocker used to sit. Or it's outside in the yard where the lawn chairs used to sit. There's no losing your awareness of it.

But it's true that some folks are far more candid than other folks. Some folks couldn't care less that a camera is running. Other folks run and hide. I think it comes down to how folks feel about themselves. If a subject is unconcerned about how he looks (or recognizes the situation as hopeless), if he knows what he's talking about and genuinely wants to tell the truth, he's gonna care less about a live camera. Camera-friendly folks tend to have the courage of their convictions. Or they're good liars.

Humor is important. I've found that humor is one of the best ways to relax my subjects. Self-deprecating humor works best for me. I don't care if I come off a little dim or stupid, especially at first. That will force the subject to work harder to save me from myself. Harry Crews thought I was a complete dimwit. He had to. I was totally unprepared.

POWELL: Larry and Mary Annie are so forthcoming about the frustrations in their marriage—drinking, the night life. Did it take prompting for these subjects to come up in conversation, or did it happen naturally?

HAWKINS: The longer I hung out, the more they loosened up. My deal with the subjects is this: you say what you want to say. Don't check yourself. And I'll run it by you before the film goes public. If you don't like it, you can yank it there. When the subjects realize they can trust me, that I'm not making some bullshit exposé in order to promote my career—that they can "unsay" anything they say—they begin to speak more freely. I would never compromise that agreement. After they saw the film Mary Annie yanked nothing. She said, "Well . . . this is our life." Larry yanked one small phrase that could've been misconstrued as a critique. Nothing important. Almost no one ever censors himself. Folks are far more likely to justify themselves once they've made a statement, no matter how off-the-wall it seems. That's how folks hang themselves. They're thinking, "I said it, and by God I meant it."

POWELL: Did you plan for Mary Annie to have such a large presence in the film?

HAWKINS: No, but then I don't really plan for anything when I begin filming. I stay more or less aloof, waiting for the material to tell me what it wants to do. It's okay to go into a documentary with an agenda, a plan, but if something better comes along, you're foolish not to go with it. You can be a good little boy or girl and follow through with your well-laid plans, but you won't be dancing with the circumstances when they arrive. The good stuff will pass you by.

The first time I went down to Oxford, Mary Annie had a fried chicken dinner ready when I walked in the door. I hung out for a couple of days before the crew arrived, just to get the lay of the land. When the actual filming began, M.A. disappeared. The second time I went to Oxford, M.A. was in a foul mood about something. She kept making all these passive-aggressive maneuvers like jumping up and stomping out of the room. Stuff like that. Okay. Larry writes all night. He's on third shift. M.A. is on first shift. So when Larry took a nap, I said to M.A., "You don't want us down here, do you?" She said, "No. It's fine." I said, "Then what is it?" "What is what?" "What's got you ticked off?" "I'm not ticked off." "Yes you are. What's got you ticked off?" Finally she said, "You think this writing stuff is so glamorous. Let me tell you, it's *not*." I said, "Jason, set up the camera," and M.A. was in the show. When Larry trudged into the kitchen after his nap, he was surprised to find his wife on camera, spilling the beans. You should've seen his face.

Mary Annie actually spoke the theme of the show while Larry was napping. It came in two parts. First she said, "When Larry started writing we never saw him." Then she said, "But when Larry writes, that's when he's the happiest. And when he's not writing that's when he's so depressed you can't stand to be around him." So I'm thinking, "You can only stand to be around him when he's not around?" You see the paradox? That's when I glimpsed the whole show—including how the stories would line up, how Mary Annie would figure into the mix, how we'd revisit over and over the conflict of Wordly Calling and Familial Duty, a conflict that stretches back at least to Odysseus. Everything became clear when she spoke that line.

POWELL: How long did it take you to conduct the interviews? How did it work? Did you stay in Oxford and see the Browns every day? Were there several sittings? Over months?

HAWKINS: I made three trips to Oxford over the course of two years. Each visit I shot as much as the film budget would allow. We ran out of money often—more money had to be raised before the next step could be taken—so the show proceeded in fits and starts. On a more positive note, the huge gaps of time between interviews allowed the family to change, giving us a much truer picture of Larry's life. Each time I visited Oxford, the mood in Larry's house was different.

The first time I visited Larry we shot the pasture and Tula interviews. We talked mostly about the craft of writing. The second time Mary Annie figured in. We shot the kitchen interviews and Larry at his desk in the dining room. The issue of marriage began to assert itself on the second trip. We also shot Larry's mother in the okra patch during the second trip. On the third visit I interviewed Mary Annie on tape and interviewed Larry in his "cool pad," attempting to plug holes in the narrative, focusing heavily on marriage. We shot three one-hour interviews over the course of three nights. We also interviewed Larry's mother in her kitchen frying okra. We picked up most of the B-roll—walking to the mailbox, building the house at Tula, fishing, etc.—on the third trip to Oxford. By then I knew what my film was about; the process had evolved from fishing to a full-blown scavenger hunt.

POWELL: What surprised you most about the Browns as you got to know them?

HAWKINS: How well their family functioned, despite complaints to the contrary. Some families agree to be dull together. Domestic gulags. Some families remain interesting but rip one another apart liked caged animals. Larry's family is both interesting and mutually supportive. I thought it was one of the most solid families I've ever seen, especially given the dynamic personalities in that household. And it's 24-7 around there. Larry is up all night and M.A. is up all day. The three kids, then sixteen to twenty-two years in age, are coming and going at all hours. Wore me out trying to keep up with them. Wore out the crew, too.

Here's an amusing anecdote: Larry had been writing all night, and at 4 A.M. (as is his habit), he left his "cool pad" to take a break, eat a dish of strawberry ice cream, and watch CNN. When he got to the living room he couldn't find a place to sit because Billy Ray's buddies were passed out all over the place. Larry yells, "That's where I draw the line, by God, when it's four in the morning and I cain't find a place to sit in my own damn living room!"

POWELL: Tell us about your actors—who's a pro and who's a local? What are the challenges of working with both?

HAWKINS: Local actors are harder to work with than professional actors. Actually I'd prefer working with a local non-actor than a local actor, because it's easier to get a non-actor to respond truthfully to the circumstances. Local actors tend to "help the show." They try to please you, and in doing so behave falsely. I mean the non-professional adults now. I'm not talking about the boys in this film, who were great. Neither boy had ever done anything on camera before.

But professionals, well, that's why they're called professionals. You pay them and they give you what you want. And they give it to you on the first take. And if you want more they'll give you that, too. The professionals I've worked with have been more focused than the non-professionals. They've been more motivated, more prepared, friendlier, less insecure, less likely to play games and, believe it or not, hungrier than the non-professionals. Certainly all of those qualities apply to Will Patton, who appears in "Samaritans."

Disney gave me Will for three days, and two of those days were travel days. He came off extremely well, though, despite the hurried schedule. A real Larry Brown character. Oh, sure. Will's a pro. I'll tell you two stories on Will. When Will walks by the outdoor ashtray [in the film], he drops a wadded cigarette pack on it. Note that he holds the pack in his outside hand, takes a half-step past the ashcan, remembers to throw away the pack, then does it by tossing it across his body and slightly behind him. He did that on purpose. Why? Because it's harder. In life we don't always hold our crumpled cigarette packs in the hand nearest the trashcan. In life we're swigging our beer when someone asks us a question. We've got to stop drinking the beer before we can answer.

POWELL: Why did you employ a still-photo technique to tell the story "Wild Thing"?

HAWKINS: For starters, I didn't have enough money to make it any other way. The same is true of the stills in the Crews show. Necessity was the mother of invention in both instances. I studied Chris Marker's *La Jetee* [1962], a science fiction film consisting almost entirely of still photos, to pick up a few tricks for *Crews*.

And I returned to the stills for "Wild Thing." I liked the black-and-white mood (actually, it's sepia). The story is so sad. The hero is so dependent on sex and female attention—he's not just flawed; he's addicted. I could've emphasized the sadness and shot the story another way. But the allure of the young woman, the erotic promise of the night, the sweetness of the countryside, I wanted to get all that across. I wanted to sell it. I wanted viewers—male viewers, anyway—to be thinking, "Sure, it's sad, but I don't blame him." I thought the black-and-white stills would help me sell the erotic promise, give the material an almost pornographic, forbidden-fruit feel.

POWELL: Your action film [in the documentary] is "Boy & Dog."

HAWKINS: Yes, Larry published "Boy and Dog" as a series of stacked sentences, five words to each sentence. The staccato sentences nudged me to present the imagery in a similar way. Instead of the usual flow of action and seamless cuts, "Boy & Dog" leans more towards "now this, now this, now this." We shot the film spaghetti-Western style in five days. I instructed the sound recordist to get what he could get, but we rarely stopped to slate sound. The result was a stand-alone silent film enhanced by Vic Chesnutt's dreamy narration, some sync-ed dialogue, foleyed effects, and Larry's original five-word sentences (in his own hand), dropped digitally onto the images.

POWELL: You said you were going for a yellowed, comic book look for "Boy & Dog."

HAWKINS: Yes, specifically the Big Little Books. I love those covers. I think they're pure pop art. We went for that look.

POWELL: But the opening shot of the dead dog is very disturbing.

HAWKINS: But you don't see him die. The dog's death creates a situation, and we filmed the situation. But not the death itself. The opening hubcap sequence is Eisensteinian montage. Through visual and audio sleight of hand we conveyed the idea of a dog being run over without actually running over a dog. The hubcap was rigged to a boom and guided by hand into a tree. Hiding the boom attachment was simply a matter of cropping out the top of the image. Getting the shot of the dog in the road was tougher than it looks, because the Mustang had to barely miss the dog (and a rolling camera on a high hat), then swerve back into his lane before the shot could take effect. It took a while to get it right. The dog is, of course, fake.

POWELL: The boy hitting the man with a brick is also disturbing. How did you achieve it?

HAWKINS: When the boy threw the brick, we ramped down a Super-8 shot to match the speed of the brick traveling over the road. The brick-through-space shot is composited from two elements—a brick suspended with low-gauge fishing line over a tilted mirror (a poor man's blue screen) and me hanging out of the sun roof of my car, shooting down at the road. Both shots were overcranked to justify the lengthy screen time. When the brick hits the driver, the screen goes momentarily red. I borrowed that idea from an old Nicholas Roeg film called *Performance* [1970]. A man is shot, and the screen goes red. When the Mustang hits the mailbox, the camera is moving towards it from the opposite side. Here is another poor man's effect. We built up one end of the dolly tracks, padded the base with sandbags, hoisted the dolly, then released it just before the Mustang entered the frame. The frame shudder upon impact is actually the dolly rolling into the sandbags.

One of my favorite shots in "Boy & Dog" is the Super-8 side mount of the approaching firetruck. We kept a stash of Super-8 cameras on the set, and anyone caught up on his duties was encouraged to pick up a camera and shoot. Someone literally taped a camera to the side of the firetruck, and it turned out to be one of the best shots in the show.

POWELL: What drew you to these stories in particular? Why did you choose them? Did you think they were representative of Larry's work? Did they lend themselves to your style of filmmaking?

HAWKINS: Chronology was the first concern. "Boy and Dog" is a boy's story, "Wild Thing" is a young man's story, and "Samaritans" is a middle-aged man's story. I had originally intended to close with "Sleep" (and still might one day), which is an old man's story. But we ran out of money and had to stop. Larry's stories tie with certain non-fiction elements, too. "Boy and Dog" links with Larry's love of dogs, with his days at the fire department, and with his willingness to experiment on the page. "Wild Thing" presents the complement to Mary Annie's "can't stand to be around him." Schneider says, "I can't stand to be home, and I'm miserable when I'm away." But you know what? I think I threw that line out. Anyway, Schneider said it. I distinctly remember him saying it. "Wild Thing" also introduces sex as the big troublemaker in Larry's stories. "Samaritans" presents a beat-up, been-there-done-that protagonist who discovers that some people just can't be helped—one of Larry's more pessimistic beliefs.

On a purely cinematic level, I wanted "Boy and Dog" to look like a yellowed comic book, I wanted "Wild Thing" to come across as a noirish sex dream, and "Samaritans," which is a dark comedy, well . . . let's just say that we shot it in a day and a half. So there wasn't a lot of attention to style.

POWELL: Let's talk a moment about the difference between mainstream film vs. independent film: what constraints are placed on a regional filmmaker?

HAWKINS: First, let's carve a distinction between independent and regional film. Independent film. Independent from what? Independent from the five major studios: the five majors and the mini-majors control almost everything you see in a mall and on television. Indies fight for what's left of the distribution pie. Studio budgets are astronomical by indie standards. Because they sink $60, $70 million into a film, they want a safe return on their investment. The best way to ensure a safe return—other than making a great film—is to make entertainment for the masses. The studios want everybody to go see their movies. They want a recognizable face in the lead, preferably a star, a happy ending, a shelf to set the box on (genre), and a clever marketing hook (log line): "In space no one can hear you scream."

Indies are usually crazier, structurally more challenging, more innovative, and more respectful of life on the fringe. Often they're closer to the lives we live, more character-driven. *Rocky* [John G. Avildsen, 1976] was an indie film. [Sylvester] Stallone was offered $300,000 to hand over his screenplay and walk away. (Burt Reynolds wanted the part, and that was long before Stallone became a household name.) Stallone refused, so the backers cut the budget to nothing. To protect their investment.

So the constraints of an indie film are almost always financial. In one form or another we're talking money and the lack of it. But that's not such a bad thing. If you can't build a set you'll find an already-existing place that serves your purpose. And if you don't have money in the budget for a set designer, you won't even dress the set. Presto! A sense of place! Sense of place by default. Poverty = Sense of Place. So your film becomes more regional because you're broke. (Assuming the place itself is regional.)

Regional films are almost always independent films, but indie films aren't always regional. *Star Wars* [George Lucas, 1977] and *Pulp Fiction* [Quentin Tarantino, 1994] were independent films. One is set in a galaxy far, far away, the other on a comic book page. *Sling Blade* [Billy Bob Thornton, 1996] is set entirely in small-town Arkansas. *Sling Blade* is definitely a regional film. David Gordon Green's films are regional. Spike Lee's *25th Hour* [2002] was absolutely faithful to New York City. (He even staged a scene overlooking Ground Zero.) Lee nailed New York City. Half of *Rocky* was shot in Philly, half in Los Angeles, but it comes off as all-Philly. Half of my show was shot in Mississippi, the other half in North Carolina. I hope it comes off as all-Mississippi. It's a matter of money. Time and money.

POWELL: You've said that regional movies have an obligation to be accurate in a way that Hollywood movies don't. How hard is it to be accurate and operate within an indie budget, work with amateurs, etc.?

HAWKINS: If you work with amateurs and less money, you're going to be more accurate to a region. But the question often becomes, should I trade accuracy for clarity? Because the difference between the local and the universal is often one of clarity. Or to say it another way, in order to make yourself clear to a large number of people, you have to sacrifice some of your local color. It's a judgment call.

I said that regional films are obligated to be accurate in a way that Hollywood films are not because we all know that Hollywood is playing to the masses. We all know that a certain amount of abbreviating and simplifying and generalizing is going on. That's the kind of cheeseburger they're serving up. You can buy it or not buy it. But you can't expect Hollywood to serve you sushi. They serve cheeseburgers.

Now if you claim to be regional, if you say, "This is homegrown," it's gotta be homegrown. And homegrown in my case doesn't mean *Southern*. Because there's no such thing as *Southern*. The Southern United States is a very large territory. A paycheck-to-paycheck accent from West Virginia sounds nothing like Charleston privilege. *Rough South* gets the thing whittled down to the working class, but even that is ultimately false. Larry Brown's Tula, Mississippi, accent sounds nothing like Kaye Gibbons's Rocky Mount, North Carolina, accent. Homegrown, regional cinema for me is Thomasville, North Carolina. The thickest accent in my town comes from the daughter of a Cambodian immigrant. She sounds far more *Southern* than me. And the strangest accent comes from Johann, the weird guy in the trench coat that works a nearby convenience store. The South is no less complicated than the rest of America.

POWELL: Students from the North Carolina School of the Arts provided the music [for the film], right?
HAWKINS: They performed it. Vic Chesnutt wrote most of it. There's a lot of [Alan] Hovhaness in there, too. And a lot of Trailer Bride.

POWELL: Will you comment on the last section from the Brown show?
HAWKINS: I call this section "Tula," and I really like the music in this section. The first track is Vic Chesnutt's watery guitar. The second track is from Alan Hovhaness's *The Flowering Peach*, and it's performed by students at the NCSA School of Music. I thought the xylophone and harp provided a nice musical metaphor for typing all night. The solo instrument was designated saxophone, but a sax would've been all wrong for this piece. My recording engineer happened to be a Julliard cellist, so he jumped in and performed the solo. The gongs—also wrong—were replaced by some snappy electric guitar noodling. I thought it worked well, though the cellist is miffed that we crank up a generator just as he begins his solo. The final track is a harp concerto by Hovhaness, performed by a School of Music student.

POWELL: I loved the shot of Larry driving [in the "Tula" section]. The camera was in the pickup bed. Do interesting shot ideas come to you at the time, or do you plan for them?
HAWKINS: That particular shot was planned for. It's a mundane shot, really, but [cinematographer Jason Dowdle] shot it beautifully. I saw it in my mind's eye and explained it to Jason, and Jason shot it. There was an unplanned element, though: while Jason was shooting Larry, a dog started chasing us. I was riding in the pickup bed, too, so I grabbed a Super-8 camera

and filmed the dog. Later I discovered that the dog belonged to Larry's mother. So now, when you see the dog running alongside, you know we're going to visit Larry's mother. Some stuff is planned for; some stuff is spontaneous. The main thing is to keep your camera loaded.

During that same visit to Oxford we filmed Larry nailing shingles to his roof at Tula. Larry took a cigarette break, and Scott, seeing a potential shot, quickly moved his camera into position. He said, "Gary, look at this." I glanced through the lens and said, "Do it," and Scott rolled camera. And that metaphorical shot—of an essentially lonely man, building a house for himself in a forest at night, away from everybody, including his family—now opens and closes the show. It's a little pat in its end position, but I love opening the show with it.

POWELL: I liked the picture of LB at his keyboard with Faulkner's quotation above. Talk about killing your darlings in filmmaking. What didn't make it into these films, and why?

HAWKINS: Although I collected thirty hours of footage for a ninety-minute show, I didn't kill too many darlings. Thirty-to-one sounds like a generous ratio, but it's really not so astounding for your average documentary. Thirty-to-one for a fiction feature, where all the action is staged, that's getting up there. Only the big studios can get away with it—or super low-budget digital features. But documentaries depend on lots of footage. It's fishing. You catch a lot of stuff, not much of it edible, so you keep fishing. At some point you've caught what you need to make a nice fish dinner. That's when you starting paring down the material. So I didn't kill too many darlings.

A lot of my darlings died, though. Sure did. Or maybe I should say they never got born. The camera wasn't running a couple of times, and if the camera's not running, it's better for the thing never to have happened. One of the most heartbreaking aspects of this line of work is all the good stuff that happens when you cut the camera off. I think Warhol said that, but it doesn't matter who said it. It's true.

POWELL: Surely you missed something . . . great?

HAWKINS: Yeah, one event that killed me above all others. It happened on my second trip to Oxford. I call it "Larry Buys a Pack of Smokes." See? My grief has a name. [Jason Dowdle] and I were sitting in the back seat of Larry's car in downtown Oxford, ready to crash after a long day. Mary Annie was riding shotgun. It was about midnight, and we were dead tired. We'd just put the camera away because we figured the day was over (always a mistake). Larry turns to Mary Annie and says, "I'm outta smokes. I need to go in the bar there and get a pack for the road." Mary Annie gets a deadly serious look on her face and says, "Larry, we're ready to go home." Larry says, "I'm just gonna run in for a pack of smokes, M.A. I'll be right back." M.A. says, "Larry . . . I mean it, now." They go back and forth a while; finally Larry breaks free and heads into the bar. While Larry is gone, M.A. sits staring at the bar, reciting to us in grim, exacting detail exactly what's going on inside the bar—how this young girl is trying to get Larry to read her new story or how that old fart wanted to buy him just one beer: the hugs, the admiration, etc. Then M.A. said, if we were lucky, Larry'd be out in twenty minutes. (A few months later I followed Larry into a bar with a camera, and all of Mary Annie's descriptions proved correct.) Seventeen minutes later Larry jogged up with his smokes and drove us home. Now what if I'd had two cameras running that night? One in the car and another following Larry? I could've cut the sequence as parallel action. I kick myself for every opportunity I missed, and I pat myself on the back for every moment I salvaged. Same as life.

You could also argue that I missed everything. After all, Larry got himself published before I heard of him, and became successful before I hustled the money together to get the film made. Most of my film looked backwards. It's hearsay. Catching the unfolding moment, that's far more dynamic.

POWELL: One more darling?

Sure. Another one that haunts me—probably because I didn't get the shot due to a camera jam—happened in M.A.'s kitchen one night. Larry and Mary Annie were arguing about an electric guitar. Larry found a Gibson at a lefty shop down in Texas, and the price was right. Mary Annie said forget it; it's not in the budget. Larry said it was. They're arguing. Okay, off to the side on a barstool, LeAnne [their sixteen-year-old daughter] is whining, "Make me a sandwich, make me a sandwich," right on top of the argument. So, absent-mindedly, Larry—still arguing—takes out the white bread, the mayonnaise, the ham and cheese, and makes LeAnne a sandwich. All the time LeAnne is whining, "Make me a sandwich, make me a sandwich." Larry doesn't even seem to know that he's making a sandwich. He's going through the motions like a factory worker. After five or so minutes of this little one-act play, Larry finishes the sandwich. He finishes the sandwich just as he and Mary Annie strike a truce. LeAnne takes one small bite of the sandwich and hurries out of the kitchen to her bedroom. I didn't know what to make of it then and I still don't, but I definitely would've included it in the show.

Once a drunken admirer hugged Larry in public. He was out with LeAnne and M.A. It was LeAnne's birthday. A drunk woman staggers out of the dark and throws herself on Larry. LeAnne springs on the woman, throws her to the ground, cusses her out, and threatens to kick her ass right there. Really. And after M.A. recounted that story, Larry capped it with, "They're like a couple of lionesses, man." And I couldn't help noticing that he said it with a twinkle in his eye, 'cause if they're lionesses, what does that make him? But I missed "LeAnne's Birthday Fight," too. Sure did. I guess I missed a lot of stuff. Probably missed all the good stuff. I don't want to talk about this anymore. I'm getting depressed.

POWELL: Finally, what audience is the film intended for? Do you think that a viewer who has not read Brown would react differently?

HAWKINS: This film is intended for everyone, but if my track record is any indication, it will play best to educated Southerners. The difference in this *Rough South* entry is Mary Annie. I think she speaks for a lot of women who have lost their husbands to work. She might also speak to a lot of men who have lost their wives to work.

It's hard to say how a viewer who has not read Larry Brown would take this show. It's hard to imagine not knowing what you know. I think what's lost in the cinematic presentation is the depth and intelligence in Larry's writing. You can only get that by reading his words on the page.

Works Cited

Baker, Jeff. Rev. of *The Rough South of Larry Brown*. Dir. Gary Hawkins. *Oxford American* 42 (Winter 2002): 43.

Brown, Larry, and Mary Annie Brown. "Re: Hawkins film." E-mail to the author. 21 Aug. 2004.

CONTRIBUTORS

Robert G. Barrier is professor of English at Kennesaw State University, where he directs the Writing Center and teaches undergraduate courses in American literature and graduate courses in rhetoric. He is also an editor for *The Kennesaw Review*, an online literary journal.

Rick Bass is the author of more than twenty books of fiction and nonfiction, most recently the short story collection *The Lives of Rocks* (Houghton Mifflin, 2006). He lives with his family in northwest Montana, where he is active with a number of conservation organizations working to protect the last wilderness lands of the Yaak Valley.

Robert Beuka is associate professor of English at Bronx Community College, City University of New York. He is the author of *SuburbiaNation: Reading Suburban Landscape in Twentieth-Century American Fiction and Film* (Palgrave Macmillan, 2004), as well as various articles on nineteenth- and twentieth-century American fiction and film. Currently working on a study of F. Scott Fitzgerald, he also reviews movies for the NPR affiliate WLIU in Southampton, New York.

Thomas Ærvold Bjerre is a Ph.D. candidate at the University of Southern Denmark. He has published essays and interviews in *Mississippi Quarterly*, *American Studies in Scandinavia*, and *Appalachian Journal*, has contributed to *Perspectives on Barry Hannah* (University Press of Mississippi, 2007) and Madison Jones's *Garden of Innocence* (University Press of Southern Denmark, 2005), and is currently co-editing a Lewis Nordan special issue of *Mississippi Quarterly*.

Jean W. Cash is professor of English at James Madison University, where she specializes in Southern literature. She is the author of *Flannery O'Connor: A Life* (University of Tennessee Press, 2002), as well as numerous articles on Southern writers, among them Edgar Allan Poe, William Styron,

and Flannery O'Connor. She is currently researching and writing an authorized biography of Larry Brown.

Robert Donahoo is professor of English at Sam Houston State University, where he teaches Southern literature, contemporary American literature, and literary theory. He has published frequently on the fiction of Flannery O'Connor, the drama of Horton Foote, American postmodernism,
and Tolstoy's *Resurrection*.

Richard Gaughran is assistant professor of English at James Madison University, where he teaches American and world literature. As senior Fulbright
lecturer in American studies, he taught Southern poetry and prose at the
University of SS. Cyril and Methodius in Skopje, Macedonia, and he has
since co-edited a collection of his translations of Macedonian short fiction,
Change of the System: Stories of Contemporary Macedonia (Magor, 2000).

Gary Hawkins, currently on the faculty of the Center for Documentary
Studies at Duke University, has written and directed six films. His second,
The Rough South of Harry Crews (1991), won a Regional Emmy and the
Corporation for Public Broadcasting's Gold Award. *The Rough South of
Larry Brown* (2002), the latest in his series about working-class Southern
writers, was named one of thirteen essential Southern documentaries by
Oxford American.

Darlin' Neal is assistant professor of creative writing and English at Mississippi Valley State University. She has published fiction and nonfiction
in *Southern Review, Shenandoah, Puerto del Sol, Mississippi Review, Night
Train, Arkansas Review, storySouth*, and several other magazines. She is a re-
cipient of a Literary Arts Fellowship from the Mississippi Arts Commission
and lives in Greenwood, Mississippi, with her dog Catfish.

Keith Perry is associate professor of English at Dalton State College, where
he teaches American literature and film. He is the author of *The Kingfish
in Fiction: Huey P. Long and the Modern American Novel* (Louisiana State
University Press, 2004) and is currently co-editing a special issue of *POST
SCRIPT: Essays in Film and the Humanities* focusing on the films of Joel
and Ethan Coen.

Contributors

Katherine Powell is the director of the Office of First-Year Experience and a lecturer in the Department of English, Rhetoric and Writing at Berry College. She is one of the founders of Berry's Southern Women Writers Conference and served as co-director of the conference from 1996–2000. She holds degrees from St. Joseph College and the Bread Loaf School of English.

John A. Staunton is assistant professor of American literature and English education at the University of North Carolina at Charlotte. His work on Larry Brown, Kate Chopin, and other American regionalist authors has appeared in *Studies in American Fiction*, *Religion and Literature*, and *Short Story Criticism*.

Jay Watson is associate professor of English at the University of Mississippi, where he teaches Southern literature and culture, literature of the Vietnam War, New Materialist theory, and law and literature. He has published articles in a number of journals and recently assembled and edited *Conversations with Larry Brown* (University Press of Mississippi, 2007). He is also the author of *Forensic Fictions: The Lawyer Figure in Faulkner* (University of Georgia Press, 1993).

INDEX

Index

INDEX

Index

INDEX